RETHINKING FOREIGN LANGUAGE WRITING

Newbury House
Teacher Development

RETHINKING FOREIGN LANGUAGE WRITING

Virginia Mitchell Scott
Vanderbilt University

HEINLE & HEINLE PUBLISHERS
I(T)P *An International Thomson Publishing Company*
Boston, Massachusetts 02116 U.S.A.

New York • London • Bonn • Boston • Detroit • Madrid • Melbourne • Mexico City • Paris •
Singapore • Tokyo • Toronto • Washington • Albany, NY • Belmont, CA • Cincinnati, OH

The publication of **Rethinking Foreign Language Writing** was directed by the members of the Heinle & Heinle French, German and Russian Publishing Team:

Elizabeth Holthaus and Stan Galek, Team Leaders
Wendy Nelson, Editorial Director
Amy R. Terrell, Market Development Director
Gabrielle B. McDonald, Production Services Coordinator

Also participating in the publication of this program were:

Publisher: Stanley J. Galek
Director of Production: Elizabeth Holthaus
Managing Developmental Editor: Amy Lawler
Project Manager: Gabrielle B. McDonald
Associate Editor: Diana Bohmer
Associate Market Development Director: Melissa Tingley
Production Assistant: Lisa Winkler
Manufacturing Coordinator: Barbara Stephan
Photo/Video Specialist: Jonathan Stark
Interior Designer: Gabrielle B. McDonald
Cover Designer: Kimberly Wedlake

Library of Congress Cataloging-in-Publication Data

Scott, Virginia Mitchell.
    Rethinking foreign language writing / Virginia Mitchell Scott.
        p.   cm.
    Includes bibliographical references.
    ISBN 0-8384-6600-1
    1. Authorship. 2. Languages, Modern—Study and teaching.
    I. Title.
PN151.S36   1995
418'.007—dc20   95-46855
                                                 CIP

Manufactured in the United States of America

ISBN: 0-8384-6600-1

10   9   8   7   6   5   4   3   2   1

TABLE OF CONTENTS

ACKNOWLEDGMENTS

My thanks go first to my colleagues at Vanderbilt University, who supported my interest in working with *Système-D*. Barbara Bowen, Franklin Brooks, Dan Church, Larry Crist, Mary-Kay Miller, Margaret Miner, and Luigi Monga willingly taught language courses in which the writing assignments required use of the software. Claude Pichois waited patiently for the results of work with *Système-D* to show in his undergraduate seminar papers. Patricia Ward gave me the necessary encouragement to finally finish my rethinking and write the last word of this book.

The bulk of my gratitude goes to the graduate teaching assistants who worked in the trenches from the beginning! This book is due in large part to their commitment to my notion that composition should be included in the elementary- and intermediate-level French courses. They have endured my thinking, rethinking, inventing, and reinventing.

My Heinle friends have been part of the rethinking from the start. Charlie Heinle, Erek Smith, Stan Galek, and Amy Terrell listened to me talk about writing for three years. Then Wendy Nelson stepped in and made it all happen.

My family and friends have waited patiently for me to finish rethinking. I have warned them that it, too, is a process and may never end. They are still with me!

Finally, I am sincerely grateful to colleagues who read this manuscript and became part of the rethinking:

James S. Noblitt, Institute for Academic Technology, University of
  North Carolina at Chapel Hill
Robert M. Terry, University of Richmond
Sally Sieloff Magnan, University of Wisconsin, Madison
Anne Nerenz, Eastern Michigan University
Jean Marie Schultz, University of California at Berkeley

FOREWORD

Rethinking is an integral part of good teaching. It is difficult to be satisfied year after year with the same approach and the same method. Good teachers continue to search for the best way to help students learn. In fact, our work as teachers is, in large part, a constant exploration of different ways to teach our students well. A colleague once said to me, "When we teach something the first time, we learn; when we teach something the second time, students learn; and when we teach the same thing the third time, no one learns!"[1]

As foreign language teachers, our job is complicated by the fact that the four skills (reading, writing, listening, speaking) are like four different subjects. While we include all four skills in our concept of teaching a foreign language, each skill requires a unique approach. We do not teach reading the same way we teach listening, and we do not teach speaking the same way we teach writing. There may be some overlap in teaching strategies for the four skills, but generally we have different techniques to help students learn each of the four skills. And, periodically we rethink our methods and change our teaching strategies.

I began to seriously rethink my approach to teaching foreign language writing during a four-hour layover in an airport with James S. Noblitt several years ago. Jim wanted to show me a software program that he had developed with his colleagues Willem J. A. Pet and Donald Solá. The program was designed to help students write in French. At the time, I did not realize that my conversation with Jim would change the focus of my thinking, my research, and my teaching. The software program he showed me included databases with abundant lexical and syntactical information; with the touch of a key we explored a bilingual dictionary, a verb conjugator, a grammar reference, a vocabulary index, and a phrases index. I wondered if my students in third-year college grammar and composition at Vanderbilt University would benefit from using this innovative software called *Système-D.* It seemed worthwhile to ask if I could try *Système-D,* as yet incomplete, but certainly ready for experimentation. Jim agreed.

The software was loaded on several computers in the microcomputer lab[2] and I took my advanced grammar and composition students for an orientation session. They were all impressed and eager to write with the support provided in the *Système-D* databases, and they did their first assignment with enthusiasm. When I read their first compositions, my anticipation turned to disappointment: I saw the same subject/verb and noun/adjective agreement mistakes, the same anglicisms, the same incomprehensible prose. *Système-D* was no miracle cure.

However, I had invested time and energy in this project, and I was not willing to give up. I decided to be frank with the students about my reaction to their *Système-D* compositions. Why was there no difference in the quality of their work? How had they used the software? What information had they looked up? The students expressed their disappointment as well. Their grades were no better than before, and they blamed the bilingual dictionary in *Système-D,* claiming that it was insufficient. In other words, the students were not searching for information in the grammar, vocabulary, and phrases indexes. Rather, the dictionary was their key resource, and they were relying on a familiar writing strategy, namely looking up words in the English dictionary, finding a match in French, and writing them down.

Those initial questions about what the students were actually doing while writing with *Système-D* made me begin to rethink foreign language writing. In my rethinking, I realized that there were a myriad of questions and very few answers: How should we teach and evaluate foreign language writing? What is good foreign language writing? What are the characteristics of good and poor writers? Is the foreign language writing process similar to the writing process in the native language? How is writing with a computer different from writing with pencil and paper? There is a good deal of research in English composition and in English as a Second Language that touches upon these questions, however, there is relatively little research in foreign language writing. Teaching with *Système-D* focused my attention on foreign language writing in general and forced me to analyze more carefully what we do when we teach writing in the foreign language classroom.

My reactions to *Système-D,* as well as those of my students, were well received by Jim and his colleagues. The databases in *Système-D* were continuously corrected and augmented, often in response to our concerns. Moreover, *Système-D* has served as a model for similar programs in other languages: *Atajo* in Spanish and *Quelle* in German. With the development of these writing assistants, computer-aided foreign language writing was added to the repertoire of instructional materials available to foreign language teachers.

The link between the commercial development of *Système-D*[3] and its pedagogical applications[4] has been productive in that real classroom needs were taken into account. Like adopting a new textbook, using *Système-D* in the French language program at Vanderbilt University forced me to reexamine the overall approach to teaching foreign language writing, the methods used to realize objectives, and the means for evaluating student work. *Rethinking Foreign Language Writing* is the result of how this technology inspired me to rethink foreign language writing and its place in the curriculum.

Notes

1. Thanks, Dan Church, for your wisdom and encouragement!

2. Thanks, Bill Longwell, for your untiring work with the software and the hardware as well as for being a champion of my cause!

3. Thanks, Charlie, Stan, Erek, and Amy, for your support over the years!

4. Thanks, Bob Terry, for your friendship, especially during our joint project writing the Teacher's Guide for the software!

INTRODUCTION

Very little is known about the nature of foreign language writing. In the fields of English composition and English as a second language, on the other hand, writing has been a subject of much inquiry. *Rethinking Foreign Language Writing* reviews pertinent theories and research about writing in English, English as a second language, and foreign language in order to further an understanding of teaching and learning foreign language writing. In discussing these fields of research, the terms *L1* and *L2* are used in a generic sense to refer to native language and second language writing, *ESL* refers to English as a second language, *EFL* refers to English as a foreign language, and *FL* refers to foreign language.

   Rethinking Foreign Language Writing is designed to be accessible to classroom teachers, at both the high school and college levels, who are interested in gaining insight into both the theoretical and practical aspects of teaching FL writing. This book can also be used as a supplementary text in a methodology course for students preparing careers in FL teaching. In addition to providing insight into FL writing, this book points specifically to the need for empirical research in the field of FL writing, and therefore serves as a source of topics for inquiry for the FL researcher.

WHAT IS "WRITING"?

Students regularly use writing at all levels of FL study to practice newly learned words and structures. Teachers generally assign writing exercises to help students practice the lexical and syntactic aspects of the target language as well as to test them on their mastery of the structures. This kind of writing is a support skill and consists of copying, taking notes, writing lists, and filling in blanks. Another kind of writing involves creating meaning through the arrangement of words, sentences, and paragraphs. This kind of writing, or composition, includes writing letters, journals, reports, academic essays, and fiction.[1] *Rethinking Foreign Language Writing* deals exclusively with this second kind of writing; therefore, the word *writing* in this book refers to composition.

WHY WRITE ABOUT FL WRITING?

Writing is given relatively little attention in the FL curriculum. Typically introduced after students have studied the target language for two or more years, writing is often relegated to a one-semester course.

   Historically, the FL teaching profession has given little sustained attention to the development of writing ability in students' target languages. Most FL professionals have taken the position that writing is a "secondary" or less crucial skill than listening, speaking, and reading . . . (Valdes, Haro and Echevarriarza, 1992, 333).

While most teachers would agree that writing is important and is an essential part of the FL learning process, it remains a low-priority skill.

Writing may be neglected because many teachers know very little about it:

Of the four skills that are discussed and (supposedly) taught with equal emphasis in our foreign language classrooms, writing is perhaps the most poorly understood and the skill that is given, in fact, the most cursory attention (Terry, 1989, 43).

Questions abound about learning and teaching FL writing: What is the nature of writing in a foreign language and how is it different from writing in the native language? How is foreign language writing related to overall language ability? Do students progress through predictable stages as they learn to write in the foreign language? How should foreign language writing be taught and what role should it play in the curriculum?[2]

Finding answers to these questions about FL writing is especially important, given the recent interest in writing in the academic setting. Current thinking holds that writing is a central part of the learning process and that there is a relationship between writing and cognitive development. The emphasis in many school programs on "writing across the curriculum" reflects an interest in the value of writing for promoting thinking and learning in all academic disciplines.

For many students, writing is a difficult skill in the native language, since it invokes more than lexical and syntactic knowledge; they must also understand principles of organization and coherence. Writing in a foreign language is certainly more challenging, given the constraints imposed by the foreign language. When writing a composition, the FL student is faced with generating and organizing ideas as well as communicating. The complex cognitive skills involved in FL writing merit careful analysis in order to gain insight into how this exercise contributes to overall language proficiency as well as to general cognitive development.

THE ORGANIZATION OF THE BOOK

Five hypotheses about the nature of foreign language writing shape the organization of *Rethinking Foreign Language Writing*. Rather than a statement of truth, each hypothesis serves as a point of departure for analyzing writing as well as for identifying questions that merit further investigation. Each chapter includes a review of literature, practical classroom implementations, and topics for discussion and research.

Chapter 1, "Writing Competence," is based on the hypothesis that writing competence is a general notion that is not language specific. In explaining this hypothesis, I suggest that a writer who is competent in L1 is likely to be competent in FL, and likewise, that a poor L1 writer is likely to be a poor FL writer. After defining the notion of writing competence, I explore several other pertinent dimensions of language competence, including the relationships between writing, reading, speaking, and linguistic competence. There are explicit examples of how teachers can implement teaching strategies that take into consideration L1 writing competence and the relationship between writing competence and competence in other language skills.

Chapter 2, "The Foreign Language Writing Process," forwards the hypothesis that the foreign language writing process differs from the native language writing process. On the surface, the language constraint appears to be the primary difference between writing in L1 and in FL. However, a closer analysis reveals that the strategies that a writer might use during the L1 writing process differ from those that the same writer might use during the FL writing process. In order to understand the concept of writing as process, I review several theoretical perspectives from which the writing process can be viewed, as well as a process model based on empirical analyses. With regard to the L2 writing process, I examine the question of accuracy, the link between writing and learning, the concept of a monitor, the role of long-term memory, and the use of translation. Furthermore, I describe the use of computer-aided research in analyzing various aspects of the FL writing process. In discussing strategies for teaching about the FL writing process, I provide a detailed description of task-oriented writing guidelines designed to guide students explicitly in the FL writing process.

Chapter 3, "Computer-Aided Foreign Language Writing," is founded on the hypothesis that computer-aided writing enhances the FL writing experience. The writing strategies used when writing with pencil and paper are quite different from those used when composing at the computer. In fact, some research suggests that using word processing may alter the nature of the writing experience. After a general discussion of what is involved in writing with a word processor, I review the theories that deal with computers and the writing process. In discussing computers and FL writing, I focus on the use of several innovative software programs for teaching FL writing. There is specific reference to aspects of these software programs that encourage effective FL writing strategies such as recursion, revising, rereading, and the appropriate use of translation. In addition, I examine the use of computers for both teaching and research in FL writing.

Chapter 4, "Correcting and Evaluating Foreign Language Writing," submits the hypothesis that correcting and evaluating FL writing are complex tasks that involve the entire writing process. Of all the dimensions of teaching writing, correction and evaluation have received the most attention. Many studies have explored how feedback affects student writing, as well as the kinds of correction that help students improve their writing. FL teachers have traditionally focused on correcting and evaluating the form, or the surface errors, of a written text. However, recent research suggests that attention to content, or ideas, is equally important. In order to understand the role that correction and evaluation plays in teaching writing, I examine the research regarding teacher feedback, peer review, and student response to feedback. I also discuss various methods for evaluating written texts, as well as for evaluating the writing process.

Chapter 5, "Teaching Foreign Language Writing," submits the hypothesis that teaching FL writing is effective at all levels of language study. In the final chapter of the book, I argue that writing needs to be fully integrated into the FL program at all levels of study. After reviewing approaches to teaching L1 and ESL writing, I examine current approaches in FL writing instruction. In addition, I review the research on teaching writing as well as the theories and research regarding writing tasks. Finally, based on the notion that students can write from the start,[3] I present an approach to teaching FL writing that consists of two fundamental principles: (1) that students must begin writing compositions from the earliest stages of language study, and (2) that they must learn to write in all four discourse modes (narrative, descriptive, expository, and argumentative).

Notes

1. In "An Introduction to the Study of Written Texts: The 'Discourse Compact'" (*Annual Review of Applied Linguistics*, 1982), Kaplan states that there are two kinds of writing: *writing without composing* and *writing through composing.* Similarly, in "Teaching and Evaluating Writing as a Communicative Skill" (*Foreign Language Annals* 22(1):43–54, 1989), Terry points out that writing as a support skill is distinct from writing as a communicative skill. The former is designed to reinforce grammatical structures, whereas the second teaches students to inform, relate, persuade, etc.

2. Valdes, Haro, and Echevarriarza ("The Development of Writing Abilities in a Foreign Language: Contributions Toward a General Theory of L2 Writing," *The Modern Language Journal* 3(76):333–352, 1992), point out that, while writing in general is now being given more attention, we know very little about FL writing. They sum up the important theoretical questions about learning and teaching FL writing: How does writing ability in a second language develop? What relationship is there between writing skills developed in L1 and those developed in L2? What relationship is there between the development of writing ability in L2 and the development of other language skills (e.g., speaking, listening)? What levels of writing skill development can be expected at different stages of L2 learning/acquisition?

3. This approach was first described by Scott in "Write from the Start: A Task-Oriented Developmental Writing Program for Foreign Language Students," R. M. Terry, (Ed.), *Dimension: Language '91*, Report of the Southern Conference on Language Teaching, 1992.

REFERENCES

Kaplan, Robert B. (1982). "An Introduction to the Study of Written Texts: The 'Discourse Compact'." *Annual Review of Applied Linguistics*, 138–151.

Scott, Virginia M. (1992). "Write from the Start: A Task-Oriented Developmental Writing Program for Foreign Language Students." In R. M. Terry, (Ed.), *Dimension: Language '91*, Report of the Southern Conference on Language Teaching.

Terry, Robert M. (1989). "Teaching and Evaluating Writing as a Communicative Skill." *Foreign Language Annals* 22(1):43–54.

Valdes, Guadalupe, Paz Haro and Maria Paz Echevarriarza. (1992). "The Development of Writing Abilities in a Foreign Language: Contributions Toward a General Theory of L2 Writing." *The Modern Language Journal* 3(76):333–352.

Chapter 1

Writing Competence

Hypothesis: *Writing competence is a general notion that is not language specific.*

Writing competence: toward a definition
>   Good writers
>   Good writing

Writing competence: L1 and L2 connections
>   Research with children
>   Writing process research

Writing competence and grammatical competence
>   Communicative competence
>   Proficiency
>   Grammar

Competence: the reading/writing connection
>   Krashen's *Input Hypothesis*
>   L1 and L2 literacy skills

Competence: the speaking/writing connection
>   Context
>   Language functions
>   Different linguistic system

Writing competence and modes of discourse
>   Two studies
>   Academic writing

A review of the findings regarding writing competence

Writing competence: the classroom implications

Case study 1

Case study 2

Conclusions

Topics for discussion and research

WRITING COMPETENCE

Hypothesis
Writing competence is a general notion that is not language specific.

This hypothesis states that a writer's knowledge about writing is not related to a particular language. Implicit in this hypothesis is the notion that a writer who is competent in the native language (L1) is likely to be competent in a second language (L2). By extension, the hypothesis proposes that a poor L1 writer is likely to be a poor L2 writer. If true, these assertions are basic in developing a theory of teaching foreign language (FL) writing. Assessing individual students' L1 writing competence could provide teachers with important information about how to teach FL writing. While there is little research about writing competence **per se**, there are studies in the fields of English, English as a second language (ESL), and FL that provide insight into the notion of writing competence. In order to explore the validity of this hypothesis, this chapter includes analyses of research in L1, ESL, and FL regarding writing competence as well as other language competencies. The classroom implications at the end of the chapter describe how L1 writing competence relates to teaching FL writing.

WRITING COMPETENCE: TOWARD A DEFINITION

What is *writing competence*? The word *competence* suggests a state of sufficiency or capability, or an ability that a person might have.[1] Krashen defines writing competence as "the abstract knowledge the proficient writer has about writing" (1984, p. 20). However, the notion of competence is not absolute; there are degrees of competence. Therefore, a competent writer is someone who has achieved a given level of ability and is able to communicate effectively and convincingly. A competent writer might also be called a "good writer." Implicit in any discussion of a good writer is the notion of "good writing." In analyzing writing competence, definitions of good writers and good writing will be explored.

□ GOOD WRITERS

Clearly, there is no standard definition of a good writer; any description is subjective. There are, however, some commonly held notions about the characteristics of a good writer. Theory and research in L1, ESL, and FL writing reveal the predominant view that good writers use effective composing strategies. The three fundamental strategies that characterize good writers are *planning, rescanning*, and *revising*.[2] In the planning phase, good writers take sufficient time to think about what they are going to write, which leads them to be more flexible and willing to modify the plan. With regard to rescanning, good writers pause frequently to reread while they are writing. As they revise, good writers make changes in content as well as in form.

In addition to using effective composing strategies, good writers give evidence of understanding the *recursive* nature of composing, whereas poor writers regard writing primarily as a fixed, *linear* process.[3] That is, good writers do not consider writing to be a fixed, linear set of steps but rather write recursively, moving between planning, rescanning, and revising at any time during the writing process. (See chapter 2 for a detailed discussion of theories and research in writing as a process.)

Another definition of good writers involves the ability to control four kinds of knowledge: knowledge of the language (morphosyntactic rules), knowledge of writing conventions (punctuation, citation rules), knowledge of subject, and knowledge of audience.[4]

□ GOOD WRITING

The strategies that good writers use before, during, and after writing tend to determine the quality of the composition. However, defining good writing is more elusive than defining good writers. Is writing good because of the choice of subject? The perspective on a given subject? The honesty or integrity of the writer? The authenticity of the writer's voice? The syntactical cohesion and accuracy? The lexical choices? The coherence between sentences and paragraphs? Furthermore, the kind of writing imposes a definition of quality: a philosophical essay would be judged by different criteria than a letter, and a literary paper suggests different content and structure than an autobiographical narrative. There are, however, general descriptions of good writing on which most writers agree. Features such as clarity, explicitness, conciseness, clear paragraph structure, and overall organization are considered important.[5] Ultimately, however, the quality of a text is based on the judgment of the reader, and the reader's own criteria become the essential measure of quality. Who, then, is the reader, and what are the reader's expectations?

In the academic setting, the reader is nearly always the teacher. (See chapter 4 for a detailed discussion of peer readers.) For this reason, most texts that define the characteristics of good writing take the point of view of the writing teacher. In *Learning by Teaching*, Murray (1983) includes six features of good writing:

1. Meaning (There must be content.)
2. Authority (The reader is persuaded that the writer knows the subject.)
3. Voice (Good writing is marked by an individual voice.)
4. Development (Good writing must satisfy the reader's hunger for information and not overestimate the reader's hunger for language.)
5. Design (Good writing has form, structure, order, focus, coherence, and gives the reader a sense of completeness.)
6. Clarity (Good writing is marked by a simplicity that is appropriate to the subject.)

In *The Language Teaching Matrix,* Richards (1990) underscores the importance of readability and identifies *coherence* and *cohesion* as the two basic aspects that determine the quality of a written text. According to Richards, coherence, or the overall semantic unity of a text, includes Canale's four general conditions: 1) development (orderly presentation of ideas); 2) continuity (consistency of facts, ideas, opinions); 3) balance (relative emphasis accorded each idea); 4) completeness (ideas must provide a thorough discourse) (p. 104). Moreover, he points out that different types of discourse, such as letters, narratives, and essays would each have different requirements for coherence. Cohesion, or the surface-level syntactic and lexical aspects of a text, is also an important aspect of writing. Richards (p. 105) cites Halliday and Hasan's five types of cohesive ties: reference, substitution, ellipsis, conjunction, and lexical.

According to Knoblauch and Brannon (1984), rhetorical conventions that describe "good writing" are superficial and false. They argue that modern theories of discourse do not include formulae, or models of expression. They make a critical distinction between skills and competence, suggesting that writing competence cannot be taught as a skill, but rather can be nurtured by encouraging the making of meaning:

> People write because it enables the making of meaning, the discovery of coherence, the communicating of valued ideas, not merely because they enjoy technical accomplishment. When teachers regard the composing process as an elaborate multiplication of skills, they are working from a pseudoconcept. They are not just overlooking the motivations that make writing worthwhile by emphasizing control of a technology; they are treating the thinking and forming processes as though they themselves were technologies, when they are not (Knoblauch and Brannon, 1984, 91).

> ... the essential ability to organize experience by means of language is also ... a human competence, not a skill. ... Teachers cannot provide students with 'skills' of thinking or 'skills' of forming assertions and connecting them as discourse. But they can create incentives and contexts for thinking and writing, so that the process of developing and strengthening composing ability may proceed (Knoblauch and Brannon, 1984, 93).

By their definition, good writing is an extension of clear thinking, and writing competence is how a writer makes meaning in written language. However, this too involves a subjective judgment, since what is clear or meaningful to one reader may not be to another.

Citing research in composition and applied linguistics, Mills (1990) concludes that readers often respond to syntactic complexity. In order to determine the syntactic complexity of a text, Mills cites Hunt's concept of *T-units*. A T-unit is defined as "one main clause plus any subordinate clause or non-clausal structure that is attached to or embedded in it" (Mills, 1990, 107). He further states that "mean T-unit length has become a standard measure of writing quality" (Mills, 1990, 108). (See chapter 4 for a detailed discussion of T-unit evaluation.)

While there are no universally accepted definitions of good writing, English composition teachers would probably agree with most of the preceding criteria. For many FL teachers, however, characteristics of good writing might be different, since form has typically taken precedence over content. FL teachers are often more interested in **how** a student says something than in **what** a student says. By this standard, grammatical accuracy and lexical choice are more important than ideas. While this view may be changing, good FL writing, especially at the early stages of language learning, is defined in terms of its syntactical correctness.

Finally, any consideration of writing competence should include both writers and writing. While there are varying opinions of what constitutes good writers and good writing, there are generally accepted standards by which writing competence is evaluated. Therefore, writing competence can be defined as what a writer knows about good writers and good writing.

WRITING COMPETENCE: L1 AND L2 CONNECTIONS

Writing competence, as defined earlier, refers to a writer's general awareness about writing as well as to the specific strategies that are used while writing. With regard to L1 writing, every student has some degree of competence. Some students may be more competent than others,[6] but all students have an individual sense of what good writing is. If writing competence is a general body of knowledge, distinct in each individual, is there a link between L1 and L2 writing competence? That is, do writers transfer their level of competence from L1 to L2?

□   RESEARCH WITH CHILDREN

An informative study involving elementary school children in a bilingual program presents data supporting the notion that there is an important relationship between L1 and L2 writing competence.

> . . . what a young writer knows about writing in the first language forms the basis of new hypotheses rather than interferes with writing in another language. Knowledge about writing in the first language can mean anything from tacit or explicit knowledge of local conventions, such as how to graphically represent one particular sound, to knowledge that written texts have different requirements than oral ones, to knowledge of what processes and strategies are used during writing (Edelsky, 1982, 227).

Although Edelsky's subjects were children working on very basic kinds of writing tasks, their capacity to demonstrate L1 writing competence and their transfer of that competence to L2 writing suggests that the same cognitive ability would be present in adult writers.

☐ WRITING PROCESS RESEARCH

The way that a writer goes about writing constitutes the writing process. As stated previously, the writing process includes strategies such as planning, rescanning, and revising. Several studies investigating the student writing process indicate that the strategies used for L1 writing are transferred to L2 writing tasks. In one study, Zamel (1983) carefully detailed the writing process of six ESL students before, during, and after writing. Although the focus of her study was to examine these strategies in order to confirm her theory that writing is a process of creating meaning, she found that the deficient strategies used by unskilled L2 writers were the same as the deficient strategies used by unskilled L1 writers. Her findings suggest that the lack of writing competence in L1 is reflected in students' L2 writing ability.

In another study, Raimes (1987) analyzed the composing strategies of ESL students to determine what strategies were common to ESL writers as well as how these strategies compared with those common to native speaker writers. She found that ESL and L1 writers had similar composing strategies. For example, like L1 writers, ESL writers spent little time prewriting or planning, and they rescanned a great deal.

> ... ESL students have internalized strategies for writing, not all of which may be facilitative, which may need to be developed, refined, or changed. They do reread the question, rehearse, plan, and rescan, but often they do so with few principles for evaluation of discourse (Raimes, 1987, 460).

In other words, ESL writers had more problems with the composing process than with their limited knowledge of L2.

In a similar study, Jones and Tetroe (1987) analyzed L1 and L2 planning strategies used by six ESL student writers. By comparing various aspects of the planning strategies for L1 and L2, they gave credence to their hypothesis that, for writing, "both good and poor strategies carry over, with little change, to the second-language task" (p. 36). They further concluded that "while second-language proficiency obviously affects the quality of the texts, it appears to have little role in constraining the planning process" (p. 55).

Friedlander's (1990) study on the effects of L1 on L2 composing provides further insight into the relationship between L1 and L2 writing competence. He states in the introduction that "a number of studies have indicated that, regardless of a language prescription, writers will transfer writing abilities and strategies, whether good or deficient, from their first language to their second language" (p. 109). All the subjects in his study were Chinese students learning to write in English. The data from his study indicate that, during the planning process, when students use the language that they associate with the topic, they will produce texts with better content. For example, when the Chinese students prepared in Chinese for writing about a Chinese event, their compositions in English were superior to the compositions of Chinese students who prepared in English before writing about a Chinese event. Likewise, when the Chinese students prepared in Chinese to write about an event they had experienced in the United States, their compositions were inferior to the Chinese students who prepared in English before writing about the American event. During planning, students generated better ideas when they used the language associated with the topic-area knowledge. Finally, this finding suggests that writing competence is a cognitive function that involves planning and generating ideas and is, to a great extent, divorced from language constraints in L2.

In a somewhat different vein, Valdes, Haro, and Echevarriarzia (1992) carried out a study that shows that students in first- and second-year college-level Spanish were able to write coherent compositions and discuss abstract topics in spite of limited language. In describing a student in the study, they state that "one can logically conclude that he is using previously acquired knowledge about writing in his first language to organize his writing in Spanish" (p. 344). The researchers argue that these findings challenge the assumptions made in the *ACTFL Proficiency Guidelines*[7] about the development of FL writing. For example, they point out that organizational development does not emerge after students have learned to copy, recombine, or create original sentences. In fact, their study suggests that students transfer concepts such as organization, cohesion, and unity of topic from L1 to the FL. Limitations in FL vocabulary and syntax do not make students disregard their knowledge about such things as paragraph construction or characteristics of different genres (p. 340). While the researchers point out that the *ACTFL Proficiency Guidelines* serve the profession well in that they have caused us to examine skill development, they do not accurately reflect actual skill development in FL writing. The authors conclude by noting that in beginning to write in a target language, students do not start at ground zero but rather build on the abilities they have acquired for writing in L1 (p. 346).

Most research points to the fact that there is a transfer of writing competence from one language to another.[8] These findings suggest that when FL students approach a writing task, they have a previously defined sense of what constitutes good writing:

> . . . it is clear that there must be common underlying proficiencies, both across languages and across modalities, that allow adult learners to draw on already developed knowledge bases and strategies as they develop literacy skills in their second language (Eisterhold, 1990, 98).

WRITING COMPETENCE AND
GRAMMATICAL COMPETENCE

Understanding the relationship between writing competence and other language competencies is vital for FL teachers. The first issue pertinent to this discussion involves the difference between writing competence and grammatical competence. As defined previously, writing competence is the knowledge a writer has about writing. Likewise, grammatical competence is the knowledge a learner has about grammar. With regard to teaching FL writing, the question is whether or not these two areas of competence are distinct. That is, is it possible for a student to be a good writer but demonstrate a poor grasp of grammar, or to be a poor writer but demonstrate a good grasp of grammar?

□ COMMUNICATIVE COMPETENCE

Scholars in the field of second-language acquisition generally acknowledge that there are several dimensions that make up overall language ability. The term *communicative competence* refers to language ability in listening, speaking, reading, and writing.[9] Canale and Swain[10] proposed an integrative model of communicative competence with four major components: *grammatical, sociolinguistic, discourse,* and *strategic*. Grammatical competence is defined as the level of mastery of the linguistic code, which includes pronunciation, spelling, vocabulary, and sentence structure. Sociolinguistic competence refers to the appropriateness of language used in a given context. Discourse competence involves the ability to communicate ideas clearly and coherently. Strategic competence consists of using effective verbal and nonverbal communication strategies to negotiate meaning. According to this model, overall language ability incorporates several kinds of competencies that operate both independently and together. While grammatical competence is included in communicative competence, it comprises only part of the whole.

□ PROFICIENCY

The word *proficiency* currently refers to the levels of ability that are described for speaking, listening, reading, and writing in the *ACTFL Proficiency Guidelines*, published in 1986 by the American Council on the Teaching of Foreign Languages, Hastings-on-Hudson, NY (1986). In an attempt to standardize the assessment of ability in the four language skills, the *ACTFL Proficiency Guidelines* describe proficiency at four basic levels: Novice, Intermediate, Advanced, and Superior. Like the model of communicative competence described previously, each level on the ACTFL proficiency scale identifies several components used for assessing language ability.

Hadley (1993, p. 14) reviews the five interrelated assessment criteria underlying the proficiency descriptions: *global tasks/functions, context, content, accuracy,* and *text type*. In this model, "global tasks/functions" refers to real-world tasks (i.e., introducing, agreeing, hypothesizing, etc.), "context" refers to the setting in which language is used, "content" refers to topics or themes, "accuracy" refers to grammatical correctness, and "text type" refers to the structure of the discourse (i.e., words, sentences, paragraphs). For Hadley, these five criteria serve as a basis for analyzing proficiency in all four skills as well as a basis for teaching. Implicit in this model is the notion that, although all five dimensions are interrelated, they are different. For example, a learner could master function and context but be deficient in accuracy, or have a high degree of accuracy but very limited functions. While one of the goals of proficiency-oriented instruction is to teach students to integrate all five areas at each level of proficiency, a student could demonstrate different levels of ability in each area. Therefore, competence in one dimension of language proficiency does not guarantee competence in another.

□ GRAMMAR

The notions of communicative competence and proficiency outlined in this chapter both include grammar, or accuracy, in the components that make up overall language ability. In FL teaching, grammar has often been considered the key to success in overall language ability. That is, if students "know" their grammar, they will succeed in all language skills. However, with regard to writing, several studies support the notion that grammatical competence alone is an insufficient condition for good FL writing. In fact, some research suggests that knowing how to write may play a more important role than grammatical competence in writing.[11]

In an article dealing with the problems of articulation between language and literature classes, Schultz (1991b) argues that the emphasis on grammar in teaching writing may have no relation to the quality of writing:

> Upper-division instructors may well react to student writing difficulties by prescribing additional grammar instruction, but ironically, research has repeatedly shown that grammar instruction has little if any impact on composition skills. A case in point would be the student who systematically receives A's on grammar tests, but who does poorly when asked to write an essay. In other words, the ability to supply the correct answer on a grammar test is not necessarily an indicator of student ability to express personal meaning in the target language (Schultz, 1991b, 412).

Knowing grammar does not appear to guarantee writing competence.

COMPETENCE: THE READING/WRITING CONNECTION

Most FL programs integrate writing instruction with other language skill development. Typical course offerings at the college level include grammar and composition or composition and conversation. In these types of courses, reading often serves as a source for discussion. That is, students talk or write about what they have read. However, in addition to providing a source of topics, reading may play a more critical role in the development of writing competence. Some research suggests that reading may improve writing and that a well-read person has more knowledge about the conventions and features of writing.

□ KRASHEN'S *INPUT HYPOTHESIS*

In *Writing: Research, Theory and Applications*, Krashen defines writing competence as "the abstract knowledge the proficient writer has about writing" (p. 20), and he suggests that a writer's abstract knowledge comes primarily from reading for interest or pleasure: "It is reading that gives the writer the 'feel' for the look and texture of reader-based prose" (p. 20). Krashen further postulates that his second-language acquisition theory holds true for the development of writing ability. The second-language acquisition theory states that language is acquired through comprehensible input, namely "when we understand messages in the second language, when we understand **what** is said or written, rather than **how** it is expressed, [and] when we focus on meaning and not form" (p. 21). Based on this theory, he suggests that writing ability in any language is acquired through extensive reading in which the focus of the reader is on the message and not on the form. However, Krashen does admit that there is no "perfect correlation between the amount of pleasure reading done and writing quality" (p. 21).

□ L1 AND L2 LITERACY SKILLS

Although many language specialists are likely to agree with Krashen's basic tenet regarding the relationship between reading and writing, there are other important variables involved in the reading-writing connection. For example, does L1 reading competence affect L2 writing? Does the level of L2 reading proficiency affect L2 writing?

> Krashen's (1984) claim that second language learners' writing competence derives from large amounts of self-motivated reading for interest and/or pleasure remains largely untested and unsubstantiated. Still, it is difficult to imagine that second language input would not play a significant role in developing literacy skills in L2, i.e., reading input presumably affects the development of writing and reading abilities and/or writing input affects the development of reading and writing abilities. The situation for second language learners is much more complex than it is for first language learners: One must take into account not only the learner's L2 language proficiency, but also the possibility of interaction of first language literacy skills with second language input (Carson, Carrell, Silberstein, Kroll, Kuehn, 1990, 247–48).

Reading in the L1 writing classroom is likely to contribute to the kind of input that will ultimately provide models from which writing skills can be learned. However, the reading-writing connections may not be the same in L2. Since second-language learners usually have well-developed L1 reading skills, but they are often limited by their language proficiency when reading in L2, there are several ways to analyze the reading-writing connection: L1 reading/L1 writing, L1 reading/L2 writing, and L2 reading/L2 writing.[12]

> Research . . . indicates that transfer of skills is not automatic, either across languages or across modalities . . . [and] they clearly indicate that the relationship between reading and writing should be exploited and that writing teachers need to be explicit in their teaching of that relationship (Eisterhold, 1990, 100).

Clearly, the reading-writing connection merits further study given its possible role in the development of writing competence in both L1 and the FL.

COMPETENCE: THE SPEAKING/WRITING CONNECTION

Is there a link between speaking competence and writing competence? Any teacher who evaluates oral and written work is aware that there can be vast differences between a student's ability in speaking and in writing. Most teachers have known students who are able to speak coherently and easily, using effective communicative strategies such as circumlocuting, enhancing, or digressing, and yet who are incapable of writing well. These students may use the strategies they find successful for oral communication, not realizing that they are often inappropriate for writing. By the same token, there are students who write well but who are not always proficient speakers. While they may feel secure and confident communicating a message in writing, they may be unsure of themselves while speaking, hesitating frequently, fearful of making mistakes. Since students do not always master both modalities equally well, in either L1 or L2, the link between speaking and writing may be tenuous.

□ CONTEXT

The fundamental difference between speaking and writing appears to be that writing is largely decontextualized. That is, writing is devoid of the kind of feedback that is available with oral messages. The relationship between speaker and listener is based upon common knowledge, whereas the shared knowledge between writer and reader is generally unknown.[13] For this reason, writing is considered to be more difficult than speaking:

> The novice writer has to learn how to make such things explicit and unambiguous, once and for all, through syntactic arrangement and lexical choice,

whereas in speech the omissions, ambiguities, and misconceptions can be clarified by action, restatement, or expansion . . . (Rivers, 1981, 292).

☐ LANGUAGE FUNCTIONS

Some writing tasks are like speech, while others are very different from speech. For example, some language functions such as narrating, informing, or persuading might be similar in speech and writing. Others, such as explaining and analyzing, may be very different. Identifying the language function in a writing task and evaluating its relationship to speech is essential in describing the link between speech and writing.[14]

In a study comparing writing and speaking in a foreign language, Dvorak (1987) found that both written and oral FL appeared to be sensitive to language function. Her study strongly suggests that written FL is very different from oral language, even for learners with limited exposure to the FL. She concludes by saying that "the development of writing skill involves mastery of a great number of subskills that progressively widen the difference between conversing and composing" (p. 89).

☐ DIFFERENT LINGUISTIC SYSTEM

Most researchers agree that writing is characterized by a more overt structure than speech:

> The general view is that written language is structurally elaborated, complex, formal, and abstract, while spoken language is concrete, context-dependent, and structurally simple (Biber, 1988, 5).

Because writing is more formal, some researchers believe that written language is a distinct linguistic system that develops separately from speaking.[15] In fact, Horning (1987) proposes that learning to write is very much like learning another language. Moreover, she argues that speech is not a primary form of language, as believed by most linguists. She considers that writing, on the other hand, may be a better representation of a person's capacity with language.

> In looking at linguistic issues such as competence and performance, Wrolstad finds that the production of oral language rarely matches linguistic knowledge. . . . Visible language performance, mostly in the form of writing, reveals one's linguistic competence more accurately (Horning, 1987, 8).

Although there is no clearly defined difference between spoken language and written language, most research gives evidence that speaking and writing are not the same. Learning to be a proficient FL speaker will not guarantee proficiency in FL writing. Likewise a student could be a proficient writer in FL without ever achieving oral proficiency. Writing competence, then, is distinct from oral competence and the two should not be considered as mirror images.

WRITING COMPETENCE AND MODES OF DISCOURSE

Does writing competence vary with mode of discourse? The four primary modes of discourse traditional to the discussion of writing are *narration*, *description*, *exposition*, and *argumentation*. Standards for a good narrative would differ somewhat from standards for a good description, just as good descriptive writing would differ from good expository or persuasive writing. However, the important question with regard to writing competence involves individual variation in different discourse modes. That is, are some writers competent when writing in one mode but less competent when writing in another?

□ TWO STUDIES

One study, involving native speakers of English, indicates that writers have different levels of ability in different language modes. Using topics requiring narration, description, and persuasion, college students representing basic, average, and honors writers participated in the research. The findings were as follows:

> Placed on a mode continuum, descriptive writing would be considered a difficult task for basic writers, an intermediately difficult task for average writers, and an easy task for honors writers. [. . .] Narrative-related skills, regardless of writing ability, were well developed, perhaps to the point of automaticity. [. . .] Whereas for basic writers persuasive writing would be placed on the 'difficult' end of the mode continuum, this type of writing would be placed close to 'intermediately difficult' for both average and honors writers (Freed, Burton, and Kelly, 1985, 291–292).

This study clearly classifies modes of discourse according to difficulty, with narration ranking as easiest, description ranking second, and persuasion ranking as most difficult.

In a similar study involving American college students studying Japanese (Koda, 1993), the results indicate that different kinds of competencies, linguistic and rhetorical, are required for different modes of discourse. A comparison of descriptive tasks and narrative tasks shows differences in linguistic performance (grammaticality and sentence structure) as well as in rhetorical features (organization, coherence).

We can infer from these studies that writers may have competence in several, but not necessarily all, modes of discourse. More importantly, we must recognize that any definition of good writing, or writing competence, involves recognizing the role of the discourse mode in written expression.

□ ACADEMIC WRITING

When students are required to write a paper in L1, the topic typically requires them to explain and persuade. Academic writing usually involves writing essays, which are analytic or interpretive in nature. Students, especially at the college level, are rarely asked to write a narrative or descriptive paper, unless they are taking a creative writing class. Writing a paper in an academic setting, therefore, often involves the two most difficult modes of discourse, namely exposition and argumentation.

In two articles dealing with teaching foreign language writing, Schultz (1991a, 1991b) discusses the fact that many teachers of FL literature are frustrated by student papers that are often very poorly written and filled with grammatical errors. Likewise, students who performed well at the elementary and intermediate levels of FL study may suddenly find that they get poor grades on their literature papers. In an attempt to explain this common occurrence, Schultz discusses the cognitive processes involved in the different modes of writing. Citing research in L1, she explains that description, narration, and exposition involve primarily linear cognitive processing, whereas argumentation draws on more complex, higher-level cognitive processes (1991a, p. 980–81). Moreover, she mentions that the linear cognitive processes necessary for describing and narrating are present in children as young as three years of age:

> . . . the cognitive infrastructures for the descriptive and narrative modes develop early and can be called upon fairly automatically for writing purposes. This tendency also holds true for exposition, which, despite its greater level of abstraction, nevertheless depends on a hierarchical presentation of supported opinion" (Schultz, 1991b, 411).

Furthermore, she makes reference to studies that support the notion that the argumentative essay requires greater and more varied cognitive skills (1991b, p. 412). Given these findings, teachers must recognize that academic writing in the FL literature class demands more of students than grammatical competence.

A REVIEW OF THE FINDINGS REGARDING WRITING COMPETENCE

The theories and research reviewed in this chapter suggest that writing competence, or the knowledge that a writer has about writing, transcends any specific language. Studies show that there is a connection between L1 and L2 writing competence, especially with regard to writing strategies such as planning, rescanning, and revising. Both the effective as well as the ineffective strategies that a writer uses are transferred from L1 to L2. Writing competence is, therefore, a body of knowledge that is generally independent from the language of expression.

In addition to being independent from a specific language, writing competence also appears to be distinct from most other language competencies. Research indicates that grammatical competence and speaking competence represent different kinds of knowledge from writing competence. Reading, on the other hand, may be related to writing competence. Studies suggest that students who read a great deal and who enjoy reading are often better writers. Furthermore, writing competence seems to vary according to mode of discourse. A writer may be competent in one mode of discourse, such as narration, but be less competent in another, such as argumentation.

These findings regarding the relationship between L1 and FL writing competence, as well as the relationship between writing competence and other language competencies, are critical to an understanding of FL writing. Any definition of FL writing must incorporate notions of general writing competence. Furthermore, students come into the FL classroom with preconceived ideas of what it means to be a good writer as well as what good writing is. Assessing their L1 writing competence and understanding their preconceptions may be the first steps in teaching FL writing.

WRITING COMPETENCE: THE CLASSROOM IMPLICATIONS

If writing competence is a general notion unrelated to a specific language, there are several implications for the FL teacher. The following suggestions can be incorporated into the FL classroom to help students at any level develop writing competence as they study the target language:

  1. *Evaluate students' L1 writing competence.*

Since students have already achieved some degree of writing competence in their native language, the first step is to assess their L1 writing. By having some sense of each student's strengths and weaknesses in L1 written expression, teachers can discern more clearly problems related to writing competence as opposed to linguistic competence. This can be done simply by asking students to write a short essay in the native language and by evaluating their essays using predetermined criteria such as those in Figure 1. After the teacher has evaluated the students' writing in L1, it is helpful to have students evaluate their own essays using the same criteria. In this way, students and teachers can compare their evaluations and begin to define writing competence in terms that both can understand.

Figure 1: Writing Evaluation Form

1. Is there a clearly stated main thesis?
   Yes_____ No_____

2. Does the writer stay with the thesis?
   Yes_____ No_____

3. Do the arguments support the thesis?
   Yes_____ No_____

4. Is the conclusion effective?
   Yes_____ No_____

5. What elements of the text are most interesting?
   _____ ideas
   _____ style (use of language)
   _____ humor
   _____ other (please specify)

6. Is this a good essay?
   Yes_____ No_____

7. How would you characterize the writer?
   _____ good / shows competence
   _____ average / shows some competence
   _____ poor / shows no competence

(Taken from pedagogical materials used by the author.)

2. *Determine what students think about writing.*

It is important to find out whether students like to write in L1. Using a questionnaire (Figure 2), it was found that students **are** interested in discussing how they feel about writing. Of the 123 elementary- and intermediate-level college French students who were given the questionnaire, 92 responded that they considered themselves good writers, while 31 said they were not good writers. Although responses varied widely, it was interesting to note that many students defined their success as writers in terms of grades they had received and teachers' opinions. Many students expressed reluctance in relying on a personal judgment of their writing competence. Furthermore, the questionnaire provided much information about students' writing preferences, concepts of the writing process, and reading habits.

3. *Define good writing.*

Before assigning a writing task, teachers should help students define the characteristics of good as well as poor writing. Through informal classroom dis-

Figure 2: Writing/Reading Questionnaire

1. Do you like to write in English? Yes_____ No_____
   If yes, what kind of writing? Check as many as appropriate.
   _____ personal letter
   _____ narration of event
   _____ description of a person or place
   _____ explanation of an idea or theory
   _____ arguing for or against an idea or theory
   other _____
   If no, why not? Check as many as appropriate.
   _____ I am not creative.
   _____ I don't know what to say.
   _____ I have gotten bad grades in the past.
   other _____

2. In your estimation, are you a good writer?
   Yes_____ No_____
   If yes, why? _____
   If no, why not? _____

3. List at least three things that you think are important when you are writing a composition in English.
   _____
   _____
   _____

4. Do you like to read? Yes_____ No_____
   If yes, what kind of texts? Check as many as are appropriate.
   _____ romantic novels
   _____ historical fiction
   _____ suspense novels
   _____ news articles
   _____ editorial essays
   _____ informative texts (i.e., about science, politics, history, environment, etc.)
   _____ poetry
   If no, why not? _____

(Taken from pedagogical materials used by the author.)

cussions, teachers can ask students to describe good and poor writing in terms of form (accuracy, lexical choices, transitional phrases, etc.) and content (clarity of ideas, organization of ideas, coherence between sentences and paragraphs, etc.). It is important for both form and content to be included in an analysis of good writing so that students understand from the start that grammatical accuracy is only one aspect of good writing. Furthermore, students should be made aware that features of good writing vary depending on the mode of discourse (narration, description, exposition, and argumentation).

4. *Define good writing strategies.*

In addition to discussing the characteristics of good writing, students should be asked to describe good writing strategies. This task is likely to be more difficult, since most students are not consciously aware of what they do when they write. When students were asked on a questionnaire (Figure 2) to list what they consider important when they are writing in L1, typical answers included:

- □ be organized and clear;
- □ have creative ideas;
- □ feel personal satisfaction;
- □ use a thesaurus and a dictionary;
- □ understand and like the topic;
- □ have correct grammar, spelling, and punctuation.

Only three students gave answers that suggested that they understood writing as a process:

- □ have an outline, try more than one opening paragraph, don't be afraid of changing your mind, have an open mind;
- □ an outline, a good grasp of what you are writing about, plenty of time beforehand to brainstorm;
- □ coherence, a broad use of language, ability to edit.

An explicit discussion of the writing strategies students use for planning, generating ideas, and revising will help students understand that good writing is often a direct result of good writing strategies. (See chapter 2 for a detailed description of teaching about writing process.)

5. *Distinguish between writing competence and linguistic competence.*

Teachers as well as students need to recognize that writing competence and linguistic competence are different. Writing competence encompasses knowledge about writing and writing strategies, which is reflected in the overall coherence of the text. Linguistic competence is knowledge of language code and is reflected in the lexical and grammatical aspects of the text. Students often consider that linguistic competence is more important in good writing. However, when students understand that linguistic competence and writing competence represent different bodies of knowledge, they are more likely to work on both competencies.

6. *Give students the opportunity to develop competence in all four modes of discourse.*

Every foreign language writing class should include assignments that require students to narrate, describe, explain, and persuade. Using simplified tasks, this can be done from the earliest stages of language learning. Chapter 5 deals specifically with teaching students to write in different discourse modes at all levels of language study.

7. *Make reading an integral part of the writing class.*

Although there is no research that deals specifically with the link between reading and writing competence in L2, teachers should capitalize on the potential influence that L2 reading might have on L2 writing. Krashen suggested that students who engaged in "voluntary pleasure reading" (1984, p. 4) proved to be the most competent writers in L1. The problem for FL students involves both the degree to which they are linguistically limited and the concept of voluntarily reading for pleasure in a classroom setting. Students in the earlier stages of language learning are unable to read extensive prose in the target language. Moreover, they are not likely to read for pleasure, unlike ESL students, who are surrounded by readily available newspapers, magazines, and fiction. What FL students can do, on the other hand, is study texts intensively to see the kinds of rhetorical devices used by native-speaker writers. This "text-model" approach can be very beneficial in helping students develop an awareness of characteristics that constitute writing competence. Furthermore, if students are exposed to texts of all kinds in all four language modes from the beginning of language study, they may acquire models for competent FL writing.

8. *Discuss the differences between spoken and written language.*

Given that writing competence is not a mirror image of oral competence, there are several assumptions that teachers should avoid making. First, students who speak well are not always good writers. Likewise, students who write well are not always good speakers. Both teachers and students should understand that oral competence does not imply writing competence. Second, students do not automatically know which lexical items and structures are used primarily in the oral mode. Since many teachers use the communicative approach to classroom language teaching, students hear a great deal of conversational language that may not be acceptable in writing. For example, functions such as greeting, introducing, and stalling for time are typically associated with spoken rather than written language. Students must be taught explicitly that certain structures are more appropriate in spoken than in written texts.

CASE STUDY 1

During the first week of an intermediate-level French course, the students were asked to write an essay in English. The teacher explained that they would be writing four compositions in French during the semester, and that the first step in learning how to write in a foreign language involved evaluating native language writing competence. All students were given the same topic: "It has been said that the mind is like a muscle and studying a foreign language increases its capacity in other areas. Do you agree with this statement? Please explain your opinion." The teacher chose this topic primarily because it would elicit expository and argumentative modes of discourse. After completing the assignment, the teacher evaluated each composition according to the criteria in Figure 1. The 23 students in the class had varying degrees of writing competence. The teacher's evaluation of their work helped them understand the notion of writing competence and its potential relationship to their success in writing in French. The following examples have been selected to show both good and poor writing competence.

Student #1 (female, third-semester college French):

Any athlete knows that when a muscle doesn't get used, or only gets used in the same repetitive pattern, it will atrophy and wither away to almost nothing. In the same manner, when the brain is never exercised, or when it is only used in one thinking pattern, it can also wither away. One way of making sure that one's brain does not atrophy is by making use of different areas of the brain and thinking in new ways. Learning a foreign language is one way to increase the capacity of the brain, both in that and other areas.

There are many ways in which learning a foreign language can improve one's aptitude in other areas. First of all, learning a foreign language forces one to look at the way that we communicate, something which is always taken for granted, in a totally different way. This type of re-examination can be useful in a broad base of subjects, including history, in which one often has to look at an event through other people's eyes, and mathematics, where re-thinking is a critical problem-solving skill. In addition, the process of learning a foreign language requires a great deal of memorization. This type of work "flexes" the brain and prepares it for other material. Finally, although a minor point, knowledge of a foreign language makes it easier to read advanced texts. Because foreign phrases pepper college texts and non-fiction works, the reader is able to get more out of the reading if he has a working knowledge of at least one foreign language.

In conclusion, the mind, like a muscle, needs to be exercised so that it can be used to its full potential. By expanding one's knowledge with pursuits like learning a new language, one can keep the mind in good shape for other endeavors.

This essay has a clearly stated thesis, good supporting arguments, and a logical conclusion. The strength of the essay lies in the ideas and the examples given to justify the ideas. This is a good essay with obvious coherence between sentences and paragraphs. The teacher told the student that she would be likely to write coherently in French and could focus on other areas, such as grammar or vocabulary.

Student #2 (female, third-semester college French):

There are two general ways in which a person is exposed to a language. The first is by hearing and seeing it being used repeatedly. The best example for this is a baby learning to speak. The baby is given new labels for objects. It is able to view life in a different way by using new names that are understood by a large population. As a result of this constant exposure, the child's sense of hearing is sharpened. The baby makes sentences because "they sound right." It's thought patterns are ordered in a new way.

The other way to learn a language is by studying it in a book. For example, the college student. Since the typical college student is only immersed in the language for about one hour a day, it is not heard or spoken easily. The language, for the time being at least, is a thought process that must take place in order to be used. This thought process is made from the same mind that processes other problems that are encountered. It gives the mind new methods for problem-solving.

Probably the most obvious way that learning something such as a language effects someone's capacities in other areas is the new ways of organizing information and studying. These ways of studying are useful in other areas.

This essay, unlike the first one, has no clear thesis, random arguments, and a conclusion unrelated to the preceding ideas. The weakness of the essay lies primarily in its faulty logic and unconnected ideas. There is very little coherence between sentences and paragraphs. In fact, one sentence is incomplete: "For example, the college student." This student was told that she should focus on organization and coherence when writing her compositions in French.

CASE STUDY 2

In order to explore the difference between writing competence and linguistic competence, a college French teacher and a high school French teacher shared their students' writing. They began by analyzing writing samples from students who had studied one year of French. Their first goal was to find students who demonstrated good writing competence despite substantial linguistic constraints. The following example is an essay written by a male high school student who had studied one year of high school French and who spent six weeks in France during the summer.

Sujet: Quel rôle joue la technologie dans la vie actuelle?

Mettez un téléphone. Téléphonez vos amis. Prenez une douche. Conduisez une voiture à votre boulot. Si vous habitez dans la vie moderne, vous avez besoin d'utiliser la technologie. La technologie joue un très grand rôle dans la vie actuelle.

Toutes les choses que les personnes font aujourd'hui utilise la technologie. Essayez d'imaginez une monde sans la technologie. Toutes les voitures ne sont pas là. Personne n'utilise des avions. La communication n'a pas des téléphones. C'est très mal.

Mais, beaucoup de personnes aiment une monde sans la technologie. Parce qu'il n'y a pas des formes de transportation, les personnes marchent et la monde a bon santé. C'est très bon. Maintenant pensez de la communication. Il n'y a pas de courrier et il n'y a pas des téléphones. Pour parler avec quelqu'un, on a besoin de marcher chez lui.

Toutes les choses que j'ai mentionné n'est pas nécessaire dans la monde moderne. Mais, sur l'autre point de vue, est-ce que nous vraiment avons besoin de la technologie? Est-ce que c'est possible que nous faisons beaucoup de problèmes à notre monde parce que la technologie existe? Est-ce que nous avons la dépression parce que nous avons la technologie? Je sais que beaucoup de personnes vraiment n'inquiètent pas de la problème.

On peut voir que la technologie joue un très grand rôle dans la vie actuelle. Encore, si vous regardez à la monde aujourd'hui, vous pouvez voir que toutes les choses utilisent la technologie.

Enfin, si la technologie est bon ou si la technologie est mal, on ne peut pas dire. On sait que la technologie est très importante et je vraiment sais que la technologie joue un très grand et important rôle dans la vie actuelle.

[Subject: What role does technology play in life today?

Put a telephone. Telephone your friends. Take a shower. Drive a car to your work. If you live in modern life, you need to use technology. Technology plays a very big role in life today.

All the things that people do today use technology. Try imagine a world without technology. All the cars are not there. No one uses airplanes. Communication has no telephones. It is very bad.

But, many people like a world without technology. Because there is not forms of transportation, people walk and the world has good health. It is very good. Now, think of communication. There is no telephones. To talk to someone, one needs to walk to his house.

All the things that I mentioned is not necessary in the modern world. But, on the other point of view, really do we need technology? Is it possible that we make many problems to our world because technology exists? Do we have depression because we have technology? I know that many people really aren't worried of the problem.

One can see that technology plays a very big role in modern life. Again, if you look to the world today, you can see that all things use technology.

Finally, if technology is good or if technology is bad, one cannot say. One knows that technology plays a very big and important role in life today.]

This student cleverly states the thesis that technology is necessary by giving examples from everyday life, such as the telephone, running water, and the automobile. He then proposes an opposing view, namely that many people would prefer a world without technology. Using the basic interrogative form *est-ce que*, he then explores the idea that technology may not be a good thing. He concludes with a broad summary statement that brings him back to his main thesis. The essay is organized, logical, and coherent, and he skillfully uses the structures and vocabulary that he has learned. However, there are a multitude of linguistic errors: incorrect word usage, gender mistakes, subject/verb and noun/adjective agreement mistakes, and many anglicisms.

The second step in analyzing the difference between writing competence and linguistic competence involved evaluating compositions written by students who had studied three years of French. The teachers' goal was to find students who showed evidence of acceptable linguistic competence and poor writing competence. The following example is an essay written by a female college freshman in a third-year French grammar and composition course.

Sujet: Lisez cet article écrit en 1887 dans lequel quelques artistes à Paris ont protesté l'érection de la tour Eiffel car ils pensaient qu'elle serait une monstruosité dans leur belle ville historique. Que pensez-vous de leur réaction?

J'ai été surprise que les écrivains, peintres, et sculpteurs ont protesté la tour Eiffel. Il me semble bizarre que les artistes en 1887 ne voulaient pas la tour Eiffel. Aujourd'hui quand quelqu'un me dit le mot "Paris", je pense immédiatement à la tour Eiffel. Je pense que la tour représente la splendeur de la ville de Paris.

L'auteur ne voulait pas l'érection de la tour Eiffel, donc il a parlé d'un ton furieux. Alors, il a dit que les artistes ont cru que la tour Eiffel allait ruiner la majesté de leur ville. Je trouve qu'il est incroyable que les artistes pensaient que la tour était laide. Le nuit, la tour Eiffel est très belle avec beaucoup de lumières. A mon avis, la tour Eiffel est un symbole de pouvoir. Il faut souligner le fait que la tour représente l'imagination et l'originalité de Paris.

Pour résumer, les réactions à la tour Eiffel en 1887 et les réactions en 1994 sont très différentes. En 1887, les artistes n'aimaient pas l'idée de la tour Eiffel parce qu'ils pensaient qu'elle allait détruire la beauté de leur culture. Mais au contraire, en 1994 beaucoup de personnes adorent la tour Eiffel, et ils voyagent pour la voir. Elle est un symbole de splendeur, d'imagination, d'originalité, et du goût unique français.

[Topic: Read this article written in 1887 in which several artists in Paris protested the construction of the Eiffel Tower because they thought that the tower would be a monstrosity in their beautiful and historic city. What do you think of their reaction?

I was surprised that the writers, painters, and sculptors protested the Eiffel Tower. It seems strange to me that the artists in 1887 did not want the Eiffel Tower. Today when someone says the word "Paris" to me, I immediately think of the Eiffel Tower. I think that the tower represents the splendor of the city of Paris.

The author did not want the construction of the Eiffel Tower, so he spoke in a furious tone. Then he said that the artists thought that the Eiffel Tower was going to ruin the majesty of their city. I find it unbelievable that the artists thought that the tower was ugly. At night, the Eiffel Tower is very pretty with lots of lights. In my opinion, the Eiffel Tower is a symbol of strength. It is necessary to underscore the fact that the tower represents the imagination and the originality of Paris.

In summary, the reactions to the Eiffel Tower in 1887 and the reaction in 1994 are very different. In 1887, the artists did not like the idea of the Eiffel Tower because they thought that it would destroy the beauty of the culture. But on the contrary, in 1994 many people adore the Eiffel Tower, and they travel to see it. It is a symbol of splendor, of imagination, of originality and of the unique French taste.]

This essay shows neither a clearly stated thesis nor any real supporting arguments. The student expresses shock at the reaction of the artists in 1887 and states that she personally likes the Eiffel Tower. Furthermore, there is little organization in the presentation of her reaction. The first two sentences of the second paragraph repeat what was said in the first paragraph and are followed by reiterations of her own admiration for the tower. In fact, the essay is characterized by its redundancy; the words "Eiffel Tower" and "tower" are repeated 13 times, once in every sentence except the final one. The most interesting idea, namely that the reactions in 1887 and in 1994 are very different, is stated in the first sentence of the concluding paragraph but is never developed. The language of expression, however, is nearly perfect. Other than a missing subjunctive (*j'ai été surprise que les écrivains . . . ont [aient] protesté*) and one gender mistake (*le [la] nuit*), the essay is grammatically correct.

After this informal study, the teacher-investigators were convinced that students could demonstrate good writing competence and poor linguistic competence as well as good linguistic competence and poor writing competence. They concluded that studying grammar and improving linguistic competence did not necessarily improve students' writing competence.

CONCLUSIONS

The hypothesis that states that writing competence is not language specific implies that a good L1 writer will be a good L2 writer. Foreign language teachers do not view themselves as L1 writing teachers and therefore tend to teach FL writing, focusing more on the surface-level structures than on the global dimensions of written texts. In fact, they are generally teaching language, not writing. In order to teach FL writing, teachers must be confident in their abilities to reach beyond language teaching and teach about writing competence.

Writing competence is something that is acquired over time. Teachers cannot teach writing competence. Rather, they can teach **about** writing competence. Students can learn to define writing competence, to identify the characteristics of good writing and good writing strategies, and to develop a general awareness that can lead to a sense of their own writing competence. Furthermore, they can be taught to think more critically about the differences among several language competencies, such as linguistic, speaking, reading, and writing competence. Helping students to develop an awareness of all the dimensions of writing competence is the first step in teaching students how to write in a foreign language.

TOPICS FOR DISCUSSION AND RESEARCH

1. Analyze the relationship between students' L1 and FL writing competence.
2. Analyze individual student differences in oral competence and writing competence.
3. Analyze individual student differences in grammatical competence and writing competence.
4. Compare the difference between students' FL writing competence in the narrative and the descriptive modes; between the narrative and the expository modes (etc.).
5. Analyze how pleasure reading in L1 affects writing in FL.

6. Determine whether reading model texts in the FL improves writing competence.

7. Evaluate how attitude about writing in L1 and in FL affects FL writing.

8. Devise a measurement instrument for assessing writing competence.

Notes

1. Noam Chomsky defined the term *competence* with regard to language as "the speaker-hearer's knowledge of his language" and *performance* as "the actual use of language in concrete situations" in *Aspects of the Theory of Syntax,* Cambridge, MA: MIT Press, 1965, (p. 4).

2. In *Writing: Research, Theory, and Applications*, Hayward, CA: Alemany, 1984, Krashen uses these terms to describe good writers. Raimes also refers to "getting ideas, getting started, writing drafts, [and] revising" in *Techniques in Teaching Writing*, New York: Oxford University Press, 1983, (p. 6).

3. In *Creative Writing in America: Theory and Pedagogy*, Urbana, Illinois: National Council of Teachers of English, 1989, Moxley describes good writers in these sames terms and rejects teaching students that writing is a linear "plan, prewrite, write, and revise" process (p. 31).

4. Kaplan uses these terms to discuss the characteristics of good writers in "An Introduction to the Study of Written Texts: The 'Discourse Compact,'" *Annual Review of Applied Linguistics*, 1982. Krashen also believes that good writers are aware of their audience rather than being centered on their own writing (*Writing: Research, Theory, and Applications*, Hayward, CA: Alemany, 1984, pp. 17–18).

5. In his book *On Writing Well*, New York, Harper & Row, 1980, Zinsser defines good writing in terms that writers can understand. He advocates simplicity, a personal style with no deliberate garnishing touches, thinking of oneself as the audience, researching words before using them, keeping paragraphs short, and making the beginning and ending as important as the middle of the essay.

6. Kaplan notes in "An Introduction to the Study of Written Texts: The 'Discourse Compact,'" *Annual Review of Applied Linguistics*, 1982 (p. 147), that "individuals from differing linguistic systems come to the writing process not only with differential control of the language and of the writing conventions but also with vastly differing presuppositions about both the process and the product."

7. See the descriptions for writing in the *ACTFL Proficiency Guidelines* published in 1986 by the American Council on the Teaching of Foreign Languages, Hastings-on-Hudson, NY.

8. In "Reading-Writing Connections: Toward a Description for Second Language Learners," in B. Kroll, (Ed.), *Second Language Writing: Research Insights for the Classroom*, New York: Cambridge University Press, 1990, Eisterhold

mentions a study by Canale, Frenette, and Belanger that found that "based on holistic scoring methods, students' L1 and L2 writing was positively correlated, suggesting a common underlying proficiency in writing ability across languages" (p. 95). She also cites Cummins's interdependence hypothesis, which supports the case for transfer of language skills, particularly in reading and writing.

9. In *Teaching Language in Context: Proficiency-Oriented Instruction*, Boston, MA: Heinle & Heinle, 1993, Hadley reviews the theories of Campbell and Wales, Hymes, Savignon, and Munby regarding communicative competence (pp. 3–4).

10. Canale and Swain's model of communicative competence is described in detail in Hadley's *Teaching Language in Context: Proficiency-Oriented Instruction*, Boston, MA: Heinle & Heinle, 1993, (pp. 6–7).

11. See studies by Jones, Jacobs, and Zamel, cited in Krapels' "An Overview of Second Language Writing Process Research," in B. Kroll, (Ed.), *Second Language Writing: Research Insights for the Classroom*, New York: Cambridge University Press, 1990 (pp. 39–41), which indicate that composing competence plays a more important role than linguistic competence in writing. See also Koda's study "Task-Induced Variability in FL Composition: Language-Specific Perspectives," *Foreign Language Annals*, 1993, 26(3):332–346, showing that while there is a relationship between linguistic competence and successful FL/L2 composition performance, linguistic competence alone is an insufficient condition for good FL composition.

12. Eisterhold discusses the affect of L1 and L2 literacy skills on writing and proposes models of inter- and intralinguistic transfer in "Reading-Writing Connections: Toward a Description for Second Language Learners," in B. Kroll, (Ed.), *Second Language Writing: Research Insights for the Classroom*, New York: Cambridge University Press, 1990.

13. Richards believes that writing is difficult to master partly due to the difference between spoken and written discourse. He states that writing is "decontextualized" and must be more explicit than spoken discourse because the "amount of shared knowledge between writer and reader is much less than that usually found between speaker and listener," *The Language Teaching Matrix*. New York: Cambridge University Press, 1990, (p. 101).

14. In *Variation Across Speech and Writing*, Cambridge: Cambridge University Press, 1988 (pp. 199–200), Biber discusses the importance of examining language functions, such as narrating, giving information, or persuading, to determine the similarity or difference between spoken and written texts.

15. Horning's book entitled *Teaching Writing as a Second Language*, Carbondale and Edwardsville, IL: Southern Illinois University Press, 1987, proposes that written language is a distinct linguistic system, very different from spoken language, and must be learned in very much the same way as a second language.

REFERENCES

Arena, Louis A., (Ed.). (1990). *Language Proficiency: Defining, Teaching, and Testing.* New York: Plenum Press.

Biber, Douglas. (1988). *Variation Across Speech and Writing.* Cambridge: Cambridge University Press.

Carson, J. E., P. L. Carrell, S. Silberstein, B. Kroll, and P. A. Kuehn. (1990). "Reading-Writing Relationships in First and Second Language." *TESOL Quarterly* 24:245–266.

Dvorak, Trisha. (1987). "Is Written FL Like Oral FL?" In B. Van Patten, T. R. Dvorak, and J. F. Lee, (Eds.), *Foreign Language Learning: A Research Perspective.* Cambridge, MA: Newbury House.

Edelsky, Carole. (1982). "Writing in a Bilingual Program: The Relation of L1 and L2 Texts." *TESOL Quarterly* 16:211–228.

Eisterhold, Joan Carson. (1990). "Reading-Writing Connections: Toward a Description for Second Language Learners." In B. Kroll, (Ed.), *Second Language Writing: Research Insights for the Classroom.* New York: Cambridge University Press.

Friedlander, Alexander. (1990). "Composing in English: Effects of a First Language on Writing in English as a Second Language." In B. Kroll, (Ed.), *Second Language Writing: Research Insights for the Classroom.* New York: Cambridge University Press.

Hadley, Alice Omaggio. (1993). *Teaching Language in Context: Proficiency-Oriented Instruction.* Boston, MA: Heinle & Heinle Publishers.

Horning, Alice S. (1987). *Teaching Writing as a Second Language.* Carbondale and Edwardsville, IL: Southern Illinois University Press.

Jones, Stan and Jacqueline Tetroe. (1987). "Composing in a Second Language." In A. Matsuhashi, (Ed.), *Writing in Real Time.* Norwood, New Jersey: Ablex Publishing Corporation.

Kaplan, Robert B. (1982). "An Introduction to the Study of Written Texts: The 'Discourse Compact.'" *Annual Review of Applied Linguistics.*

Knoblauch, C. H. and Lil Brannon. (1984). *Rhetorical Traditions and the Teaching of Writing.* Upper Montclair, NJ: Boynton/Cook Publishers, Inc.

Koda, Keiko. (1993). "Task-Induced Variability in FL Composition: Language-Specific Perspectives." *Foreign Language Annals* 26(3):332–346.

Krapels, Alexandra R. (1990). "An Overview of Second Language Writing Process Research." In B. Kroll, (Ed.), *Second Language Writing: Research Insights for the Classroom.* New York: Cambridge University Press.

Krashen, Stephen. (1984). *Writing: Research, Theory, and Applications.* Hayward, CA: Alemany.

Kroll, Barbara (Ed.). (1990). *Second Language Writing: Research Insights for the Classroom.* New York: Cambridge University Press.

Matsuhashi, Ann (Ed.). (1987). *Writing in Real Time: Modeling Production Processes.* Norwood, New Jersey: Ablex Publishing Corporation.

Mills, Carl. (1990). "Syntax and the Evaluation of College Writing: A Blind Alley." In L. A. Arena, (Ed.), *Language Proficiency: Defining, Teaching, and Testing.* New York: Plenum Press.

Moxley, Joseph M. (1989a). *Creative Writing in America: Theory and Pedagogy.* Urbana, Illinois: National Council of Teachers of English.

———. (1989b). "Tearing Down the Walls: Engaging the Imagination." In J. Moxley, (Ed.), *Creative Writing in America: Theory and Pedagogy.* Urbana, Illinois: National Council of Teachers of English.

Murray, Donald M. (1982). *Learning by Teaching.* Montclair, NJ: Boynton/Cook Publishers.

Raimes, Ann. (1983). *Techniques in Teaching Writing.* New York: Oxford University Press.

———. (1987). "Language Proficiency, Writing Ability, and Composing Strategies: A Study of ESL College Student Writers." *Language Learning* 37(3):439–467.

Reed, M., J. Burton and P. Kelly. (1985). "The Effect of Writing Ability and Mode of Discourse on Cognitive Capacity Engagement." *Research in the Teaching of English* 19:283–295.

Richards, Jack C. (1990). *The Language Teaching Matrix.* New York: Cambridge University Press.

Rivers, Wilga. (1981). *Teaching Foreign-Language Skills.* Chicago: University of Chicago Press.

Schultz, Jean Marie. (1991a). "Mapping and Cognitive Development in the Teaching of Foreign Language Writing." *French Review* 64 (6):978–988.

———. (1991b). "Writing Mode in the Articulation of Language and Literature Classes: Theory and Practice." *The Modern Language Journal* 75 (4):411–417.

Valdes, Guadalupe, Paz Haro, and Maria Paz Echevarriarza. (1992). "The Development of Writing Abilities in a Foreign Language: Contributions toward a General Theory of L2 Writing." *The Modern Language Journal* 76(3):333–352.

Zamel, Vivian. (1983). "The Composing Processes of Advanced ESL Students: Six Case Studies." *TESOL Quarterly* 17:167–187.

Zinsser, W. K. (1980). *On Writing Well.* New York: Harper & Row.

Chapter 2
The Foreign Language Writing Process

Hypothesis: *The foreign language writing process differs from the native language writing process.*

The L1 writing process
> Theoretical perspectives
> A process model
> Generating ideas
> Revising
> Recursive writing
> Constraints in the writing process
> An argument against prescriptive approaches

The ESL writing process
> The question of accuracy
> Research perspectives
> The *Monitor Theory*

The FL writing process
> Models for the process approach
> Research with *Système-D*
> Revising and *Système-D*

The writing process: the classroom implications

Case Study

Conclusions

Topics for discussion and research

THE FOREIGN LANGUAGE WRITING PROCESS

Hypothesis
The foreign language writing process differs from the native language writing process.

The concept of writing as "a process" means that writing is a succession of actions undertaken to bring about some desired result.[1] These actions may include planning, generating ideas, organizing, analyzing, synthesizing, and revising. In order to carry out these actions, all writers use strategies of some kind in both their native language and in a second language. The writing process in L1 and L2, therefore, consists of a set of actions and the strategies used to complete those actions.

Recent research attests to the complexity of the writing process. Writing is clearly not a simple act, but rather an intricate set of steps and choices. Furthermore, there is no such thing as a natural or normal process for writing. Each writer has a unique approach and uses different strategies to produce a text. However, student writers are not always aware of the strategies that they use for either L1 or L2 writing. Their attention is typically focused on the product, or the text, and not on the process, or the cognitive strategies that they use while writing. It is likely that many student writers engage in the complex process of writing in both L1 and L2 without a clear sense of the strategies that may be effective or ineffective.

While writers may transfer what they **know** about writing from L1 to L2, as discussed in chapter 1, they may not **do** the same thing when they write in L1 as when they write in L2. The hypothesis governing the organization of this chapter postulates that the L1 and the FL writing processes are different. More specifically, it suggests that when writers undertake a writing task in L1, they use different strategies than when they undertake a writing task in the FL. While the set of actions involved in the writing process, such as planning, generating ideas, organizing, revising, etc., may be the same in L1 and FL, the strategies necessary to carry out those actions may differ when writing in the FL. That is, **how** students plan or generate ideas in L1 may be different from how they plan or generate ideas in the FL. In order to understand the differences between the L1 and the FL writing process, this chapter will review the theories and research about the writing process in L1 and in ESL, ultimately pointing to a theory of the FL writing process.

THE L1 WRITING PROCESS

In English composition theory, the process of writing is currently being given much attention. The act of writing and the dynamics of composing represent relatively new areas of inquiry; however, studies undertaken during the past two decades have increased our understanding of this complex field of study. Rather than focusing only on the product, teachers are recognizing the importance of trying to analyze and understand writing as a dynamic process:

> Recently . . . the focus of research on composition has shifted. Rather than investigating what students write, teachers and researchers are beginning to study the composing process itself. They are now working under the assumption that before we know how to teach writing, we must first understand how we write (Zamel, 1982, 196).

A review of the recent theories and empirical research on the writing process in English composition points to the importance of this field of inquiry.

☐ THEORETICAL PERSPECTIVES

A theory central to an understanding of the writing process is the idea that writing is an activity that brings about the discovery of meaning. That is, in seeking to express ideas clearly, the writer finds new associations between thoughts, ideas, and opinions.

> As a fundamental mode of thought and self-expression, writing integrates, organizes, connects, and stimulates perception and learning . . . [it is] an **integrative** and **generative** process of discovering and shaping meaning (Moxley, 1989, 26).

Murray (1980), one of the first scholars to define writing as "discovery," states that "writing is a significant kind of thinking in which the symbols of language assume a purpose of their own and instruct the writer during the composing process" (p. 3). He identifies three fundamental stages of writing: *rehearsing, drafting*, and *revising*. Within each of these three stages, he considers that there are four forces that interact quickly, often at a nearly subconscious level, as the writing evolves: collecting, connecting, writing, and reading. He contends that all of these operations occur constantly and often simultaneously during the writing process.

The concept of writing as an activity of discovery precludes any notion that a text is a preconceived or static message. By this definition, the writing process is dynamic, with the writer and text interacting actively. As a writer sets about the task of writing, the recurring question is "How can/should I say this so that I make myself understood?" The subsequent searching for ways to organize, synthesize, restate, and clarify invokes cognitive strategies and composing behaviors that are both actions and reactions in a quest for meaning.

☐ A PROCESS MODEL

While theories about writing can be helpful to teachers in that they show how process-oriented writing can be viewed in a variety of ways,[2] real insight about writing can only come from studying what writers actually do when they write. Based on an analysis of think-aloud protocols done by writers, Flower and Hayes (1981) proposed a very comprehensive problem-solving model of the L1 writing process.[3] Their model includes *planning, translating,* and *reviewing.* They describe planning as the process of forming an internal, relatively abstract representation of the knowledge that will be used in writing. Generating ideas, organizing, and goal setting are involved in the planning process. Translation is described as the process of putting ideas into language. Since the images, or kinetic sensations, in a writer's mind may not be directly linked to syntactical language, the writer engages in a kind of translation in order to concretize the ideas. As an example of translation, the Flower and Hayes point out the complex processes involved in trying to capture the movement of a deer on ice in language (p. 373). Reviewing, which involves evaluating and revising, can occur at any time during the act of writing.

While Flower and Hayes believe that there is a hierarchical ordering of the processes involved in writing, they do not consider the overall process to be a sequence of stages activated in a linear fashion. In their view, the process of writing involves a set of optional actions that a writer may choose to use during the act of writing:

> Writing processes may be viewed as the writer's tool kit. In using the tools, the writer is not constrained to use them in a fixed order or in stages. And using any tool may create the need to use another. Generating ideas may require evaluation, as may writing sentences. And evaluation may force the writer to think up new ideas (Flower and Hayes, 1981, 376).

In addition to planning, translating, and reviewing, Flower and Hayes describe complex subprocesses that may come into play throughout the writing process. The subprocesses that are most commonly discussed are *generating ideas, revision,* and *recursiveness.*

□ GENERATING IDEAS

Typically, generating ideas is the first step in writing a composition. Deciding what to say about a topic is often more difficult for writers than determining how to say it. Writers may generate ideas in a variety of ways, such as making notes, reading, or discussing ideas. Long-term memory and task requirements play key roles in idea generation. That is, the writer devises a plan based on the assignment, and this plan involves the retrieval and organization of information stored in long-term memory.

In a study on idea generation, Caccamise (1987) focused on the constraints imposed by *long-term memory, topic familiarity, the writing task,* and *the audience.* With regard to long-term memory, she describes an internal constraint imposed upon writers by their pre-existing experience and knowledge of the world:

Individuals produce an idea and, depending on their knowledge base, elaborate on it, develop it in depth, forming a cluster of closely related ideas. Then they move on to another idea which begins a whole new cluster of closely related ideas. This process is engaged recursively until the subjects decide that they have exhausted the topic (Caccamise, 1987, 242).

Moreover, in analyzing how writers approach a given topic, she found that the subjects were able to generate more ideas when dealing with a familiar topic. Concerning the writing task, she found that when given a specific topic, subjects demonstrated a lower rate of idea generation (ideas per minute) than when they were given a general topic. Finally, as for the audience, she found that the subjects were constrained by trying to decide what ideas retrieved from long-term memory were most appropriate:

> These results suggest that attempting to account for intended audience during the idea-generation phase is achieved only at the cost of the quality of the ideas themselves because (not surprisingly) knowledge of intended audience does not appear to be stored with subject matter. A model of efficient writing, then, should probably recommend that when writing for unfamiliar audiences one should first generate ideas with total disregard for intended audience; later, recast the ideas to reflect the needs of the intended audience (Caccamise, 1987, 246).

□ REVISING

Another component of the writing process crucial to successful writing is revising. This process involves reading, examining, changing, and correcting the text. In a study of revision strategies, Faigley and Witte (1981) propose a model based on two kinds of changes that writers can make when revising their texts: *surface changes* and *meaning changes*. Surface changes include such things as spelling, tense, modality, punctuation, additions, deletions, and consolidations that do not alter the meaning, or the gist, of the whole text. Meaning changes include additions, deletions, substitutions, permutations, distributions, and consolidations that alter the meaning, or summary, of the whole text. Faigley and Witte compared the revision strategies of three groups of writers: inexperienced students, advanced students, and expert adults. Their results indicate that these three groups of writers revise their texts differently. Specifically, the data show that inexperienced writers make more surface changes and fewer global meaning changes than expert writers.

Matsuhashi (1987b) argues that it is important to observe revisions as they occur in real time, since it reveals the traces of the writing process and can illustrate a writer's shifting focus of attention and pattern of decision making. She points out that revision is not only the final editing that is usually associated with the third part of the "think-write-rewrite" model but also an ongoing process of repair:

> Revision is clearly a complex phenomenon, initiated by a range of creative impulses, reflecting not only repair but a constant reevaluation of the evolving text and the writer's mental representation of that text (Matsuhashi, 1987b, 201).

She also points out that to inexperienced writers, revision can feel like a trap rather than an opportunity because their attention is focused on low-level problems of generating and inscribing the text when they are under the pressure of real-time processing. She suspects that this problem is due primarily to an inability to look beyond the text to consider the mental representation of the text as a whole.

In a study on methods for facilitating revision, Matsuhashi (1987b) found that the presence of the text played a key role in the writers' ability to revise. The subjects who were asked to "revise" by rereading their essay, putting it aside, and then listing five new things to incorporate into the text, performed better than those who were simply told to revise their essay or those who were told to add five new things to their essay.

> When the writer plans additions to an unseen text . . . the plans are based on a mental representation of the text. The opportunity to plan—free from both the presence of the text and from the efforts of prose production—offers an incentive to work exclusively with the idea structure of the text (Matsuhashi, 1987, 204).

□ RECURSIVE WRITING

All research points to the fact that writing is a recursive, nonlinear process. That is, writers move backward and forward in the text, adding and deleting, and repeating certain steps during the writing process. For example, a writer might continue to modify an introductory paragraph during the entire writing process in an attempt to achieve coherence in meaning. According to Perl (1980), the two most obvious recursive elements are rereading little bits of discourse and returning to a key word called up by the topic. Perl also refers to a third recursive element in writing, which is more difficult to define, since it involves a non-verbal sense or feeling that a writer experiences during writing:

> . . . the move is not to any words on the page nor to the topic but to feelings or non-verbalized perceptions that **surround** the words, or to what the words already present **evoke** in the writer. The move draws on sense experience, and it can be observed if one pays close attention to what happens when writers pause and seem to listen or otherwise react to what is inside of them (Perl, 1980, 365).

Perl maintains that this elusive recursive move involves "retrospective structuring" and "projective structuring." Retrospective structuring entails constructing tangible meaning in words from a sense or a feeling, similar to Flower and Hayes's notion of "translation." Projective structuring is the writer's ability to make meaning intelligible and compelling to others. Perl believes that these two processes are central in composing, the former relying on the ability to go inside oneself, the latter relying on the ability to go beyond oneself.

□ CONSTRAINTS IN THE WRITING PROCESS

The research in L1 writing clearly indicates that writing is an active and complex process. This process, which engages the writer fully in multiple and simultaneous acts, is demanding, often difficult, and potentially stressful.

> As a dynamic process, writing is the act of dealing with an excessive number of simultaneous demands or constraints. Viewed in this way, a writer in the act is a thinker on a full-time cognitive overload (Flower and Hayes, 1980, 33).

According to Flower and Hayes (1980), these constraints, which affect both what a writer writes and how a writer goes about doing it, are *knowledge, written speech,* and *the rhetorical problem.* Knowledge is the information stored in memory as well as the integration of bits of information into a coherent whole. The writer must retrieve knowledge and create a comprehensible arrangement of what is known. Since writers may be writing about something that they have neither thought about nor spoken about, they clarify for themselves and for the audience the analysis and the synthesis of this knowledge through writing. Written speech refers to the linguistic and discourse conventions peculiar to written prose. The rules that a typical writer has about written discourse include being specific, repeating ideas for emphasis, referring back for coherence, not repeating words or phrases in close proximity, etc. The rhetorical problem consists of the writers' purpose, their sense of the audience, and their imagined roles. This dimension, according to Flower and Hayes, "should direct the entire process of generating knowledge and language" (1980, p. 40) and can be the task that frustrates writers the most.

In discussing how a writer might juggle these constraints, Flower and Hayes (1980) believe that human beings are not able to handle a large number of simultaneous demands on attention. These simultaneous demands create "cognitive strain," which refers to the demands placed on short-term memory or conscious attention. They suggest that in order to juggle converging constraints and to reduce cognitive strain, writers may use some of the following strategies:

- □ ignore a constraint, such as concern about the audience
- □ divide and subdivide the problem, reducing it to manageable segments
- □ set priorities

- □ use a familiar routine or well-learned procedure
- □ plan not just what to say, but also take into account the real purpose (i.e., write a French composition for a grade)
- □ plan how to compose (i.e., free-write first, then organize ideas, then stop for a day, then rewrite, etc.) (Flower and Hayes, 1980, 40)

□ AN ARGUMENT AGAINST PRESCRIPTIVE APPROACHES

Given the theories about writing as a process, teachers are likely to want students to concentrate on the composing process in the writing class. This focus on the process approach to teaching writing has raised some concern. For example, Selzer (1984) supports the process models and theories of composition, but he questions the validity of implementing a prescriptive approach to teaching composition. He believes that each student writer may have several different composing styles or habits that may vary according to the writing tasks. He also maintains that students who appear to be using inferior planning or revising strategies may be doing so, not out of ignorance, but because the assignment may have been unimportant or uninteresting. Furthermore, Selzer argues that when students are required to follow a prescriptive model of composing strategies, their writing may ultimately suffer. Since most real-life writing is different from academic writing because of the audience, the writer's familiarity with the subject, the time constraints, and the importance of the assignment, teachers should prepare students to use a variety of composing strategies.

> Instead of prescribing a single composing model and instead of making assignments appropriate only to that model, teachers need to concentrate on expanding and directing students' composing repertoires, in much the same way they expand and direct students' stylistic repertoires . . . Students need to be introduced to new overall composing sequences and to various inventing, arranging, and revising tactics that they have never tried but that may prove useful in certain circumstances (Selzer, 1984, 282–283).

THE ESL WRITING PROCESS

Theories and research in L1 writing have been the primary basis for most theories in ESL writing. The *process approach*, or the view that writing is an activity comprising multiple actions and strategies, is prevalent in ESL composition instruction as in L1 composition instruction. Moreover, ESL writing, like L1 writing, is considered to be an act of discovering and creating meaning.[4] Silva (1990) describes ESL writing as "purposeful and contextualized communicative interaction, which involves both the construction and transmission of knowledge"

(p. 18). In fact, this view of writing, or the *cognitive view*, which holds that students identify the problem, plan, explore, and arrive at a conclusion, has had a primary effect on ESL composition research and teaching.[5]

□ THE QUESTION OF ACCURACY

While the process-nature of writing is currently an issue of importance in ESL composition theory and research, the focus on language (or accuracy) plays a far greater role in ESL than in L1. Zamel has pointed out that in ESL, the focus on the product—or the written composition—has been greater than in L1 composition theory or practice given the attention to grammar and accuracy:

> ESL teachers concerned with language acquisition and error analysis emphasize, even more than other writing teachers, correctness and form (Zamel, 1982, 196).

> ESL writing continues to be taught as if form preceded content, as if composing were a matter of adopting preconceived rhetorical frameworks, as if correct language usage took priority over the purposes for which language is used (Zamel, 1983, 167).

□ RESEARCH PERSPECTIVES

As stated previously, most theories of the ESL writing process are based directly on theories from L1. Likewise, the research questions for the ESL writing process are similar to those from L1. Researchers in ESL are interested in how ideas are generated and developed and how the writer revises the content and the form of the text. Research indicates that, despite the language constraint, the writing process in ESL is often similar to writing in L1 in that it is a recursive, nonlinear process. Some studies show that there is a difference in writing processes between skilled and unskilled ESL writers; however, most of them engage in the discovery and creation of meaning by planning, rereading, and revising.

Zamel's (1982) study involved an interview with eight proficient ESL writers from different language backgrounds who were no longer enrolled in ESL writing courses and who were successfully completing their university writing assignments. Her findings indicate that the students were most influenced by what happened before the actual writing began. Classroom discussions as well as familiarity with the topic were cited as very important. Some students reported having "internal dialogues" to determine how to proceed; others said that they read the composition aloud to an imaginary listener to assess its clarity; and nearly all the students stated that formal outlines were rarely, if ever, used. Moreover, students indicated that they needed time to think about what they were writing, both before and during the actual writing. A surprising finding of the study was that the most proficient writer admitted that she wrote her composition in her own language, and then translated it into English. The student claimed that her flow of thought was uninterrupted in her own language and therefore her expression was not inhibited (p. 201). While Zamel does not discuss the use of translation as a viable composing strategy, she suggests that it is not necessarily an ineffective strategy:

> This student, in resorting to translation, however, did not in fact contradict any of the experiences reported by the other students; rather it corroborated the fact that writing and creating seem to be simultaneous and reciprocal (Zamel, 1982, 201).

In another study, Zamel (1983) investigated the degree to which ESL students experienced writing as a process of discovering and creating meaning and how writing in a second language affected this process. By observing students as they wrote, recording what they wrote, and conducting interviews at the end of the study, Zamel was able to describe several characteristics of ESL composing strategies. One of the major findings was that planning and generating ideas did not precede writing but rather were ongoing processes, thus showing that students writing ESL compositions were involved in "the constant interplay of thinking, writing, and rewriting" (p. 72). These findings corroborate those in the L1 writing process research, giving evidence that L1 and ESL composing strategies are very similar. In fact, she found that the linguistic problems were of little concern to the students. The development of their ideas did not stop when they encountered lexical and syntactic difficulties; rather, they devised strategies to avoid being sidetracked by any linguistic difficulties. These strategies included leaving blank spaces, circling the problem word, or writing the word in the native language. Zamel's study suggests that skilled ESL writers intuitively recognized the importance of first making meaning and then working on linguistic accuracy.

In a study of ESL students with different levels of language proficiency, Raimes (1987) used audiotaped think-aloud protocols to analyze several aspects of their composing strategies. Raimes reports that the students showed evidence of planning, rehearsing, rescanning, rereading the topic, and revising. While she found that they did very little planning, they frequently used rehearsing to complete an idea after writing a few words, they rescanned sentences they had just written, they referred to the topic mostly in the prewriting stage, and they revised and edited during the writing process and not at the end as a final cleanup operation. She noted that rehearsing was a more important composing strategy than revising. Coincidentally, Raimes also found that a specified purpose and audience had no observable effect on the subjects' composing strategies. She suggests that more is needed than just surface wording of the assigned topic in order to shift students' awareness away from the teacher/evaluator as reader.

□   THE *MONITOR THEORY*

In a different vein, Jones (1985) explores the use of a *monitor* as it relates to the writing process. The *Monitor Theory*, as proposed by Krashen, posits that language learning, as opposed to language acquisition, involves a conscious knowledge of the rules, and that learned FL competence is available only through a monitor, that checks and corrects output.[6] Krashen further proposes that some students may be monitor overusers, editing their speech to such a degree that they are unable to achieve fluency. Other students may be monitor underusers, speaking freely but completely unconcerned by errors. The ideal situation would be to promote optimal monitor use, allowing sufficient editing without provoking excessive concern for accuracy. In relating the monitor theory to second-language writing, Jones suggests that overuse of the monitor can be an important source of nonlinguistic difficulty:

> The problem is that the writer relies on conscious knowledge to evaluate the grammaticality of the sentences she produces, and this conscious "monitoring" of syntactic form takes precedence over other parts of the process (such as generating ideas and connecting them, and organizing them for the audience). Underuse of this monitor may also affect composing . . . (Jones, 1985, 97).

In a study comparing the composing processes of two students, one a monitor overuser and the other a monitor underuser, Jones videotaped his subjects during the act of writing, and determined that monitor use could be studied by analyzing the subjects' pauses and revisions. The results of his research show that the monitor overuser paused more frequently and for longer periods than the monitor underuser and seldom revised the text once it was written down. The monitor underuser paused less frequently and for shorter periods and made many editing changes in the text. Jones states that even though the monitor overuser performed better on grammatical tests than the underuser, their texts had a similar number of errors. These results suggest that monitoring does not lead to improved writing and may in fact be a detriment. Heavy monitoring takes time due to frequent stops and starts, and it also interferes with the overall unity of the text, since attention is given primarily to short chunks and surface features. Jones's study gives evidence that when writers monitor heavily, they work with only limited amounts of text, pause frequently to polish short segments, and move forward very slowly. By contrast, writers who do not use the monitor are more likely to write longer pieces of text, revising later.

THE FL WRITING PROCESS

Most theories that we have about FL writing are based largely on research in L1 and ESL writing. FL writing is also considered to be a complex process that involves various steps and cognitive strategies that are necessary to achieve a comprehensible product. However, there is very little research on the FL writing process. Since teachers often design writing assignments to practice and evaluate the students' command of grammatical structures, they may not have much experience with the processes involved in composing and communicating in writing. Many questions remain unanswered about the FL writing process, and there is a great need for theories and empirical research in foreign language that can point to a theory of the FL writing process and to the development of credible approaches to teaching FL writing.

□ MODELS FOR THE PROCESS APPROACH

There are several models for teaching FL writing that are similar to the process models in L1 and ESL writing instruction. Hewins (1986) proposes a five-step model that is designed to engage students in the process of writing with minimal teacher intervention:

1. prewriting: talking, brainstorming for ideas and vocabulary
2. first draft: students write straight through using available vocabulary
3. feedback: comments on content only from peers or teacher
4. second draft: student revises and rewrites based on peer and/or teacher comments
5. proofreading: student writer and peer read, concentrating on errors (Hewins, 1986, 223)

She insists, furthermore, that the writing assignment should be relevant to the students' lives, and should include a specified audience and a reason for writing.

Like Hewins, Barnett (1989) presents a model for teaching students to engage in the process of writing. Students are directed to make notes about their ideas, to organize their notes, to write a first draft without being overly concerned with grammar or vocabulary, to write a second draft several days later, paying more attention to grammar and vocabulary, and to type a final version to hand in. Although these models are somewhat linear and prescriptive, following a prewrite-write-rewrite format, they represent an initial attempt to view FL writing as a process that involves more than manipulating grammatical structures.

□ RESEARCH WITH *SYSTÈME-D*

Recently, *Système-D* (Noblitt, Solá, and Pet, 1992), has become a tool for research. *Système-D* is a writing assistant that provides students of French with access to a bilingual dictionary, a verb conjugator, a reference grammar, a vocabulary index, and a phrase index. In addition to the dictionary and the indices that students can consult while writing, there is a tracking device that records student inquiries. Every time a student looks up a word, an expression, an example, or a verb conjugation, the tracking device lists the inquiries in chronological order. The list, or log, provides a way of seeing how students go about writing. Figure 1 shows a sample log with a code explanation.

In a pilot study, Bland et al. (1990) and Noblitt and Bland (1991) investigated the use of the **Système-D** tracking device. By studying the kinds of lexical inquiries that students made, they suggest that the tracking device can be an

---

Figure 1: Sample *Système-D* Log with Code Explanation

SAMPLE LOG

1. 16:37:52		B:COMP1		
2. 16:40:23	DE	born	be born	*naître*
3. 16:40:57	DEX	(example)	be born	*naître*
4. 16:41:30	DEC	(conjugate)	be born	*naître*
5. 16:41:45	DT	(Passé Composé)	*naître*	be born
6. 16:43:31	DF	foyer	home	
7. 16:45:02	IVN	(note)	personality	
8. 16:48:34	IGN	(note)	*avoir* EXPRESSIONS	
9. 16:53:26	IPN	(note)	describing people	
10. 16:59:55		B:COMP1		

CODE EXPLANATION

1. Logged on to write COMP1 at time indicated.
2. Looked up *born* in the English dictionary and got a match. (DE = Dictionary English.)
3. Looked at example of word used in a sentence. (DEX = Dicitionary English example.)
4. Looked at summary conjugation screen for *naître*. (DEC = Dictionary English conjugate)
5. Looked at the expanded screen for verb in *passé composé*. (DT = Dictionary tense.)
6. Looked up *foyer* in French dictionary and got a match. (DF = Dictionary French.)
7. Looked at the "personality" screen in vocabulary index. (IVN = Index vocabulary note.)
8. Looked at *avoir* EXPRESSIONS in grammar index. (IGN = Index grammar note.)
9. Looked at "describing people" in phrase index. (IPN = Index phrases note.)
10. Logged off at the time indicated.

(Taken from pedagogical materials used by the author.)

important tool for exploring the learners' mental conception of L2 as well as the language learning process. In another study using the tracking device, Scott and New (1994) investigated certain aspects of the FL writing process. The study involved 21 intermediate-level students of French who were given a variety of writing assignments, each one including specific directions to seek information from the grammar, vocabulary, and phrase indexes in *Système-D.* Before the students actually wrote, the teacher discussed the topics and the information available in the databases with the students. When the students handed in their compositions, the log of inquiries was attached.

By analyzing the logs of student inquiries as well as the corresponding compositions, Scott and New were able to describe specific features of the FL writing process. While they did not take into account the kinds of strategies that preceded the writing task, such as planning and generating ideas, they devised an evaluation instrument, shown in Figure 2, that reports the strategies used by students writing in French with *Système-D.*

Figure 2: *Système-D* Log Analysis

1=NEVER	2=SELDOM	3=AVERAGE	4=OFTEN	5=VERY OFTEN

Section A:

Adherence to guidelines	1	2	3	4	5
Example inquiry	1	2	3	4	5
Conjugation inquiry	1	2	3	4	5
French dictionary inquiries	1	2	3	4	5
Circumlocution in French	1	2	3	4	5
Circumlocution in English	1	2	3	4	5
Browsing	1	2	3	4	5
Error avoidance	1	2	3	4	5
Recursive approach	1	2	3	4	5
Final revising	1	2	3	4	5

Section B:

English dictionary dependence: ____low ____avg ____high

Quality of lexical inquiries: ____low ____avg _____high

Time on task: _____ lines / _____ minutes

(Taken from Scott and New, 1994.)

One of the most frequently used strategies that they analyzed was dictionary use. Most students were clearly English-French dictionary dependent and rarely looked up examples of the lexical items used in context. This finding was particularly interesting in light of the fact that students whose compositions were considered good, both stylistically and grammatically, showed less English-French dictionary dependence. Furthermore, some good writers showed creative use of the French-English dictionary, testing hypotheses that they had about a word they had heard or read previously. Another significant observation was that most students seemed to begin at the beginning and write continuously until the end of the composition, rarely editing the work already written. Only one student showed clear evidence of recursive, or nonlinear, writing. Her composition and corresponding log revealed that she was constantly in the process of rereading and revising her composition. The case study at the end of this chapter analyzes this student's writing process in detail.

□ REVISING AND *SYSTÈME-D*

The preliminary findings of the research with the **Système-D** tracking device show that this approach provides a method for analyzing some components of the FL writing process. However, this approach has certain limitations. For example, the log does not indicate what students are doing when they are not looking up information in the databases. Important aspects of the writing process, such as pause time and textual additions and deletions, are not documented on the log.

In a study designed to provide further information about the FL writing process, New (1994) videotaped students while they were writing with **Système-D.** As expected, students focused almost entirely on revisions for form, such as spelling, word choice, and verb conjugations. The students rarely made clausal or sentence changes. Moreover, they revised their texts more when writing than they did when asked to revise a composition that they had written during a previous writing session. New concluded that students perceived a finished text as "fixed" and less easily adaptable to later revisions. With regard to pause time, students spent an average of three hours for a writing session with as much as one hour of the session spent not writing. Postwriting questionnaires indicate that the students were rereading their work during the pause time. It is interesting to note that, despite a relatively long period of time spent not writing, the majority of the revisions were for form rather than content.

THE WRITING PROCESS: THE CLASSROOM IMPLICATIONS

As noted previously, teaching FL writing has typically been viewed as another way to work on grammar and accuracy. However, research in the writing process (or the entire repertoire of strategies that writers use before, during, and after they write) has changed our view of writing. This new perspective is changing the way that teachers teach writing, namely shifting the focus from the product to the process. In fact, textbooks in L1, ESL, and FL indicate that this shift in focus has already taken place. Students are directed to identify and use effective strategies as part of the composition assignment.

While there is little research that specifically studies the FL writing process, there is much information to be gleaned from research in L1, ESL, and FL. It would be clearly unwise to propose a single prescriptive approach to teaching FL writing, however, all of the theories and research in L1, ESL, and FL writing process strategies give us a solid foundation from which to suggest classroom practice. The following suggestions point to a new way of teaching about the FL writing process.

1. *Teach **about** the FL writing process.*

Every student will have a different set of writing strategies based on both formal and informal past experiences, and will go about the writing process in a slightly different way. For this reason, the instructional approach must take individual student differences into account.

> Course design . . . should include instruction and practice with strategies: how to deal with . . . their own merging text, how to generate ideas on a topic, how to rehearse ideas, and how to consider the options prior to devising a plan for organizing their ideas. Students need to learn, too, how to rescan their texts and which questions to ask to revise and edit more effectively. Often students exhibit these processes but their strategies are not efficient. The students make a plan, they read, they question, they rescan their text, they search for errors—but all in a very general, almost haphazard way (Raimes, 1987, 460).

Teaching FL writing involves explicit instruction about the writing process so that students learn to develop their own effective FL writing strategies.

2. *Discuss the L1 writing process.*

Students are not likely to be aware of the processes that they use to write in L1 and are even less likely to be conscious of the processes they use for FL writing. In fact, the language constraint imposed by the target language is probably the only aspect of the FL writing process that students are aware of. Therefore, the first step in teaching the FL writing process is to have students identify their own L1 writing strategies so that they will recognize the complexity, the challenge, and the frustration involved in the L1 writing process. The questionnaire in Figure 3 will help students analyze and articulate what they do when they write in L1.

Once students are aware of the strategies they use for writing in L1, they are more likely to want to explore strategies that may be unique to the FL writing process. By using the questionnaire in Figure 4, teachers can direct students' attention to effective and ineffective strategies for writing in the FL.

3. *Teach writing as discovery.*

The importance of writing in FL takes on new meaning in light of the notion that writing is an act of discovery.[7] Theories that describe writing as a kind of thinking activity that brings about the discovery of meaning suggest that language, or words, can function as a stimulus for configuring meaning in new

---

Figure 3: Writing Process Questionnaire

When writing in your **native language** . . .

1. Do you get your ideas mostly from thinking, reading, or discussing?
   Explain:

2. Do your ideas take the shape of **images** or **words**?
   Explain:

3. Do new and different ideas come to you before or during writing?
   YES _____ NO _____
   Explain:

4. Do you make a formal outline before beginning to write?
   YES _____ NO _____
   Explain:

5. Do you reread your work while writing?
   YES _____ NO _____
   Explain:

6. Do you imagine who your audience is?
   YES _____ NO _____
   Explain:

7. Do you revise or change your work?
   YES _____ NO _____
   Explain:

8. Do you prefer writing with pencil and paper or with a computer?
   Explain:

(Taken from pedagogical materials used by the author.)

ways. In teaching FL writing, the writing process can be approached as an activity during which the target language becomes the stimulus for ideas and discovery.

When students are given a composition topic, they have a natural tendency to generate elaborate ideas. These ideas may be in images or in the native language but are unlikely to be in the target language. Under these circumstances, writing becomes a tedious task of translating the images and the native language into meaningful FL. And, as most teachers know, this process can have unfortunate results. In FL writing, words and expressions in the target language should become the guiding principle as students engage in planning, generating ideas, and writing. By using FL words and expressions as a means of generating ideas, student writers will be engaged in two kinds of discovery: the discovery of language in a specific sense and the discovery of ideas. For example, after being assigned a composition topic, students should be instructed to make lists of

---

Figure 4: Foreign Language Writing Process Questionnaire

When writing in a **foreign language** . . .

1. Do you write down your ideas in your native language or in the foreign language?
   Explain:

2. Do you use your textbook while you are writing?
   YES _____ NO _____
   Explain:

3. Do you use a grammar reference while you are writing?
   YES _____ NO _____
   Explain:

4. Do you use a dictionary while you are writing?
   YES _____ NO _____
   Explain:

5. Do you translate from your native language to the foreign language while you write?
   YES _____ NO _____
   Explain:

6. Do you revise and correct grammar errors?
   YES _____ NO _____
   Explain:

7. Do you revise the ideas and content?
   YES _____ NO _____
   Explain:

(Taken from pedagogical materials used by the author.)

verbs, adjectives, or adverbs that they think will be useful in expressing their ideas. Given this task, their focus is narrowed and they are likely to engage in "language play," such as looking for synonyms or antonyms. As they engage in this activity, they are likely to learn new words and expressions as well as to discover previously unforeseen ways of thinking and writing about the topic.

4. *Provide a new perspective on grammar and writing.*

If, as suggested previously, teachers explicitly teach students to use the target language and engage in the process of discovery while writing, they will create a natural link between grammar and writing. However, the link will not be in the traditional terms of good grammar = good writing. Rather, the link will be in terms of grammar (i.e., language) = discovery. In other words, grammar should be thought of in conjunction with the writing process and not the writing product. Students can be taught to shift their focus from thinking of writing as a linguistic exercise in which quality is measured by the degree of accuracy, to thinking of writing as an activity in which linguistic information can help them shape their ideas.

When Zamel (1982, 206) states that "extensive research has shown that grammar study may have little to do with composing," she is suggesting that teaching grammar and teaching composition are not the same thing. While this is a legitimate point, it does not necessarily mean that curriculum changes need to be made to separate these two areas of study. A course that combines the study of grammar and composition can be very effective in that it can teach students to understand the crucial distinction between learning grammar and learning effective writing strategies. Research tells us that inexperienced ESL and FL writers are focused on linguistic accuracy, nearly to the point of obsession. In a grammar and composition course, teachers have the opportunity to explicitly teach students to avoid this fixation on the product and to use grammar as a tool during the writing process.

5. *Redefine "creative" writing.*

When we move away from viewing writing as a kind of grammar exercise, we often adopt the idea that composition is creative writing. However, the word *creative* is problematic in that it often means that students are relying on "inspiration" of some sort. Some research indicates that students often subscribe to the "think-it-say-it" model of composing, perhaps even believing in a mythical good writer who would know exactly what to say.[8] Therefore, when they cannot think of anything to say, or when they are not inspired by some mythical source, they believe that they are poor writers.

In order for students to learn to be good FL writers, they need to understand creative writing in appropriate terms. The kind of creativity that we typically associate with poets or novelists is not at all what we want FL students to attempt. In FL writing, we want students to create personal meaning with the target language, not to engage in free-flowing creative thought. If teachers can remove the burden of creativity and teach the art of discovery, of engaging in creative play with language, students will be more likely to succeed.

6. *Design writing assignments that engage students in the writing process.*

Since the writing assignment is often considered to be a grammar exercise, the topic is chosen to elicit certain linguistic features. A typical assignment might be to "summarize your daily activities" (reflexive verbs) or "describe your favorite family member" (adjectives) or "tell about your vacation last summer" (past tenses). However, students are capable of recognizing the real focus of this kind of writing assignment, namely linguistic accuracy. Research tells us that the quality of a composition is more directly related to the composing strategies used by the writer than to the mastery of linguistic structures. Therefore, the composition assignment represents the first step in leading the student writer away from a concept of writing as a linguistic exercise and toward an exploration of the process-nature of FL writing.

Many new textbooks include writing assignments that are designed to teach students how to engage in the process of FL writing. Generally, students are directed to do various prewriting tasks, such as making lists or outlines, and then are reminded to reread their work. It is important to note that these assignments often follow a plan-write-revise model, which may suggest to students that writing is a linear process. Teachers need to help students develop effective strategies for each phase of the writing process.

A *task-oriented approach* to writing assignments addresses the process-nature of FL writing from a different vantage point.[9] In this approach, an assignment consists of a situation, or context, and specific tasks for meeting the requirements of the situation.[10] Figure 5 shows a task-oriented writing guideline.

At first glance, this task-oriented approach does not appear to engage students in the FL writing process because it signals the grammar, vocabulary, and phrases necessary to carry out the assignment. However, indicating the linguistic dimensions of the writing assignment serves as a link between a language and a process exercise. Rather than discouraging the process-nature of writing, the tasks can engage students in several aspects of the FL composing process. First, they decrease the cognitive demands on the students by providing an outline that includes specific reference to helpful grammatical and lexical information. Second, the tasks serve as a point of departure for brainstorming and idea generation in FL, consequently discouraging direct translation. Furthermore, the outline frees students from overall concerns of coherence and allows them to work on cohesion within sentences and paragraphs. Finally, the link between language function and linguistic structure within tasks helps students work equally on meaning and form, thereby avoiding an exclusive focus on accuracy.

7. *Discuss the intended audience.*

Another consideration inherent in assigning a composition topic is the intended audience. Assignments such as writing letters, newspaper articles, or academic essays are realistic and implicitly include an intended audience. In fact, many teachers assign compositions that explicitly give the intended audience, such as another student in the class or a fictitious pen pal. While some studies indicate that a composition topic that includes a purpose and an audience has no effect on the students' composing strategies,[11] other studies have shown that specifying an audience may inhibit the process of generating ideas.[12] Regardless, students writing in a FL have so many demands that further adding to those demands by designating an audience may prove to be detrimental rather than beneficial. Students should perhaps be guided to tailor their text to a specified audience **after** it is written.

Figure 5: Task-Oriented Writing Guideline

SITUATION: You are writing an informative article about American children for a French magazine.

TASKS:

1) *Comment est une famille américaine?*
   Describe a typical American family.
      *PHRASES: Writing an essay; Describing people
      *VOCABULARY: Family members
      *GRAMMAR: Adjective agreement; Adjective position

2) *Comment sont les enfants américains?*
   Write what a typical American child does each day, telling what he or she does, doesn't do, how he or she looks and dresses.
      *PHRASES: Linking ideas; Weighing alternatives
      *VOCABULARY: Clothing; Games; Sports
      *GRAMMAR: Negation; Nouns after *c'est, il est*

3) *Quand j'étais enfant . . .*
   Describe how you were as a child, what you did, the holidays and traditions that you liked, etc.
      *PHRASES: Sequencing events
      *VOCABULARY: Personality; Time expressions
      *GRAMMAR: *Imparfait; Passé composé*; Verbs with auxiliary *être*

4) *Les enfants sont . . .*
   Conclude with a generalization about children.
      *PHRASES: Writing an essay

*indicates the categories in ***Système-D***

(Taken from pedagogical materials used by the author.)

8. *Assess the time necessary to carry out the writing task.*

When we talk about writing and time, we are referring to the actual time involved in the whole writing process, from the moment the topic is assigned until the finished product is turned in to the teacher. There is no question that time has an effect on the strategies used by a writer. If there is a time constraint, the writer is likely to use different kinds of strategies than if there is unlimited time. However, it is most likely that students think of the time involved in writing a composition only as the time spent engaged in the physical activity of writing. In teaching writing, the productive use of time is essential. Teachers must allot time for thinking about a topic, discussing it with peers or with the teacher, and making notes that link ideas to the target language. During the actual writing, they will need time for pauses to think, reread, or just rest, as well as time to revise.

9. *Teach students effective strategies for generating ideas.*

The first step in writing is generating ideas, a process that invokes complex cognitive skills. As students try to decide what they will write about, they use long-term memory to retrieve information about the topic. In L1 writing, this long-term memory retrieval is likely to be related to the topic. That is, ideas come from stored knowledge and experiences directly related to the topic. These ideas may be stored in long-term memory in the form of language, or they may be stored as concepts and kinetic images not yet formulated in words. Moreover, if the topic is familiar to the writer, there will be more ideas than if the topic is unfamiliar.

In FL writing, idea generation and the use of long-term memory are far more complex. First of all, students are unlikely to distinguish consciously between long-term memory information on the topic and information on the language of expression. In fact, the writer may consider the linguistic information, or grammar, stored in long-term memory more important than the ideas on the topic. This confounding of topic information and grammar information in long-term memory may impede the idea-generation phase of the FL writing process. Furthermore, if the topic is culturally related and somewhat unfamiliar to the writer, generating ideas will be even more difficult, since the writer will have less related information stored in long-term memory. Finally, since ideas are not always initially formulated in words, students are doubly challenged: they must first translate their feelings, images, or ideas into words, and second, those feelings, images, and ideas must be expressed in the target language.

Since generating ideas in FL writing can be a very complex activity, students require explicit guidance in this undertaking. In the prewriting phase, when students are engaged in some kind of brainstorming activity, they must be taught to distinguish between ideas on the topic and language of expression. At lower levels of language proficiency, there are two basic approaches to guiding students in generating ideas. One possibility is to allow students to generate ideas in L1 and then to help them identify the linguistic structures that will transfer their ideas into the FL. For example, if students are asked to write an essay about an important social issue (i.e., racism, pollution, drug abuse, etc.), they could begin by identifying their opinions on the topic in their native language. Making notes and organizing ideas helps students focus on generating ideas that are relevant and interesting to them. After generating ideas in L1, they need explicit guidance in determining how to communicate their ideas without translating directly from L1 to the FL. Figure 6 shows a worksheet designed to be used in the target language to help students work on the linguistic aspects of their essay after they have generated ideas in L1.

Figure 6: Sample Worksheet for Writing an Essay

(Designed for use in target language)

Topic of the essay:

Ten key words in the essay:

Express your opinion using the following expressions:
In my view . . .
It is clear / evident that . . .
It appears that . . .

Link two ideas with several of the following words:
and, but, therefore, so, consequently, although, nevertheless

Compare two ideas with several of the following expressions:
X is comparable to Y.
X is similar to Y.
X is like / unlike Y.
similarly, X and Y are . . .
on one hand X is . . . whereas on the other hand Y is . . .

Contrast two ideas with several of the following expressions:
Unlike X, Y is . . .
In contrast to X, Y is . . .
Y contradicts X in that . . .

Conclude your essay with one of the following expressions:
In summary . . .
In conclusion . . .
Finally . . .

(Taken from pedagogical materials used by the author.)

Another approach to guiding students during the idea generation is to use familiar lexical items and linguistic structures in the FL to generate ideas. For example, if students are asked to write a description of their own personality, teachers can use triggers from the FL to guide students in generating ideas. Figure 7 shows a worksheet designed to be used in the target language to help students generate ideas in the FL. Finally, regardless of the approach, teachers must recognize that idea generation in FL writing is a far more complex process than idea generation in L1. Teachers need to play an active role in helping students in this initial phase of the FL writing process.

Figure 7: Sample Worksheet for Generating Ideas

(Designed for use in the target language)

Topic: Describe your personality.

Underline the adjectives that describe you best:

intellectual	athletic	quiet
naïve	boring	loud
lazy	enthusiastic	anxious
serious	intelligent	calm
crazy	dull	depressed
optimistic	hopeful	diligent
realistic	active	perfectionistic
pessimistic	adventuresome	loving

Use the dictionary to find five more adjectives that describe you:

Use some of the following expressions as you describe yourself:

always	rarely	often
occasionally	never	regularly
in the morning	during the day	at night
with my friends	with my parents	on a date
when I'm tired	when I meet someone	at a party
when it's rainy	when it's sunny	on a trip

(Taken from pedagogical materials used by the author.)

10. *Address the issue of translation honestly.*

Translating from the native language to the target language may be the most natural, spontaneous strategy that students use when writing in the FL. For some students, whose overall language competence is very high, translation can be an effective strategy.[13] However, all teachers have come across sentences such as *Quoi est droit pour vous n'est pas droit pour moi* ("what's right for you is not right for me"), suggesting that for most students translation can be disastrous. For this reason, teachers generally consider translation the most ineffective writing strategy possible.

Even though teachers discourage translation, students "cheat" and rely on it in writing when other strategies seem to fail. Why is translation such a natural strategy and why is it so difficult? Translation is natural because most students think of the FL as being "another version" of L1. They often believe that there is an exact match for every word in L1 rather than understanding that there are culturally and linguistically different ways of expressing meaning in the FL. Moreover, translation is difficult because of the complex cognitive processes that are involved when writing in the FL. The term *translation*, as defined by Flower and Hayes (1981), refers to translating ideas and images into language. They explain that "the writer's task is to translate a meaning, which may be embodied in key words . . . and organized in a complex network of relationships, into a linear piece of written English" (p. 373). When students write in the FL, just as in L1, they activate the cognitive processes involved in translating ideas into language. However, for the FL student, this often means translating ideas into L1 and then translating L1 into the FL. In order to help students confront this challenge, teachers can focus on the idea-generation phase of the writing process, using familiar words and expressions in the target language to guide students in their writing. Teachers may not be able to stop students from translating, but they can talk openly with students about why translation is, or is not, an effective FL writing strategy.

11. *Teach students to revise.*

The word *revise* carries many meanings for both teachers and student writers. It could suggest rereading for linguistic, or surface errors, or it may mean adding and deleting content material in an attempt to refine the clarity of the text. Furthermore, it could be an activity that is done after writing or one that is ongoing throughout the writing process. In any case, the teacher needs to specify what is required of the students with regard to revision.

When students are taught to revise their compositions, there are several effective strategies that can be taught explicitly. First, they should learn to reread their text frequently while they are writing. This rereading should be slow and deliberate rather than skimmed, especially at the lower levels of proficiency. That is, students should read aloud, or rehearse, either in their heads or by voicing.

Rehearsing is an important composing strategy for editing what is already on the page as well as for generating new ideas.[14]

Second, students should reread their text for content and organization as a separate activity from rereading their text for linguistic accuracy and clarity of expression. Research shows that students rarely edit the content, but rather focus on changes in the form. With regard to form, students need explicit direction as they do a close reading of their work in order to learn to check for common linguistic errors such as subject-verb agreement, noun-adjective agreement, tense use, etc. (See chapter 5 for further details about evaluating errors.) Modifications of the content are far more difficult and require the writer to generate new ideas or to rethink the development of the ideas. Matsuhashi's (1987) research suggested that the presence of the text can be a distraction. She found that when students are actually faced with the text as they are trying to revise the content, they are often less successful than when they put the text aside and make notes on areas that they want to change. Finally, teachers must decide whether a formal rewriting of the composition should be part of the students' work. If a formal rewriting of the composition is required, students should be given credit for a first draft to ensure that they put an equal amount of effort into both versions of their text.

12. *Develop an awareness of a monitor.*

Krashen's (1982) theory of the monitor posits that learned competence is available only through a monitor, or editor, that checks and corrects output. The monitor theory is usually used in reference to oral competence and describes how individuals differ in their reliance on the monitor: overusers rely heavily on the monitor, resulting in hesitant speech, while underusers do not monitor their speech and therefore make frequent errors. Research shows that the monitor plays a role in writing as well and that writers may be monitor overusers or underusers.[15] As in speech, heavy monitoring does not necessarily result in better writing.

According to Krashen (1982), the two conditions necessary for monitor use are time and focus on form. Since the act of writing allows students more time than speech, and since writing is often perceived as an exercise in form, or structure, students are likely to engage in heavy monitor use during the FL writing process. In fact, monitor overuse in the writing mode may well be perceived by students as a natural and necessary part of the FL writing process. Monitor overuse may also lead to frustration; students may think that if they cannot write correctly in the FL, they cannot write at all.

Teachers can help students avoid heavy monitor use during writing in two ways. First, they can discuss the concept of monitor use in FL learning. An awareness of the concepts of monitor overuse, underuse, and optimal use in FL learning can provide students with tangible ways to evaluate their own language learning behaviors. Second, teachers can encourage students to practice freewriting during which they focus only on the flow of ideas and not on accuracy. Students need to be given the opportunity to experiment with writing without fear of reprimand for surface errors. Monitor overuse may trap the student in the revising phases of the writing process and prevent them from moving freely between other phases such as generating ideas, writing, rereading, and revising. Teachers can help students develop an awareness that monitor use is potentially detrimental to the writing process.

13. *Include a writing conference in the instructional approach.*

The writing conference can take place either before or after a teacher has read a student composition. When the conference occurs prior to reading a composition, it is typically very student-centered, since the teacher has limited knowledge about what the student wrote. The students are likely to want to explain what they wrote as well as any problems they may have encountered while writing. This kind of conference can be a positive and productive experience for both student and teacher. A conference that occurs after the teacher has read a student's composition can also be very beneficial. In this situation, the teacher is likely to ask questions and make suggestions for improvement. It is important to ask open-ended questions that promote cooperation, such as "Can you tell me more about this?" rather than questions that feel like a trap, such as "Do you think that this is clear?"[16] When teachers demonstrate genuine interest in their students' writing, students are more likely to invest themselves seriously in their work. Moreover, when students are questioned about how they actually went about writing a composition, they become increasingly aware of the importance of using effective composing strategies. The writing conference, therefore, is likely to have an influence both on the writing product and the writing process.

CASE STUDY

A graduate teaching assistant at Vanderbilt University[17] decided explore the FL writing process through informal postwriting conferences with her intermediate-level French students. All students in the course were required to use ***Système-D*** and had to turn in their compositions with the corresponding log of inquiries. (The ***Système-D*** tracking device logs inquiries that students make to the database while writing. See Figure 1 for a sample log and interpretation of the code.) First, using the instrument designed to interpret the log shown in Figure 2 (Scott and New, 1994), the TA analyzed each student's composition and its corresponding log of inquiries. The example that follows is part of one student's composition and log. The numbers 1–14 in the composition correspond to the numbers on the log.

Nous sommes allés à Boulder en avion. J'avais (5) peur pour une moment, parce que l'avion a agité (7) quand nous avons atterri (6). De toute facon, Boulder est une belle ville (1), et elle a beaucoup de divertissements (2). La ville est entourée par (3) les Rockies, qui sont très magnifique (4). Il y a une grande université, L'Université de Colorado. La ville n'est pas trop grande, et les gens (10) y sont tres sympathique. Le temps faisait beau. Il faisait (12) soleil, et assez chaud.

Pendant nos vacances en Boulder, ma famille et moi avons fait une nouvelle activité (14) chaque jour. Nous avons visité (8) le bureaux de niveaux (9) américain, les musées, et nous avons mangé à beaucoup de restaurants. Et puis nous sommes allés aussi (11) voir une pièce au théâtre de l'université. Mon père et mon frère aimaient grimper (13) sur les montagnes, pendant ma mère et moi aimaient faires les courses. A mon opinion, Boulder est une ville fantastique . . .

Log:					
	19:28:43	DE	place	seat, place	*asseoir*
1.	19:29:14	DE	city	city, town	*ville*
	19:29:26	DEN	(note)	city, town	*ville*
2.	19:31:01	DE?	amusements	amuse	*divertir*
	19:31:25	DFS	(scroll)	*divertissements*	diversion
3.	19:36:38	DE	surrounded	surrounded	*entouré*
	19:37:12	DE	by	by	*par*
4.	19:38:39	DF	*magnifique*	*magnifique*	magnificent
	19:40:26	IVN	Means of transportation		
5.	19:42:51	DF	*avoir*	*avoir*	have
	19:43:04	DFC	(conjugate)	*avoir*	have
	19:43:19	DT	(*Imparfait*)	*avoir*	have
6.	19:43:53	DF?	*decollier*	*décoller*	unstick, take off
	19:44:09	DE	land	land	*atterrir*
7.	19:45:50	DE	shake	wave, shake	*agiter*
	19:46:02	DEC	(conjugate)	wave, shake	*agiter*
8.	19:54:19	DF	*visiter*	*visiter*	visit
	19:54:30	DFC	(conjugate)	*visiter*	visit
9.	19:56:06	DE?	standards	level, standard	*niveau(x)*
10.	20:04:15	DF	*gens*	*gens*	people
	20:04:21	DFN	(note)	*gens*	people
11.	20:09:17	DE	also	also	*aussi*
12.	20:15:39	IPN	(note)	Describing weather	
	20:17:20	DFC	(conjugate)	*faire*	make, do
	20:17:42	DT	(*Imparfait*)	*faire*	make, do
13.	20:20:39	DE	climb	climb	*grimper*
14.	20:29:05	DF?	*activite*	*activité*	activity

(Taken from Scott and New, 1994.)

By comparing this composition and log, the TA made the following notes about this student's writing process:

It appears that this student seeks information in the databases and uses it to piece together her intended meaning in a completely nonlinear fashion:

The words *ville* (1) and *divertissements* (2) are at the beginning of the log, but they don't appear in the composition until the third sentence. The words *entourée par* (3) and *magnifique* (4) appear in the fourth sentence. At this point, the student looks up "means of transportation" and probably finds the word *avion*, which is used in the first and second sentences. To describe her reaction to the plane flight, she finds the imperfect conjugation of *avoir* and writes *j'avais peur* (5) in the second sentence. Then she searches for a way to say "to land," first looking up *decollier* and getting a match, but then choosing to use *atterrir* (6) in the second sentence. She goes back and adds *l'avion a agité* (7), which is grammatically incorrect but very meaningful. *Visité* (8) and *niveaux* (9) in the second paragraph indicate that she continued to describe what she did before adding the description about *les gens* (10) at the end of the first paragraph. She looks up *aussi* (11) and uses it in the third sentence of the second paragraph and then accesses information on describing weather and uses that in the last two sentences of the first paragraph (12). She looks up *grimper* (13) and uses it in the second to last sentence and then finds the word *activité* to use in the first sentence of this paragraph.

There is also evidence of other strategies:

She circumlocutes in both English and French. She looks up "place" and is not happy with the match *asseoir* and uses "city" instead. Later she uses her intuition and looks up *decollier* in French and gets the closest match, *décoller*, but chooses to use "land", or *atterrir*, instead. This may also be evidence of error avoidance.

The student takes the time to read information screens. After looking up "city" and *gens*, she reads the notes to see these words used in context. She is also willing to check the conjugation screens for several verbs to verify that she is spelling them correctly.

After analyzing all the students' compositions and logs, the TA scheduled postwriting conferences to discuss her reactions. She indicated such things as overuse of the dictionary, the value of browsing in the databases for generating ideas, and the importance of revising throughout the writing process. She found that the students were very interested in talking about their writing. For example, they discussed when and why they consulted the dictionary, whether the examples of words used in context were helpful, and whether it was useful to browse in the databases. Although the postwriting conferences were very time consuming, the

TA concluded that using the log and the log evaluation helped students gain insight into their FL writing process and motivated them to work on their writing.

CONCLUSIONS

Research in the L1, ESL, and FL writing process points to several notions about teaching writing. First of all, teaching about the process is teaching writing. The entire writing process, from getting an assignment to handing in a finished product, involves many phases and complex cognitive strategies. Each writer uses strategies that are, to some degree, unique and that result from both experience and learned behavior. The strategies that a writer uses are directly related to the writing outcome: good writers use effective strategies, whereas poor writers use ineffective strategies. Therefore, teaching effective writing strategies will directly influence the writing product.

The second notion about teaching writing follows logically, namely that teaching effective writing strategies is essential. However, in order to teach effective strategies, we must first identify them. Research in L1 composition documents the complexity of the writing process and indicates the strategies used by good writers. Many of those effective strategies are directly transferable to ESL and FL writing. However, some strategies, such as those used for generating ideas, translating those ideas into words, and revising the text take on different characteristics during the FL writing process. While the FL writing process may be similar to the L1 writing process in many ways, there are strategies that are unique to the FL writing process. Teachers must help students identify effective strategies as they teach about the FL writing process.

Finally, teaching FL writing is teaching a unique kind of problem solving. As students write, they must tackle the problems involved with expressing meaning clearly and accurately in the FL. Teaching students how to manage both the form and content of their writing is traditionally part of the composition curriculum. However, teaching students the art of solving problems that are specific to the FL writing process is a new notion. FL teachers and students are faced with a new challenge: the FL writing process is as important, if not more important, than the FL composition itself.

TOPICS FOR DISCUSSION AND RESEARCH

1. Have students generate ideas from a topic given in FL and from lexical/ grammatical stimuli in FL. Compare the quality and quantity of the ideas generated from the topic stimulus with those generated from the linguistic stimulus.

2. Give students a writing topic in FL that is related to the target culture and that is somewhat unfamiliar. Have one group generate ideas in L1 and another in FL. Compare the quality and quantity of ideas generated by the two groups. Repeat the experiment using a topic that is familiar and related to the L1 culture.

3. Analyze how/when students use translation from L1 to the FL as a writing strategy.

4. Assess the quality of compositions for students who have been engaged in a writing conference with their teacher and students who have not had direct interaction with their teacher.

5. Analyze how and to what degree students revise their texts when they write in FL.

6. Examine how one might determine whether a writer is a monitor overuser, underuser, or optimal user. Analyze the FL writing process of each kind of monitor user.

7. Analyze the differences in the writing process of novice, intermediate, and advanced students of FL.

Notes

1. The term *process* as it relates to writing has never been clearly defined. Susser ("Process Approaches in ESL/EFL Writing Instruction," *Journal of Second Language Writing* 3(1):31–47, 1994) points out that the term has often been used incorrectly to refer to a theory or theories of writing. He clarifies that process is a component of many different theories of writing, including expressionist and cognitive theories.

2. In "Competing Theories of Process: A Critique and a Proposal," *College English* 48(6):527–542, 1986, Faigley identifies three basic ways of viewing process-oriented writing: the *expressive* view, which stresses that writing is a discovery of the true self, the *cognitive* view, which describes writing as problem solving, and the *social* view, which holds that writing, rather than being an act of private consciousness, is a representation of the individual as a constituent of a culture. In "What Composition Theory Offers the Writing Teacher," in L. A. Arena, (Ed.), *Language Proficiency: Defining, Teaching, Testing*, New York: Plenum Press (1990), Dyer recognizes Faigley's three views of writing and adds two more: the *tagmemic* view, which considers writing as an invention involving four stages and three heuristics to deal with them, and the *dramatistic* view, which looks upon writing as an invention involving act, scene, agent, and purpose.

3. In their study "A Cognitive Process Theory of Writing," *College Composition and Communication* 32(4):365–387, Flower and Hayes determined that the act of writing involves a process of solving problems and the model includes

three major elements: the task environment, the writer's long-term memory, and the writing process.

4. Murray ("Writing as Process: How Writing Finds Its Own Meaning," in Timothy R. Donovan and Ben W. McClelland, (Eds.), *Eight Approaches to Teaching Composition*, Urbana, IL: National Council of Teachers of English, 1980) and Moxley ("Tearing Down the Walls: Engaging the Imagination," in J. M. Moxley, (Ed.), *Creative Writing in America: Theory and Pedagogy*, Urbana, IL: National Council of Teachers of English, 1989) describe native language writing as an activity that brings about the discovery of meaning.

5. In "L1 Composition Theories: Implications for the Developing Theories of L2 Composition," in B. Kroll, (Ed.), *Second Language Writing: Research Insights for the Classroom*, New York: Cambridge University Press, 1990, Johns discusses the effect of the cognitive view on approaches to teaching ESL writing.

6. The most complete description of Krashen's monitor theory can be found in his book *Principles and Practice in Second Language Acquisition*, New York: Pergamon Press, 1982.

7. See note 4 for references to theories about writing and the discovery of meaning.

8. Flower and Hayes discuss creative writing in "The Dynamics of Composing: Making Plans and Juggling Constraints," in L. Gregg & E. Steinberg, (Eds.), *Cognitive Processes in Writing*, Hillsdale, NJ: Lawrence Erlbaum, 1980, p.32.

9. For more information about task-oriented writing, see Scott "Task-Oriented Creative Writing with *Système-D*" (*CALICO Journal* 7(3):58–67, 1990) and "Write From the Start: A Task-Oriented Developmental Writing Program for Foreign Language Students" (in Robert M. Terry, (Ed.), *Dimension: Language '91*. Valdosta, GA: Southern Conference on Language Teaching, 1992).

10. See Scott and Terry "Teacher's Guide: *Système-D* Writing Assistant for French," Heinle & Heinle Publishers, 1992, for task-oriented exercises for writing at all levels of language study.

11. See, for example, Raimes's study, which provides evidence that a composition topic that includes a purpose and an audience has no effect on the students' composing strategies ("Language Proficiency, Writing Ability, and Composing Strategies: A Study of ESL College Student Writers," *Language Learning* 37(3):439–467, 1987).

12. According to Caccamise ("Idea Generation in Writing," in A. Matsuhashi, (Ed.), *Writing in Real Time: Modeling Production Processes*, Norwood, NJ: Ablex Publishing Corporation, 1987), research shows that specifying an audience inhibits idea generation.

13. In "The Composing Processes of Advanced ESL Students: Six Case Studies," *TESOL Quarterly* 17(2):165–187 (1983), Zamel found that some good

writers **do** write their compositions in their native language and then successfully translate the work to the foreign language.

14. Raimes discusses the concept of rehearsing as part of the revising process in "Language Proficiency, Writing Ability, and Composing Strategies: A Study of ESL College Student Writers," *Language Learning* 37(3):439–467, 1987.

15. In "Problems with Monitor Use in Second Language Composing," in M. Rose, (Ed.), *When a Writer Can't Write*, New York: The Guilford Press, 1985, Jones studies monitor use in ESL writers and states that heavy monitoring during the writing process takes time and does not lead to improved writing.

16. In a study on how instruction fits into the writing process, Freedman and Katz examined the student-teacher interaction and its influence on composing. By focusing specifically on the comments and questions made by both a teacher and a student during a conference prior to reading the composition, they assessed the effectiveness of this kind of a conference. Their results show that overall structure of the conference follows a predictable pattern, including primarily teacher initiation, student response, and teacher evaluation. They found this kind of verbal interaction to be more student-centered than in the usual teaching-learning situation, and therefore ultimately a positive experience for the student. They further identified two kinds of teacher questions: exam questions for which the teacher has the answer and real questions for which there is no predictable answer. They suggest that real, or open-ended, questions are more productive, since they encourage collaborative problem solving rather than teacher-directed solutions. ("Pedagogical Interaction During the Composing Process: The Writing Conference," in A. Matsuhashi, (Ed.), *Writing in Real Time: Modeling Production Processes*. Norwood, NJ: Ablex Publishing, 1987.)

17. Elizabeth New, currently an Assistant Professor of French at the University of North Texas, spent many hours analyzing student compositions and corresponding logs during her Ph.D. studies at Vanderbilt University. Her work provided much insight into the FL writing process.

REFERENCES

Barnett, Marva A. (1989). "Writing as Process." *The French Review* 63(1):31–44.

Bland, Susan Kessner, James S. Noblitt, Susan Armington & Geri Gay. (1990). "The Naïve Lexical Hypothesis: Evidence From Computer-Assisted Language Learning." *Modern Language Journal* 74:440–450.

Caccamise, Donna J. (1987). "Idea Generation in Writing." In A. Matsuhashi, (Ed.), *Writing in Real Time: Modeling Production Processes*. Norwood, NJ: Ablex Publishing Corporation.

Chomsky, Noam. (1965). *Aspects of the Theory of Syntax*. Cambridge, MA.: The M.I.T. Press.

Donovan, Timothy R. and Ben W. McClelland. (1980). *Eight Approaches to Teaching Composition*. Urbana, IL: National Council of Teachers of English.

Dyer, Patricia. (1990). "What Composition Theory Offers the Writing Teacher." In L. Arena, (Ed.), *Language Proficiency: Defining, Teaching, Testing*. New York: Plenum Press.

Faigley, Lester and Stephen Witte. (1981). "Analyzing Revision." *College Composition and Communication* 32(4):400–414.

Faigley, Lester. (1986). "Competing Theories of Process: A Critique and a Proposal." *College English* 48(6):527–542.

Flower, Linda and John R. Hayes. (1980). "The Dynamics of Composing: Making Plans and Juggling Constraints." In L. Gregg & E. Steinberg (Eds.), *Cognitive Processes in Writing*. Hillsdale, NJ: Lawrence Erlbaum.

———. (1981). "A Cognitive Process Theory of Writing."*College Composition and Communication* 32(4):365–387.

Freedman, Sarah Warshauer and Anne Marie Katz. (1987). "Pedagogical Interaction During the Composing Process: The Writing Conference." In A. Matsuhashi, (Ed.), *Writing in Real Time: Modeling Production Processes*. Norwood, NJ: Ablex Publishing Corporation.

Gregg, Lee W. and Erwin R. Steinberg (Eds.). (1980). *Cognitive Processes in Writing*. Hillsdale, NJ: Lawrence Erlbaum.

Hayes, John R. & Linda S. Flower. (1980). "Identifying the Organization of Writing Processes." In L. Gregg & E. Steinberg (Eds.), *Cognitive Processes in Writing*. Hillsdale, NJ: Lawrence Erlbaum.

Hewins, Catherine. (1986). "Writing in a Foreign Language: Motivation and the Process Approach." *Foreign Language Annals* 19:219–223.

Johns, Ann M. (1990). "L1 Composition Theories: Implications for the Developing Theories of L2 Composition." In B. Kroll, (Ed.), *Second Language Writing: Research Insights for the Classroom*. New York: Cambridge University Press.

Jones, Stan. (1985). "Problems with Monitor Use in Second Language Composing." In M. Rose, (Ed.), *When a Writer Can't Write*. New York: The Guilford Press.

Kowal, Sabine and Daniel C. O'Connell. (1987). "Writing as Behavior: Myths, Models, Methods." In A. Matsuhashi, (Ed.), *Writing in Real Time: Modeling Production Processes*. Norwood, NJ: Ablex Publishing Corporation.

Krapels, Alexandra R. (1990). "An Overview of Second Language Writing Process Research." In B. Kroll, (Ed.), *Second Language Writing: Research Insights for the Classroom*. New York: Cambridge University Press.

Krashen, Stephen. (1982). *Principles and Practice in Second Language Acquisition*. New York: Pergamon Press.

Kroll, Barbara (Ed.). (1990). *Second Language Writing: Research Insights for the Classroom*. New York: Cambridge University Press.

Matsuhashi, Ann (Ed.). (1987a). *Writing in Real Time: Modeling Production Processes*. Norwood, NJ: Ablex Publishing Corporation.

———. (1987b). "Revising the Plan and Altering the Text. In A. Matsuhashi, (Ed.), *Writing in Real Time: Modeling Production Processes*. Norwood, NJ: Ablex Publishing Corporation.

Moxley, Joseph M. (1989). "Tearing Down the Walls: Engaging the Imagination." In J. M. Moxley, (Ed.), *Creative Writing in America: Theory and Pedagogy*. Urbana, IL: National Council of Teachers of English.

Murray, Donald M. (1980). "Writing as Process: How Writing Finds Its Own Meaning." In T. R. Donovan and B. W. McClelland (Eds.), *Eight Approaches to Teaching Composition*. Urbana, IL: National Council of Teachers of English.

New, J. Elizabeth. (1994). "Revision Strategies in French as a Foreign Language: Case Studies in Computer-Aided Writing." Ph.D. dissertation, Vanderbilt University.

Noblitt, James S. and Susan K. Bland. (1991). "Tracking the Learner in Computer-Aided Language Learning." In B. Freed, (Ed.), *Foreign Language Acquisition Research in the Classroom*. Lexington, MA: D.C. Heath.

Noblitt, James S., Willem J. A. Pet, and Donald Solá. (1992). *Système-D*. Boston, MA: Heinle & Heinle Publishers.

Odell, Lee. (1980). "Teaching Writing by Teaching the Process of Discovery: An Interdisciplinary Enterprise." In L. W. Gregg and E. R. Steinberg, (Eds.), *Cognitive Processes in Writing*. Hillsdale, NJ: Lawrence Erlbaum.

Perl, Sondra. (1980). "Understanding Composing." *College Composition and Communication* 31:363–369.

Raimes, Ann. (1987). "Language Proficiency, Writing Ability, and Composing Strategies: A Study of ESL College Student Writers." *Language Learning* 37(3):439–467.

Rose, Mike (Ed.). (1985). *When a Writer Can't Write*. New York: The Guilford Press.

Selzer, Jack. (1984). "Exploring Options in Composing." *College Composition and Communication* 35(3):276–284.

Scott, Virginia M. (1990). "Task-Oriented Creative Writing with *Système-D*." *CALICO Journal* 7(3):58–67.

——— . (1992). "Write From the Start: A Task-Oriented Developmental Writing Program for Foreign Language Students." In R. M. Terry, (Ed.), *Dimension: Language '91*. Valdosta, GA: Southern Conference on Language Teaching.

——— and Robert M. Terry. (1992). *Teacher's Guide: Système-D Writing Assistant for French*. Boston, MA: Heinle & Heinle Publishers.

——— and Elizabeth New. (1994). "Computer Aided Analysis of Foreign Language Writing Process." *CALICO Journal* 11(3):77–90.

Silva, Tony. (1990). "Second Language Composition Instruction: Developments, Issues, and Directions in ESL." In B. Kroll, (Ed.), *Second Language Writing: Research Insights for the Classroom*. New York: Cambridge University Press.

Steinberg, Erwin R. (1980). "A Garden of Opportunities and a Thicket of Dangers." In L. W. Gregg and E. R. Steinberg (Eds.), *Cognitive Processes in Writing*. Hillsdale, NJ: Lawrence Erlbaum.

Susser, Bernard. (1994). "Process Approaches in ESL/EFL Writing Instruction." *Journal of Second Language Writing* 3(1):31–47.

Zamel, Vivian. (1982). "Writing: The Process of Discovering Meaning." *TESOL Quarterly* 16(2):195–209.

——— . (1983). "The Composing Processes of Advanced ESL Students: Six Case Studies." *TESOL Quarterly* 17(2):165–187.

Chapter 3
Writing and Computers

Hypothesis: *Computer-aided writing enhances the FL writing experience.*

WRITING AND COMPUTERS

Hypothesis
Computer-aided writing enhances the FL writing experience.

Computers are not new in the field of FL teaching. For more than a decade, many teachers have used computers to help students learn linguistic structures. Software with discrete point exercises to practice such things as verb conjugations and vocabulary provides students with immediate feedback and reduces tedious grading for teachers. Various authoring programs that allow teachers to design their own software to reinforce or test discrete language structures have further helped take mechanical language manipulation out of the classroom.

While using computers for FL drill work is not a new idea, the notion that students can use computers to write compositions is gaining favor in FL programs. Computer labs and word processing programs are available at many high schools and colleges, and some FL teachers are beginning to take advantage of these resources. However, questions remain about the benefits of using word processing for FL writing. In order to describe how computer-aided writing can enhance the FL writing experience, this chapter will examine theories and research in the use of computers for writing in L1, ESL, and FL.

COMPUTERS IN THE ACADEMIC SETTING

Writing with computers, or using word processing programs, has become an integral part of our academic lives. Teachers have access to computers for writing instructional materials or for writing scholarly research papers. Most students today are computer literate and have already used some kind of word processing for their course work. In fact, the notion of literacy is beginning to include computer literacy. Yet, when we talk about integrating computers and word processing into the writing curriculum, teachers often want to know whether students actually write better with a computer. There is, to some degree, a demand that research provide data to validate the use of word processing over traditional pencil-and-paper approaches to teaching writing. However, teachers who use computers to teach writing recognize that there is little relevance in comparing work done on the computer and work done in a traditional noncomputerized setting. They maintain that we live in the computer age, and that it is no more possible to step backward away from computers than it is to retreat to a time before typewriters:

> Early research on word processors and writing tried to discover whether word processors helped or hindered writers. More recent research, however, understands that the question is now moot. Word processors are here; they are part of the writer's, and of the writing teacher's, environment. We will not, most of us, most of the time, choose to return to the pen, or to the typewriter (LeBlanc and Moran, 1989, 111).

No longer is there a question about whether computers will be used for instructional purposes. Rather, the question now is how the computer will be used to enhance learning in the schools (Montague, 1990, 17).

Computers have clearly found a place in the academic setting. Both high schools and colleges seek funding to equip computer labs for use in the humanities, and many teachers have integrated the use of computers into the writing program.

□ A WRITING REVOLUTION

In many ways, computers have revolutionized the act of writing. Word processing has given writers the opportunity to write more quickly, to correct typing errors nearly effortlessly, to facilitate revising at the sentence as well as the global level, and to save a text for later modification. For some writers, composing at the computer is a great improvement over the tedious task of writing with a pencil, crossing out or erasing words and sentences, drawing arrows to relocate paragraphs, adding paragraphs marked with asterisks on separate sheets of paper, and finally, rewriting or typing the finished product. For other writers, composing at the computer can be difficult. One reason for this difficulty may be that they are unable to actually see or reread what they have written without scrolling to different screens. These writers may miss the physical presence of their text in various phases of the writing process. Regardless of how writers feel about composing at the computer, there is no doubt that the computer environment has changed the way that writers go about writing.[1]

If computers have, in fact, revolutionized writing, they may also revolutionize the way we teach writing. However, as teachers begin to consider using computers to teach writing, it is important to be aware of various factors involved with writing and computers and to make informed decisions. Teachers must study the technology, evaluate the different software programs, assess the computer literacy of the writers, identify the skill level of the writers, and examine how the software affects the writing process.[2] Computers will revolutionize the teaching of writing only if it is clear that they can improve the experience for both students and teachers.

COMPUTERS AND WRITING IN L1

For more than a decade, publishers and computer companies have invested in developing software programs that are designed to teach writing. Concurrently, English teachers have been examining the use of computers and experimenting with composition and word processing. Given that the process-nature of writing is a predominant concern, teachers are primarily interested in how computers can enhance the writing process. As we explore the use of computers in L1 writing, we will focus on theoretical considerations in designing software, methods for assessing available software, and research on computer-aided writing and the writing process.

□ DESIGNING COMPUTER PROGRAMS

Many teachers do not feel that they have the necessary expertise to author computer programs. However, most schools have a computer specialist who may be able to design a program tailored to a teacher's pedagogical needs. Therefore, being able to articulate those needs is important. In discussing how to create successful writing software, Selfe (1986, 7–8) states that teachers should begin by identifying student writing problems, using the following four categories: 1) process problems, such as planning and revising, 2) attitude problems, such as commitment and fear, 3) mechanical problems, such as spelling and agreement, and 4) logic problems, such as organizing paragraphs and topic sentences. In addition to classifying writing problems, Selfe believes that teachers should systematically identify their own assumptions about writing and composing as well as their assumptions about teaching writing.

In a similar vein, Kellogg (1989) discusses computer aids that facilitate the processes and products of writing. Specifically, he suggests that software should be developed according to a psychology of writing and should address writing problems such as *attentional overload*, *idea bankruptcy,* and *affective interference.* Attentional overload, or a writer's attempt to plan, translate, and review all at the same time, can be alleviated by a program that helps the writer focus on only one or two processes at a time. Idea bankruptcy, or the failure to generate usable ideas, can be reduced by software that helps create, clarify, and order concepts. Affective interference, or the anxieties that impede successful writing, can be relieved by software that reinforces and encourages the writer. Kellogg describes several computer programs that serve these functions, however, he concludes by stating that using computer aids to enhance writing is a valuable but still elusive goal.

□ FOCUS ON THE WRITING PROCESS

Computer programs for writing are especially interesting if they can help the writer during various phases of the writing process. Any word processing program can facilitate the revising process because additions and deletions are simple and quick. However, there is an increasing interest in how computers can address some of the more difficult phases of the writing process:

> For the most part, the popular word processing programs of today support "bottom up" processes for the mechanics of writing, such as spelling and word choice. This support takes the form of spell checker, dictionary, and thesaurus subprograms. . . . The wave of the future, however, is the development

of subprograms that support "top down" writing processes such as idea generation, organization, and goal specification. These subprograms will facilitate writers' efforts to search for and retrieve ideas from rich, domain-specific knowledge bases. . . . The integration of subprograms for managing top-down and bottom-up subprocesses represents a major advance in word processing, paving the way for the creation of computer writing environments with full cognitive support (Glynn et al., 1989, 4–5).

In keeping with the challenge to explore how computer programs can provide support for top-down writing processes, Schwartz (1989) discusses several ways that any word processing program can enhance a writer's experience. She discusses several features of the writing process, including coming up with ideas, forming ideas, organizing ideas, editing, and polishing. For coming up with ideas she proposes "invisible writing," during which the student turns down the contrast on the monitor so that the text cannot be seen. After writing for a designated time period, the student can turn up the contrast and review and edit the ideas. For forming ideas, she suggests an activity that involves engaging in a debate on disk. Two or more students are given a short time period to type their opinions on a given topic and then pass the disk on to the next student, who can support the argument or disagree. An activity for organizing ideas consists of having students reread their texts and them having them put an asterisk in front of the controlling sentences in each paragraph. Then the students save the text under a new file name and delete everything except the sentences that have an asterisk. The "starred" sentences form a kind of abstract from which the students can organize their thoughts, later incorporating the ideas from the original text.

While ordinary word processors can provide support for the writing process, there are teachers who are interested in programs that are designed specifically to address process problems.[3] Smith and Lansman (1989) describe the design of a computer writing environment (WE) that corresponds to the cognitive processes of writers. In developing WE, the researchers began with a description of cognitive modes, or ways of thinking, that writers utilize in order to execute different aspects of the entire writing task. They identify the following modes: *exploration, situational analysis, organization, writing, editing (global organization), editing (coherence relations), editing (expression)*. For each of these modes, they define constituents: *processes, products, goals,* and *constraints*. For example, for the exploration mode, the processes include recalling, clustering, associating; the products include making clusters, or networks, of related concepts; the goals include externalizing ideas; the constraints are described as flexible, informal.

When using WE, the cognitive modes of the writers are supported by various aspects of the software design. For example, for the exploration mode, writers are able to note individual concepts, cluster associated ideas, and make relational structures by creating small boxes and linking them in ways considered appropriate. The environment tailored to the organizational mode allows the writer to construct a coherent hierarchical structure of concepts and ideas. The environments for writing and editing are similar to conventional word processing, however, they are linked to the other environments for exploration and organization so that the writer may move freely from idea generation to planning to writing and editing. Furthermore, WE includes an automatic tracking function that "produces a detailed transcript for a session in which each action performed by the user is recorded, along with the time and other relevant information. . . . These data constitute a concurrent protocol that is gathered unobtrusively and in a machine-readable form, ready for analysis" (Smith and Lansman, 1989, 50). While researchers do not yet have data to analyze the effectiveness of WE, the premise upon which the software is conceived provides insight into the potential for creating computer programs that may help student writers engage effectively in several phases of the writing process.

☐ RESEARCH ON COMPUTER-AIDED WRITING

Recent research on writing with computers suggests that various aspects of the writing process may be significantly altered when students write with computers. Cochran-Smith et al. (1991) studied elementary school children learning to write with word processing, and found that "word processing was not just a writing tool, but was indeed a 'pedagogical instrument' that shaped the ways teachers and children constructed learning contexts for writing that in turn shaped children's theories and practices of writing" (1991, 9). Based on an analysis of the effect of word processing on composing, the researchers make five propositions about writing:

1. In classroom or computer laboratory situations, using word processing affects the composing processes of student writers. Students make more surface-level and meaning-level revisions, are less likely to plan before writing and more likely to let the text "evolve," tend to carry over composing strategies used in pencil-and-paper writing, such as writing in a linear and sequential fashion rather than recursively, and can enhance their composing strategies with instructional intervention.

2. When students use word processing in classroom or computer laboratory situations, the quality and quantity of their written products is affected. Students' skills in typing as well as their general familiarity with word processing are important factors in analyzing written products. Moreover, using word processing in and of itself does not improve writing quality.

3. Student writers respond positively to the use of word processing.

4. When students begin to use word processing, there is an initial learning period, the length of which is dependent in part on the prior typing and writing experiences of the student.

5. The ways that word processing is used for writing in individual classrooms, the social organization of classroom learning environments, and the goals and strategies of individual teachers are interactively related. (Cochran-Smith et al., 1991, 22–67).

While the subjects of this study were elementary school children,[4] the research findings have clear implications for the writing classroom in general.

One of the most significant questions in computer-aided writing involves the extent to which the computer environment affects a writer's writing process. That is, do writers go about the writing process differently when they use a computer? In a study of experienced writers not accustomed to composing at the computer, Bridwell-Bowles et al. (1987) found that all the subjects had to modify and often abandon familiar scribal (pencil-and-paper) composing strategies when using the computer. Outlining, jotting ideas in diagram form with arrows, and even shuffling papers were important parts of the writing process for some writers, and composing at the computer required them to adopt new composing strategies. However, the subjects became increasingly accustomed to using word processing throughout the course of the study and found ways to approximate their familiar scribal revision patterns. At the beginning of the study, they spent between 8 percent and 12 percent of the time composing combined with editing. However, by the last writing session they were spending 27 percent of their time combining text production and editing. The researchers also found that the subjects spent only an average of 15 percent of their time actually writing, about 9 percent of their time pausing and producing text, and all subjects revised more with the computer. In addition to altering the writing process, they found that subjects wrote an average of 200 more words with the computer than with scribal methods. The results of their research suggest that composing and computers may have an effect on the composing strategies of future writers:

> One point to make about the implications for computer composing is that students, for whom composing on a computer may be commonplace in the future, may develop altogether different styles of composing as a result of what the machine can do for them. . . . The size of the revision is the critical issue, however. There is no question that revising the surface features and format of a text is easier; but to use the computer for large-scale revision, real "re-seeing" and "re-composing," may require word-processing features that do not yet exist for planning (e.g., integrated graphics for planning; multiple, high-resolution screens that allow the writer to see several pages at once; the ability to print parts of a file while working on other parts of it) (Bridwell-Bowles et al., 1987, 104).

Williamson and Pence (1989) designed a study to determine: 1) if word processing coupled with writing instruction increases the quantity and type of text changes that students make, and 2) if students who use word processing produce higher-quality texts than students who do not learn to write with a word processor. The subjects were 184 students who scored well enough on the

Verbal SAT or the Test of Standard Written English (TSWE) to be considered more advanced than basic writers. One half of the group used word processing, and the other half used traditional scribal methods. Their findings indicate that students in the word processing sections wrote longer essays and took more time to complete their essays than the students in the pencil-and-paper sections. Moreover, they found that students in the word processing sections showed improvement in the quality of their essays over time. However, the study also showed that while the students in the word processing sections made more surface-level revisions in their texts, there was no significant difference between the groups in word-, phrase-, clause-, and sentence-level revisions.

The most notable aspect of Williamson and Pence's study is the video analysis of different revising models used by students in the word processing sections. They found three general models of revising: *linear*, *intermittent*, and *recursive*. Linear revisers composed entire drafts quickly, making few text changes while writing, and revised their texts in subsequent drafts. Intermittent revisers were similar to linear revisers, but periodically stopped to revise their texts, scrolling back to the preceding paragraph or sentence. Recursive revisers wrote slowly, composing for shorter periods of time between revisions, seemed to be constantly rereading, and only scrolled back several lines. Furthermore, recursive revisers seemed to be closely focused on the point at which the text was being generated, attempting to clarify their message before proceeding and working primarily on content rather than surface meaning. The researchers suggest that the recursive style of revision is the most effective, with intermittent and linear revisers being less effective. They concluded that writing with a computer was beneficial to certain kinds of writers:

> Word processing facilitates the intermittent and recursive revisers because it frees them from the linear conception of writing that is an artifact of writing on paper, and it frees them from the messiness of recursive revision strategies on paper (Williamson and Pence, 1989, 122).

□ CONFLICTING IDEAS

While some studies suggest that word processing enhances the writing process, others disagree. Haas (1989) disputes the notion that writing with a computer generally improves writing processes. She focuses particularly on planning, or the reflective activity about both the global and the sentence-level aspects of the text that occurs before and during writing. In a study using ten experienced writers and ten student writers, Haas compared planning processes in three writing conditions: pencil and paper, word processing, and a combination of pencil and paper and word processing. Her findings clearly show that all the writers planned significantly less when using word processing than when using pencil and paper. The results further indicate that there was less conceptual planning (global) but more sequential planning (sentence-level) with word processing. Subjects reported being overly attentive to sentence-level concerns when using word processing, perhaps due to the fact that they only saw a limited amount of their text on the screen. Finally, when the subjects were able to use both pencil and paper and word processing, the study shows vast differences in planning strategies. Some planned and wrote out the entire text by hand and then typed it on the computer, making word and sentence-level changes, while others never used pencil and paper at all.

Like Haas, Harris (1985) concluded that using a computer did not necessarily alter or improve the writing process. Harris investigated the effect of word processing on revising, specifically revisions of meaning and organization. Her subjects were six college freshmen from both an honors English course and an advanced composition course who already knew how to type and were familiar with computers. Her findings include that students revise the printouts of their work, subsequently using word processing to make the indicated changes, and that there is no evidence that the computer facilitates recursive writing. Ultimately, she concluded that teachers cannot assume that using word processing will make students revise their work more thoroughly or effectively.

Hawisher (1987) concurs with the findings of Harris, stating that students revised significantly more with pen and typewriter than with word processing:

> The results of this study do not support the claim that a computer is a more effective revising tool than pen and typewriter, if one measures effectiveness by the frequency of revision and by the quality ratings assigned to the final drafts. At the same time, the results do not suggest that word processing is a less effective tool than conventional methods for students (Hawisher, 1987, 156).

□ THE NETWORKED CLASSROOM

The networked writing classroom has recently garnered a great deal of attention. In this setting, each student sits at a computer and exchanges messages and reactions with other students as they write on a given topic. Teachers are encouraged, and even enthusiastic, about how actively students become engaged in writing when they can respond and react to their classmates. They seem more willing to explore issues and to express themselves clearly and concisely when their peers have immediate access to their prose. This forum may serve as a kind of elaborate prewriting activity during which students can brainstorm with their peers, generate ideas, and organize their thoughts. Moreover, the audience is real and immediate. However, networked writing doesn't duplicate the kind of writing that is done as a solitary act of composition.

□ FUTURE CHALLENGES

Relatively little empirical data are available regarding how computer-aided writing affects the writing process. Several studies indicate that writers are influenced in significant ways when they use computers. In fact, it is possible that computer-aided writing may have an impact on the cognitive development of young student writers and alter the writing process of adult writers. Research must continue to inform us about how the writing process can be facilitated by computer-aided writing. However, the real challenge for the future lies in formulating theories about computers and writing that can inform our teaching. The issues raised by research in computer-aided writing do not call into question whether teachers should use computers to teach writing, but rather **how** teachers should use computers to teach writing. As researchers and teachers continue to examine this issue, they not only make headway in software design and use, but also refine our thinking about the writing process and teaching writing.

COMPUTERS AND WRITING IN ESL

Following the lead of colleagues in English, many ESL composition teachers have been experimenting with computers in the writing class. The issues in ESL writing are similar to those in English composition: teachers are interested in understanding how computer-aided writing affects both the writing process and the writing product.

□ VARIABLES THAT CAN AFFECT RESEARCH OUTCOMES

It is important to continue to assess the value of using word processing to teach writing. While there is no reason to contemplate a return to the precomputer era, it is critical to have a clear sense of the positive and negative aspects of computer-aided writing. There is a good deal of research in L1 and in ESL regarding the effectiveness of computer-aided writing, however, Pennington (1993) notes that there are several crucial variables that can have a significant impact on research outcomes. The first consideration is the students, especially given the diverse population of many ESL classes. Depending upon their backgrounds, previous training, or culturally determined attitudes and learning styles, using computers to write will have varying results. Another variable is the teacher. The teachers' attitudes, knowledge of computers, and goals for the computer writing class will have an effect on how the students respond to writing with computers. Pennington further adds the setting, the length of time of instruction with computers, the nature of the instruction, and finally, the type of software used for writing as additional variables that are important to consider when assessing the value of computer-aided writing.

□ COMPUTERS AND REVISION

Computers make revising easier and quicker. In fact, adding, deleting, and inserting are often considered the most beneficial features of computer-aided writing. However, in a study of ESL students by Phinney and Khouri (1993), results showed that language proficiency was less important than computer experience in determining how students revised with a computer. Furthermore, they found that the students showed typical negative writing behaviors, such as premature editing, avoidance behavior, and a concern with form over content. The most significant finding involved the fact that the computer did not seem to affect the way the students wrote.

> The results underscore the need for early and continued exposure to writing on computers if we expect our students to adapt their strategies to writing on the computer in English (Phinney and Khouri, 1993, 271).

□ TEXT ANALYZERS

Text analysis is one of the most popular and the most controversial computer writing aids in ESL composition instruction. Using various kinds of analyses, such as finding grammatical errors, word choice, and style problems, the programs are designed to offer the writer suggestions for changing and improving a text. Brock's (1993) study of the effectiveness of three English text analyzers shows that there can be several difficulties for ESL students. He found that text analyzers are often wrong and offer incorrect advice, that ESL writers are unlikely to know when the program is wrong, and that the programs were ineffective in addressing content-level problems. Brock concludes that, while computer-aided writing can be very successful for ESL students, text analyzers should be used with great care.

COMPUTERS AND WRITING IN FL

While computers and word processing may have revolutionized writing in English and ESL, FL writing programs are not typically known for their use of computers. For many FL teachers, there is a problem with gaining access to computer labs often reserved for other disciplines. However, schools with sufficient funding are beginning to modernize language labs and incorporate computers for various kinds of computer-aided instruction.

There does not seem to be any particular theoretical perspective among teachers of FL writing regarding the use of computers. Generally, if computers are accessible, they are likely to use them; likewise, if there are no computers available, it is not considered a critical issue. However, given the research on computers and writing in L1, it appears that writing with pencil and paper is very different from writing with a computer. The various phases of the writing process, such as planning, generating ideas, editing, and revising, require different strategies in the computer setting. Moreover, using computers for teaching writing is likely to alter the instructional approach. As in the field of English composition, questions regarding the effects of word processing on writing and on writing instruction in the FL merit careful study.

□ USING WORD PROCESSING

The most obvious advantage to using word processing in FL composition instruction is rewriting. Once a composition has been typed onto a data disk, rewriting and making corrections on grammar and expression is a less tedious task. In fact, both teachers and students often feel that incorporating corrections in a second or even third draft of a composition is an important part of the FL learning process. Any word processor can facilitate this aspect of the writing process and make revising and rewriting a potentially more rewarding experience.

However, computers can be used for more than rewriting. Teachers are beginning to use common word processing programs to engage students in other phases of the writing process. For example, Greenia (1992) designed a computer-facilitated advanced writing program in Spanish that can be used with any word processing program. According to his model, each student in the course receives a diskette on which the teacher has created a set of files. Some files are already full, such as the Course Description file and the file with samples of model texts. Most files are empty, such as the Work in Progress file (that may be designated as private space that the teachers can promise not to inspect), the Completed Assignment file, a Dialogue Journal file (that the teacher reads and reacts to but does not correct), and a file for special exercises created by the teacher. His model encourages students to grapple with process problems, such as generating ideas through freewriting, editing, and revising. He also includes many suggestions for increasing the volume of student writing, expanding the variety of writing assignments, and easing the teacher's grading load. Little or no paper is involved, since students hand in diskettes and the teacher can record comments and suggestions directly on the diskette. This kind of model can change the dynamics of the FL writing class and inspire students to experiment with written expression in several different ways.

□ SOFTWARE FOR FL WRITING

For more than a decade, some FL teachers have been interested in developing and using software that is designed specifically for writing in FL. These programs are typically language specific and include features that support writing in the target language. For example, Harvey (1986) designed Computer-Assisted Composition Instruction (CACI) for students of Spanish that includes support for *prewriting, writing,* and *revision.* During the prewriting phase, students use the word processor to freewrite ideas, giving little or no attention to form. After writing a rough draft, students exchange disks and read each other's work, commenting on the content and organization of the composition. During a 50-minute class period, students can read and comment on as many as three drafts. At this point, the students review their own compositions, looking for grammatical errors. The teacher may supervise this surface revision process by calling attention to typical errors such as subject/verb or noun/adjective agreements. The students may also use the text analyzer feature of the software. Finally, the students revise the content and organization of their compositions.

The most notable software programs for teaching FL writing are *Système-D* for French (Noblitt, Pet, and Solá, 1992),[5] *Atajo* for Spanish (Dominguez, Noblitt, and Pet, 1993), and *Quelle* for German (Kossuth, Noblitt, and Pet, 1995). Each of these language-specific programs includes a bilingual dictionary, a verb conjugator, and databases with lexical and grammatical information. *Système-D* was the first of these three programs to be developed, and served as the model for *Atajo* and *Quelle*.[6] The software is available in both DOS and Windows versions as well as on a Macintosh platform.

All three programs are founded on a similar theoretical principle, namely that students need several kinds of resources to write in the target language. As students write, they work with a split screen, one half of which is writing space, while the other half displays the information retrieved from the databases. Figure 1 shows a screen from *Système-D* that displays information on "writing a letter (informal)" at the top and the student's text at the bottom. Figure 2 shows a screen from *Atajo* with several windows: the writing window (top), a window with the vocabulary categories (center), a reference lookup window (lower right center), and a window with words related to computers (bottom). Students can choose to keep their texts in the half-screen format or to view them on the full

---

Figure 1

```
=========================== INDEX NOTES ===========================
 F1 Help                                                   F10 Main
              Editor        Dictionary        Index
              F2            F3                F4
=================================: :===============================
                    Writing a letter (informal)
LA LETTRE
  Informal Openings

    ┌─────────────────────────────────┬──────────────────────┐
    │ Cher ami, Chère amie,           │ Dear friend,         │
    │ Cher Paul, Chère Anne,          │ Dear Paul,...Anne,   │
    │ Mon cher cousin, Ma chère cousine│ Dear cousin,        │
    └─────────────────────────────────┴──────────────────────┘

                                                              >>>
───────────────────────────────────────────────────────────────
    Cher ami,                                                   ¶

         Je m'appelle Kim et je suis une étudiante.  J'aime le
    français!  J'aime la biologie aussi.                        ¶
       ▪
───────────────────────────────────────────────────────────────
              ============ FILE: B:GINNY (line   1) ============
```

Figure 2

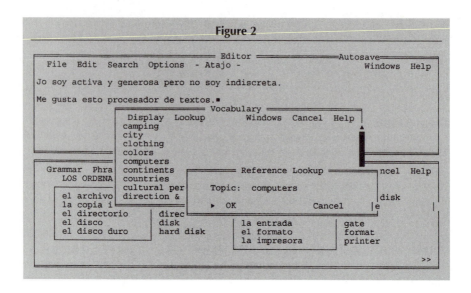

screen. In either format, students can toggle back and forth between the information screens and the text they are writing.

The main sources of information are located in two databases: the bilingual dictionary and the index. The dictionary, while not exhaustive, includes words taken primarily from lists in elementary and intermediate textbooks. Figure 3 shows how the bilingual dictionary appears on the *Système-D* screen. The word *étudier* has been looked up in French, and the English correspondent "to study" appears. Students have the opportunity to see examples of this verb, as indicated

Figure 3

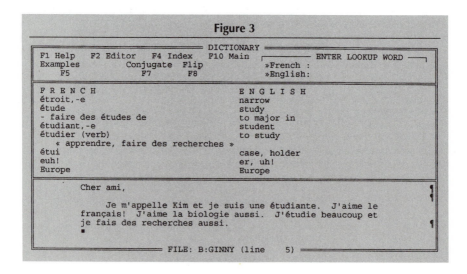

on the menu at the top of the screen. Another menu option is Conjugate. From the Verb Summary screen, students can type the number that corresponds to the tense that they want, and a full conjugation screen of the verb in question will appear in the tense requested.

Many dictionary entries have expanded notes that show students a given word used in context, other words that may be related to it, as well as idiomatic expressions with the word. For example, when students look up the word "car" in *Système-D* they find *auto «voiture (véhicule à moteur à quatre roues)»*. The expanded notes on "car" include vocabulary words such as *le volant, le moteur, le pneu*, and ten idiomatic expressions related to driving, including *faire un tour en voiture, conduire, tomber en panne*, and *faire le plein d'essence.*

The second database that serves as a source of information is the three-part index that comprises grammar, vocabulary, and phrases. The Grammar Index contains brief informational screens for one hundred grammar points found in typical elementary and intermediate textbooks. Moreover, students do not need to know grammatical terminology. For example, if students using *Système-D* type the word *que*, they will find several screens, each representing a different way to use *que*: comparison, conjunction, interrogative pronoun, relative pronoun. The information given in the Grammar Index serves as a brief review and not as an exhaustive presentation of language structures. The Vocabulary Index includes more than one hundred categories organized in semantic fields. Figure 4 shows some of the adjectives in *Atajo* listed under "personality." The Phrases Index includes more than fifty categories listed in functional terms such as "apologizing," "comparing and contrasting," "describing people," and "writing an essay."

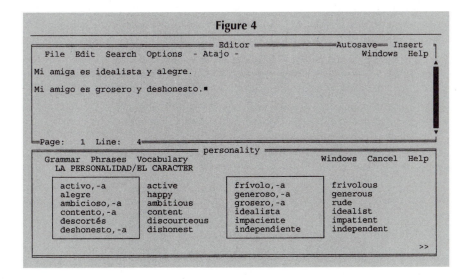

Figure 4

Finally, software programs designed specifically for FL writing can heighten students' interest in the subject. Using a new medium for writing can be motivating in itself. In addition, computer writing assistants that facilitate both locating and retrieving linguistic resources can enhance the writing experience in general. However, since computer-aided FL writing is relatively new, there is little research to inform our teaching. There are still many unanswered questions about the long-term effects of using computers to write in the FL. As teachers begin to explore the use of computer writing assistants, they must continue to evaluate and rethink how this new technology can best serve to teach FL writing.

COMPUTER-AIDED WRITING: THE CLASSROOM IMPLICATIONS

When teachers use computers for writing in FL, they must rethink many aspects of teaching and evaluating writing. What are the advantages and disadvantages of asking students to use computers for writing in FL? Will teachers' expectations be different? Will the FL writing process be enhanced? There is no question that several dimensions are altered when teachers change the writing medium from scribal to computer: the physical dimension (the location and accessibility of the computer), the affective dimension (motivation, anxiety, and past experience associated with computer work), and the cognitive dimension (strategies such as planning and revising). As FL teachers explore the possibilities with computer-aided writing, it is important to consider the following suggestions:

1. *Become active in securing the use of computers for writing.*

Teachers and administrators may not consider computers necessary for FL writing instruction. However, given that a definition of literacy may now include computer literacy, FL teachers have the right to assert that computers belong in the FL program. All teachers, regardless of their discipline, should have access to computers. In pleading the case for computers for teaching FL writing, there are several valid arguments. First, research has shown that students enjoy writing with computers, and that they are likely to write more when they use word processing. Given the movement toward writing across the curriculum, any added opportunity to write and learn should be encouraged. Second, studies of the writing process indicate that editing and revising are greatly facilitated with word processing. When students write in FL, they need the capacity to revise and rewrite their work, since accuracy is often an important aspect. Third, there are software programs available for teaching FL writing, and schools have a responsibility to explore that dimension, just as they are responsible for keeping abreast of new texts and approaches. FL teachers should consider their discipline as worthy of computers as any other discipline.

2. Articulate feelings and attitudes about writing with computers.

Many teachers and students have had the opportunity to use computers both at home and in the academic setting. Typewriters, and in some instances pencil and paper, have been replaced by computers. However, when it comes to writing with a computer, everyone has a different reaction. Positive reactions to computers and word processing may be directly related to a person's typing ability. Good typists may feel at ease composing at the computer because their fingers move rapidly enough to keep up with their thoughts. Poor typists may feel that the flow of their thoughts is interrupted by their clumsy hunt-and-peck typing skills. In FL writing, the use of accents may further hinder typing speed and frustrate the writer. Teachers and students need to evaluate their keyboard ability as it relates to writing with computers.

In addition to talking about how a writer's typing skills can affect the success or failure of using computers to write, teachers and students should discuss how to use a computer while writing. For some, it is natural and easy to write with a computer. These writers can compose at the computer, moving back and forth in their texts, constantly rereading, revising, and writing. For others, the computer only represents a different way to type something that has already been written by hand. For these writers, all the rereading and revising is done on paper, and the computer may only serve to refine the spelling or punctuation in their texts. Other writers may show a combination of pencil-and-paper and computer writing. Both teachers and students should explore the strategies that they use when writing with a computer.

A final consideration is the setting. The location of the computers that students will use to write may be crucial to their attitude. Some FL programs may have access to computer labs in which students write in sound-proof cubicles, while others may have computer classrooms that provide little privacy. For some students writing must be a solitary, quiet activity, whereas others are less sensitive to sound and disturbances. In order to maximize the success of computer-aided writing, teachers and students should consider their individual attitudes about all the aspects of writing with computers.

3. Assess students' computer literacy.

In addition to evaluating attitudes, teachers should assess their students' computer literacy. With regard to writing, computer literacy refers to students' knowledge of word processing functions. A basic understanding of word processing includes familiarity with backspacing, deleting, blocking, moving, saving, and printing. Some students may have little or no experience with computers and writing, and will require extra help in mastering the basic concepts. Most students today have had some kind of computer experience. However, regardless of basic computer literacy, every student is likely to have had varied experiences with word processing as well as with computer platforms. Every word processing program available on the market has different commands for different functions. Moreover, some students will be familiar with the Macintosh platform, others with the IBM platform, either DOS or Windows. Some students will have used a mouse, while others will be accustomed to using function keys. Finally, teachers need to be aware of all the possible factors that may affect the success of a computer writing program.

4. *Become familiar with the program that students will be using.*

Teachers are rarely computer experts. The hardware, including computers of various sizes and memory capacities, monitors, printers, and cables, may seem forbidding. The software, while generally less intimidating, may come with directions for loading and use that are incomprehensible to the novice. However, good help is nearly always available in the academic setting, and it can be beneficial to ask for a lesson in the basics of computers.

Knowing about computer hardware can be helpful, although it is not essential. However, having a thorough knowledge of the software that students will be using to write is imperative. Some teachers may feel that if they have acquired good software for teaching writing, and if the students seem to have learned how to use it, they do not need to be experts in the software themselves. In fact, many teachers are content to remain ignorant, relying on the software and on their students' computer expertise. Generally students know when teachers are unfamiliar with the software. Under these circumstances, the students' commitment to the software is likely to reflect the teacher's lack of familiarity. Software is like a textbook and should be treated accordingly. Teachers should not recommend any kind of pedagogical tool to their students, including computer software, if they are not committed to achieving a good degree of proficiency with the tool themselves.

5. *Require students to use computer-aided writing.*

Once a teacher has made the decision to use computers for writing, the new approach should be fully integrated into the writing program. Just as texts and other instructional materials are course requirements, the software for writing should be an integral part of the course. If teachers tell students that the software is optional, there is a great likelihood that very few students will use it. To illustrate this point, 41 students in 2 sections of a third-year French composition class at Vanderbilt University were told that using **Système-D** would be helpful, but that it was optional. Thirty-three students had been required to use the software for at least one semester prior to enrolling in the composition class. An informal survey of student attitudes showed that all of the students that had used **Système-D** liked it and felt they had benefitted from using it in their previous courses. The students who had never used it expressed interest in learning more about it. However, only three students used the software, all of whom were doing very poorly in the course and hoped to improve their grades. The teacher concluded that students have so many demands on their time that unless using the software was required, they would make do without. If the software is required, students typically use it willingly.

    6. *Develop a plan for implementation.*

Teaching FL writing with computers can be a rewarding experience for teachers and students if there is a clearly defined plan for implementation. The following case study provides an example of a successful implementation plan.

CASE STUDY

Since 1989, elementary- and intermediate-level students of French at Vanderbilt University have been using **_Système-D_** to write their compositions. Through extensive work with this writing assistant, the teachers have developed an implementation plan that defines 1) the pedagogical principles upon which instruction is based, 2) the best approach to orienting students to the software, 3) the kinds of assignments that are best suited for the software, 4) the methods for holding students accountable for their work, and 5) the evaluation of the software.

    1. *Pedagogical principles.*

The first step in implementing a computer-aided approach to teaching FL writing involves defining the pedagogical principles upon which the software is founded. That is, the teacher must have a clear sense of what theories about learning undergird the design of the software. According to Montague, when we teach with computers we are obliged to examine our fundamental theories about learning:

> A theory of educational computing requires a fundamental conceptualization of the nature of learning. Learning, as a reciprocal process, requires that the learner be challenged by the learning environment and cognitively engaged in the learning activity. . . . The shift is away from learning facts to understanding the structures of information and developing skills in finding, synthesizing, and interpreting information. (Montague, 1990, 18–19).

Teachers must not only examine their own theories about learning, as Montague states, but must also analyze how the software supports their theories.

A cursory analysis of the organization and presentation of material in *Système-D* suggests a philosophy of learning based on the notion that FL students are naturally curious and want to engage in expressing themselves in the target language. Rather than being limited to using familiar words and structures, *Système-D* allows students to explore databases with information that may be unfamiliar.

A closer examination of the software reveals that it facilitates several fundamental aspects of the writing process. First, it permits the student writer to edit and revise with relative ease given the Cut, Paste, and Delete functions. Second, it helps students to engage in both *bottom-up processing* and *top down-processing*. Bottom-up processing involves the mechanics of writing, such as word choice and spelling. This aspect of the writing process is supported primarily by the dictionary and its abundant examples of how words are used in context as well as what their grammatical functions are.

Top-down processing entails generating ideas, planning, and organizing. Generating ideas is supported predominantly by the information in the three-part index. When writing in FL, students should be discouraged from generating complex ideas and then searching for words in the target language to express those ideas. Rather, they should be guided explicitly to use familiar words and phrases in the target language during idea generation.[7] The *Système-D* indexes are designed to give students ready access to many words and expressions that can help them generate ideas. For example, if students are asked to write a description of themselves, they might begin by looking up "describing people" in the Phrases Index. Under this category, there are sentences such as *Il/Elle a les cheveux longs/courts*, *Il/Elle est grand(e)/petit(e)*, and *Il est jeune/vieux*, as well as suggestions to look in other indexes such as "nouns after *c'est, il est*" and "personality." In the "personality" category there are adjectives including *optimiste, pessimiste, paresseux-se,* and *sportif-ve*. All of these words and structures can trigger associations and help the student brainstorm about the topic.

With regard to planning and organizing, *Système-D* does not provide explicit support for these aspects of top-down processing. That is, it does not include ways for students to identify topic sentences, to cluster and link associated ideas, or to construct a coherent hierarchy of concepts and ideas. However, the information provided in the Phrases Index can serve as an organizational structure. For example, the phrases for "sequencing events," "linking ideas," "weighing alternatives," or "writing an essay" include expressions that implicitly direct students to plan and organize. Expressions such as *d'abord, et puis, en somme, pourtant,* and *de plus* provide a framework for planning and organizing a text. Finally, if students are guided explicitly to use these words and phrases as stimuli for generating and organizing ideas, they are likely to engage in a kind of language play in the creation of meaning.

In an informal experiment comparing the quality of ideas generated while using *Système-D* with the quality of ideas generated in a pencil-and-paper setting, results showed that students generally wrote more in the computer setting. All students were in first-year college French. Ten students wrote with

Système-D and 14 students wrote with pen and paper. The 24 students in both conditions had recently studied descriptive adjectives and leisure activities as part of the regular course curriculum, and the writing task required that they use familiar material: "Write four things about yourself to describe your personality, including what you like and/or dislike." Students in both conditions made similar mistakes, such as noun/adjective and subject/verb agreement. However, students using the computer wrote an average of 14 descriptions of themselves, while the students using pencil and paper wrote an average of 7 descriptions of themselves. The following writing samples are from two students in the computer setting[8] and two students in the pencil-and-paper setting.

Example #1—Computer (16 descriptions)

Je suis américaine. Je suis une étudiante et je travaille aussi. Je suis sportive et je joue au football, hockey, et tennis. Je suis patient. Je ne suis pas desagréable. J'ai les yeux bleu. J'ai les chevaux brune. Je ne suis pas petite. Je suis grande. J'ecoute la musique rock, jazz, rock classique, et country western. Je n'ecoute pas la musique métal hurlant. Je ne danse pas la musique métal hurlant soit.

[I am American. I am a student and I work also. I am athletic and I play football, hockey, and tennis. I am patient. I am not disagreeable. I have blue eyes. I have brown hair. I am not short. I am tall. I listen to rock music, jazz, classic rock, and country western. I don't listen to screaming metal. I don't dance to screaming metal either.]

Example #2—Computer (17 descriptions)

J'ai les yeux bleus et les cheveux bruns. Je suis timide. Je n'aime pas parler beaucoup, mais j'aime écrire! Je suis une idéaliste. J'etudie beacoup, mais je n'etudie pas trop. Je suis travailleuse et intelligent. J'aime la littérature, mais je deteste la mathématiques. Je ne suis pas enérgique. Je suis fatiguée trop. Je n'aime pas le lundi. Je suis une étudiante, mais je ne suis pas trop studieuse.

[I have blue eyes and brown hair. I am timid. I don't like to talk a lot, but I like to write! I am an idealist. I study a lot, but I don't study too much. I am a hard worker and intelligent. I like literature, but I hate math. I am not energetic. I am tired too much. I don't like Mondays. I am a student, but I am not too studious.]

Example #3—Pencil and paper (7 descriptions)

Je suis actif et j'aime beaucoup les sports. Je suis de Georgia mais je deteste la chaleur. J'aime beaucoup le cinéma et le théâtre. De temps en temps, je suis vaniteux.

[I am active and I like sports a lot. I am from Georgia but I hate the heat. I like the movies and the theater a lot. Every now and then, I am vain.]

Figure 5: Système-D Version 2.1

REFERENCE INDEX FOR GRAMMAR

ADJECTIVE AGREEMENT
ADJECTIVE AGREEMENT (number)
ADJECTIVE POSITION
ADVERB FORMATION
ADVERBS OF TIME
avoir EXPRESSIONS
CAUSATIVE faire
COMPARISON que
COMPOUND PAST TENSE Passé composé
COMPOUND TENSES Temps composés
INDEFINITE ARTICLE un, une; des
CONDITIONAL Conditionnel
CONJUNCTION que
CONTRACTIONS à & de + DEF. ARTICLE
DEFINITE ARTICLE le, la, l'; les
DEMONSTRATIVE ADJ. ce, cette; ces
DEMONSTRATIVE PRONOUNS ce, cela, ça
DEMONSTRATIVE PRONOUNS celui, celle
DIRECT & INDIRECT OBJECTS
DIRECT OBJECTS le, la, l'; les
faire EXPRESSIONS
FAMILIAR FORMS tu te toi ton ta tes
FORMAL FORMS vous, votre, vos
FUTURE PAST Futur antérieur
FUTURE TENSE Futur
FUTURE WITH aller: Futur immédiat
IMPERATIVE Impératif
IMPERSONAL il
IMPERSONAL il + ADJECTIVE
INDEFINITE PERSONAL PRON. on, soi
IINDIRECT OBJECT lui, leur
INFINITIVE Infinitif
INTERROGATIVE ADJECTIVE quel
INTERROGATIVE ADVERBS
INTERROGATIVE est-ce que
INTERROGATIVE PHRASE n'est-ce pas
INTERROGATIVE PRON lequel, laquelle
INTERROGATIVE PRONOUN que, quoi
INTERROGATIVE PRONOUN qui?
LOCATIVE PRONOUN y

PAST CONDITIONAL Conditionnel passé
PAST IMPERFECT Imparfait
SUBJUNCTIVE Subjonctif passé
PRON. (1&2 pers. summary)
PRON. (3rd pers. summary)
PLUPERFECT Plus-que-parfait
PLURAL OF NOUNS
POSSESSION WITH de
POSSESSION WITH à
POSSESSIVE ADJ. leur, leurs
PRONOUN vous
POSSESSIVE ADJ. mon, ma; mes
POSSESSIVE ADJ. son, sa; ses
POSSESSIVE ADJ. ton, ta; tes
POSSESSIVE ADJECTIVES (summary)
POSSESSIVE ADJS. notre, votre
POSSESSIVE PRON. le mien, le nôtre
POSSESSIVE PRON. le sien, le leur
POSSESSIVE PRON. le tien, le vôtre
PRECEDING ADJ. beau, belle
PRECEDING ADJ. nouveau, nouvelle
PRECEDING ADJ. vieux, vieille
PREPOSITION + REL. PRON. lequel
PREPOSITIONS OF LOCATION
PREPOSITIONS WITH TIMES AND DATES
PREPOSITIONS à, en WITH PLACES
PRESENT TENSE Présent
PRONOUN en
PRONOUN nous
PRONOUNS elle la lui
PRONOUNS elles les leur
PRONOUNS il le lui
PRONOUNS ils les leur eux
PRONOUNS je me moi
PRONOUNS tu te toi
REFLEXIVE CONSTRUCTION WITH se
REFLEXIVE PRONS. me te se nous vous
REFLEXIVE VERB s'en aller
REFLEXIVE PRONOUN ce qui, ce que
RELATIVE PRONOUN dont

NEGATION WITH ne ... pas	RELATIVE PRONOUN qui, que
NEGATION WITH ne ... personne, rien	SEQUENCE OF TENSES WITH si
NEGATION WITH ne ... plus, jamais	SIMPLE PAST TENSE Passé simple
NOUNS AFTER c'est, il est	SUBJUNCTIVE Subjonctif
NUMBER un, une	VERB + de + INFINITIVE
NUMBERS FOR BUILDING FLOORS	VERB + INFINITIVE
PARTICIPLE AGREE. participe passé	VERB + à + INFINITIVE
PARTICIPLE AGREE. participe présent	VERB SUMMARY
PARTITIVE du, de la, des	VERBS WITH AUXILIARY avoir OR être
PASSIVE VOICE WITH être, se	VERBS WITH AUXILIARY être

Example #4—Pencil and paper (6 descriptions)

J'aime beaucoup le ski. J'aime beaucoup la musique. Je suis généreuse et sympatique. Je ne suis pas vaniteuse et paresseuse.

[I like skiing a lot. I like music a lot. I am generous and nice. I am not vain and lazy.]

Finally, the organization and content of the **Système-D** databases represent an approach to teaching writing that is compatible with our pedagogical theories about teaching and learning FL writing. Students can engage in an interactive process of making meaning in the FL while also finding support for planning, organizing, generating ideas, editing, and revising.

2. *Orienting the students.*

In order for students to learn how to use **Système-D**, they participate in a 45-minute orientation session that is divided into three 15-minute parts.[9]
Part 1: During the first 15 minutes, the teacher guides the students in browsing through the bilingual dictionary and the three-part index. By telling students to look up *faire* in the dictionary, they readily see how quickly and easily they can see words used in context, explore the idiomatic usages of the word, and gain access to the verb conjugation feature. After showing students the dictionary, the teacher explains that the dictionary is **not** the most important source of information for writing compositions in the FL.[10]
In guiding students to explore the three-part index, the teacher begins by giving students a printed copy of the categories in each of the indexes, as shown in Figures 5, 6, and 7. Then, beginning with the Grammar Index, the teacher shows how simple it is to gain access to grammatical information. Explaining that students do not need to know grammar terms like "relative pronoun" or "interrogative adjective," the teacher asks students to type *dont* and then *quel* to illustrate the point. When showing students the Vocabulary Index, the teacher asks students to look up "automobile" so that they see all the related words, such

Figure 6: Système-D Version 2.1

REFERENCE INDEX FOR VOCABULARY

animals	mail
arts	materials
automobile	meals
bathroom	means of transportation
bedroom	meat
body	medicine
bread	menu
calendar	money
cheeses	months
city	monument
classroom	musical instruments
clothing	nationality
colors	numbers
computer	numbers (ordinal)
continent	office
countries	pastry
days of the week	people
delicatessen	personality
direction & distance	poultry
dreams and aspirations	problems
drinks	professions
education	quantity
electronic products	restaurant
entertainment	rooms
fabric	seafood
face	seasoning
family members	seasons
fish	sickness
flowers	sports
food	store
fruits	studies, courses
furniture	table setting
games	taste (dishes)
garden	telephone
geography	time expressions
hair colors	time of day
health	toilette
house	trades, occupation
housing	traveling
housing ads	university
insects	upbringing
kitchen	vegetables
languages	women's clothing
leisure	working conditions
living room	

Figure 7: Système-D Version 2.1

REFERENCE INDEX FOR PHRASES

Accepting	Introducing
Advising	Inviting
Agreeing	Leaving
Apologizing	Linking ideas
Appreciating (food)	Making a judgement
Asking for a favor	Making an appointment
Asking for an opinion	Making something work
Asking for information	Offering
Asking for the date	Persuading
Asking permission	Pointing out a person
Asking the price	Pointing out an object
Attracting attention	Reassuring
Comparing & contrasting	Refusing or declining
Congratulating	Repeating
Describing health	Requesting or ordering
Describing objects	Self reproach
Describing people	Sequencing events
Describing weather	Stating a preference
Disagreeing	Telling Time
Disapproving	Thanking
Encouraging	Warning
Expressing an opinion	Weighing alternatives
Expressing exasperation	Welcoming
Expressing intention	Writing a letter (formal)
Giving directions	Writing a letter (informal)
Greetings	Writing a news item
Holiday greetings	Writing an essay
Hypothesizing	

as *le volant, le frein,* and *le moteur,* as well as verbal expressions related to driving, such as *faire un tour en voiture, conduire,* and *tomber en panne.* In the Phrases Index, the teacher shows students a simple information screen, "congratulating", and a more sophisticated screen, "writing an essay". The teacher points out that the three-part index is the most valuable source of information.

Part 2: During the next 15 minutes, the teacher gives a task-oriented dictation. All students begin by going to the Editor, which will require that they insert their personal data disk. Then the teacher tells them to type the following text while also giving them directions:

Bonjour! Je m'appelle (name). *Je suis un(e) étudiant(e).* Call up the accent screen and practice several different accents. *Je suis* (nationality). Look up "nationality" in the Vocabulary Index and type the appropriate nationality. Look up "writing a letter" (informal) in the Phrases Index and insert an appropriate beginning and ending for a letter to a French friend named *Natalie*.

Part 3: In the final 15-minute phase of the orientation, students learn to save their work, to format their texts (i.e., line spacing), and to print. Since every computer lab has different machinery, the teacher must be familiar with the setting in advance.

During the next class meeting, the teacher briefly reviews the orientation session and gives the first composition assignment.

   3. *The writing assignments.*

In order for students to benefit from writing with **Système-D**, the writing assignments are designed to encourage them to use the information available in the database. Typically, the writing assignment is related to the course content. To illustrate this point, we will imagine that food is the topic that students are studying. Beginning with the categories in the Phrases Index, the teacher first decides what kind of writing she wants the students to do. For example, for narrative writing, she will want students to look up information under "sequencing events"; for descriptive writing, students could use "describing people" or "describing weather"; for expository writing students could consult "comparing and contrasting" or "weighing alternatives"; for persuasive writing students can look at "writing an essay" or "expressing an opinion."

Once the desired mode of discourse has been identified, the teacher designs a writing prompt. For example, a topic about food that is both descriptive and persuasive might involve convincing the reader that a certain kind of food is good. The Vocabulary Index includes many different categories having to do with food, such as "bread," "fruits," "meat," etc. Some of the grammatical structures that will be helpful include "definite article," "indefinite article," "negation," etc. The final writing assignment could appear as follows:

<u>Situation:</u> You are writing a helpful brochure for the French exchange students that have come to your school. Take the position that 1) the food at school is great and they should eat it, or 2) the food is terrible and they should not eat it.

<u>Tasks:</u> Consult the following categories in the **Système-D** index to help you express your ideas:

PHRASES: Expressing an opinion, Writing an essay, Describing health, Weighing alternatives, Warning

VOCABULARY: Fish, Food, Fruits, Meat, Pastry, Seafood, Vegetables

GRAMMAR: Present tense, Verb + infinitive, Verb + *de* + infinitive, Verb + *à* + infinitive, Partitive

---

Figure 8: Composition Evaluation

Part A: USE OF THREE-PART INDEX IN *SYSTÈME-D*

1. VOCABULARY

Inadequate, repetitious	1	2
Adequate, errors in usage	3	4
Broad, clear, expressive		5

2. PHRASES

Inadequate, repetitious	1	2
Adequate, errors in usage	3	4
Broad, clear, idiomatic		5

3. GRAMMAR

Many repeated errors	1	2	
Some errors	3	4	
Few, isolated errors		5	TOTAL ____/15

Part B: THE TEXT

1. CONTENT

Minimal information/ideas	1	2
Adequate information/ideas	3	4
Creative information/ideas		5

2) ORGANIZATION

A series of unrelated sentences	1	2
Some coherence between sentences	3	4
Good coherence between sentences and paragraphs		5

3) ACCURACY

Accuracy is poor; generally incomprehensible	1	2	
Accuracy acceptable; generally comprehensible	3	4	
Accuracy good; completely comprehensible		5	TOTAL ____/15

OVERALL COMPOSITION SCORE: ____/30

(Taken from pedagogical materials used by the author.)

Figure 9: *Système-D* Questionnaire for First-timers

General computer questions:

1. Have you used a computer to write compositions in English?   YES ___ NO ___

2. Do you enjoy using a computer to write?   YES ___ NO ___

3. Do you compose at the computer?   YES ___ NO ___

4. What features of computer writing do you consider most beneficial?

Questions relating to *Système-D*:

1. Was the orientation session helpful?   YES ___ NO ___
   Explain:

2. Did you find the software user-friendly?   YES ___ NO ___
   Explain:

3. What features in **Système-D** did you use while writing? Check all that apply.

   _____ dictionary   _____ grammar index

   _____ verb conjugator   _____ vocabulary index

   _____ other   _____ phrases index

   Explain:

4. What did you like most about the software?

5. What did you like least about the software?

6. Please note any other reactions/criticisms that you have about writing with this software.

(Taken from pedagogical materials used by the author.)

(See chapter 5 for a more detailed discussion of writing prompts.)

4. *Student accountability.*

Since we require students to use *Système-D* to write their compositions, they are held accountable for doing so. Students who spend a good deal of time browsing through the indexes and using the information in their compositions are rewarded for their efforts, regardless of how good or bad their final composition may be. Figure 8 shows a composition evaluation instrument that is designed to measure how effectively students exploit the information in the three-part index as well as the quality of their final composition. Chapter 4 provides a detailed discussion of various methods for correcting and evaluating FL compositions.

5. *Evaluating the software.*

The success of **Système-D** is, in large part, due to how students feel about using it. In evaluating the software, we ask students to identify generally how they use computers to write and then to comment on how they feel about using the software. Figure 9 is a questionnaire designed to assess how students react after using the software for the first time.

When this questionnaire was given to 98 students of French from two universities,[11] several patterns emerged. With regard to computer use in general, all of the students surveyed indicated that they had used computers for English composition, and all but 4 reported that they liked to write with computers. In addition, 72 students wrote that they composed at the computer, while 26 indicated that they did not. As for the use of **Système-D**, all students noted that the software was easy to use and was helpful for writing in French. The bilingual dictionary was the most frequently used feature, although many students noted that it was too limited. Several students indicated that the best aspect of the software was that the information was easy to access and took much less time than looking up all the information in a textbook. Finally, this questionnaire is helpful in identifying problems with computer-aided writing in general as well as positive and negative reactions to the software.

CONCLUSIONS

The fact that computers are here to stay is indisputable. Following the lead of our colleagues in English composition, some teachers are experimenting with using computers to teach FL writing. Teachers may choose to use a conventional word processing program or one of the writing assistants designed specifically for FL writing. Regardless of what teachers choose to do, FL programs have the option to participate in the technology revolution and to take part in helping students become computer literate.

Research shows that writing with computers can be a catalyst in changing a writer's writing process. In L1 writing, this fact can pose a special problem, since students often have a set way of going about writing a composition with pencil and paper. That is, depending upon the writing task, students generally have established strategies for planning, generating ideas, and revising. Using computers for writing in L1 can mean that students have to make radical changes in the strategies they use during the writing process. FL writing, on the other hand, is a different issue because the FL writing process is different from the L1 writing process. First, the FL writing process may not be established. Second, students may use ineffective or inappropriate strategies for writing in the FL. When teaching FL writing, teachers need to teach about the FL writing process and how it may be different from the L1 writing process. (See chapter 2 for a discussion of the FL writing process.) The computer environment provides a good opportunity for implementing a process-oriented approach to teaching FL writing. In fact, computer-aided FL writing can enhance both bottom-up and top-down processing. Revising and correcting surface-level features of the text as well as generating ideas, and working toward overall textual coherence can be facilitated by computer-aided writing.

Finally, we want FL students to enjoy writing. Given that writing is often a difficult task in the native language, teachers face the challenge of motivating students to approach the FL writing task with a positive attitude. Teachers typically use all available tools for encouraging students to learn the FL. Computer-aided writing is a teaching tool that can facilitate learning as well as engage students in the FL writing process.

TOPICS FOR DISCUSSION AND RESEARCH

1. Compare the attitudes and feelings of students who are at ease composing at the computer and those who prefer composing with pencil and paper.

2. Compare the time and quality of planning in the scribal mode and in the computer mode.

3. Compare peer editing when students exchange disks and when they exchange papers.

4. Use videotape to analyze various phases of the writing process in computer-aided writing.

5. Examine how the databases in **Système-D, Atajo,** and **Quelle** engage students in idea generation.

6. Compare the logs and compositions of students who use the databases in **Système-D, Atajo,** and **Quelle** and those who do not.

Notes

1. Pennington ("A Critical Examination of Word Processing Effects in Relation to L2 Writers," *Journal of Second Language Writing* 2(3):227–255), 1993) lists four areas in which research has indicated how word processing has had a positive effect on the writing experience: the quality of written work (higher holistic and analytic ratings of compositions), the writing activity (longer compositions and more experimentation with language), revision behavior (greater number and types of revisions, both discourse-level and meaning-level), and the affective outcome (less apprehension, greater objectivity, more collaboration among peers). She further notes that there are several studies that show

no positive effects and, in some cases, disadvantages in computer-aided writing.

2.   In "Computers and Composition Studies: Articulating a Pattern of Discovery" (in Hawisher and LeBlanc, (Eds.), *Re-imagining Computers and Composition*, Portsmouth, NH: Boynton/Cook, 1992), Neuwirth and Kaufer discuss four interconnected processes involved in building knowledge in computers and composition studies: 1) identifying writers (novices, experts, etc.) and a writing task, 2) building a theory- and research-based model of the writing task, 3) designing technology to alleviate writing problems (planning, generating ideas, revising), and 4) studying the technology in use to build knowledge and refine the model.

3.   In "Computer-Based Creative Problem Solving" (in W. Wresch, (Ed.), *The Computer in Composition Instruction*, Urbana, IL: National Council of Teachers of English, 1984), Rodrigues and Rodrigues focus their attention on prewriting, an aspect of the writing process they consider to be especially important. They point out that computer programs for writing should make it possible for students to be explicitly directed to engage in invention strategies. For example, they propose a program that contains a menu of problem-solving approaches, including features such as simple analogy, two-dimensional matrix or chronological flowchart (p. 44).

4.   See also Daiute's study involving children writing with computers entitled "Can the Computer Stimulate Writers' Inner Dialogues?" in W. Wresch, (Ed.), *The Computer in Composition Instruction*, Urbana, IL: National Council of Teachers of English, 1984. The software that Daiute used had 14 different kinds of text analyses and comments, such as highlighting overly long sentences and asking if a paragraph has a clear focus. The results showed that this kind of prompting can stimulate children to reflect on their own writing and improve it. The young students talked to themselves about their writing and made more changes in their texts.

5.   Burston reviews the use of **Système-D** in "Using **Système-D** in a Classroom Environment" (*CALICO Journal* 8(4):51–57, 1991), and states that students can benefit from using this software if it is fully integrated into the curriculum and if the instructor is actively involved in the process.

6.   **Quelle** is still in development, and therefore the examples given are from **Système-D** and **Atajo**. All three computer writing assistants are designed according to the same format.

7.   The notion that generating ideas in FL writing should be achieved through use of target language stimuli is presented in Scott's "Write From the Start: A Task-oriented Developmental Writing Program for Foreign Language Students" (in R. M. Terry, (Ed.), *Dimension: Language '91*, Report of the Southern Conference on Language Teaching, 1992). This idea is also discussed in some detail in chapter 2.

8. Special thanks go to the students in first-year French at the University of Richmond for participating in this study.

9. Scott and Terry's *Teacher's Guide:* **Système-D** *Writing Assistant for French* (Boston, MA: Heinle & Heinle Publishers, 1992) describes in more detail how to orient students to the software.

10. Close attention to the logs of inquiries that students make to the **Système-D** databases as well as informal conversations with the students have led us to conclude that nearly all students consider the bilingual dictionary the most important resource when they write.

11. Elementary and intermediate students of French at Vanderbilt University and at the University of Richmond filled out this questionnaire after using **Système-D** for the first time.

REFERENCES

Bridwell, Lillian, Geoffrey Sirc and Robert Brooke. (1985). "Revising and Computing: Case Studies of Student Writers." In S. W. Freedman, (Ed.), *The Acquisition of Written Language: Response and Revision.* Norwood, NJ: Ablex Publishing Corporation.

Bridwell-Bowles, Lillian, Parker Johnson and Steven Brehe. (1987). "Composing and Computers: Case Studies of Experienced Writers." In A. Matsuhashi, (Ed.), *Writing in Real Time: Modeling Production Processes.* Norwood, NJ: Ablex Publishing Corporation.

Britton, Bruce K. & Shawn M. Glynn, (Eds.). (1989). *Computer Writing Environments: Theory, Research, & Design.* Hillsdale, NJ: Lawrence Erlbaum.

Brock, Mark N. (1993). "Three Disk-Based Text Analyzers and the ESL Writer." *Journal of Second Language Writing* 2(1):19–40.

Burston, Jack L. (1991). "Using **Système-D** in a Classroom Environment." *CALICO Journal* 8(4):51–57.

Cochran-Smith, Marilyn, Cynthia L. Paris and Jessica L. Kahn. (1991). *Learning to Write Differently: Beginning Writers and Word Processing.* Norwood, NJ: Ablex Publishing Corporation.

Daiute, Colette. (1984). "Can the Computer Stimulate Writers' Inner Dialogues?" In W. Wresch, (Ed.), *The Computer in Composition Instruction.* Urbana, IL: National Council of Teachers of English.

Dominguez, Frank, James S. Noblitt, Willem J. A. Pet. (1993). *Atajo.* Boston, MA: Heinle & Heinle Publishers.

Glynn, Shawn M., Denise R. Oaks, Linda F. Mattocks and Bruce K. Britton. (1989). "Computer Environments for Managing Writers' Thinking Processes." In B. K. Britton & S. M. Glynn, (Eds.), *Computer Writing Environments: Theory, Research, & Design.* Hillsdale, NJ: Lawrence Erlbaum.

Greenia, George D. (1992). "Computers and Teaching Composition in a Foreign Language." *Foreign Language Annals* 25(1):33–46.

Haas, Christina. (1989). "How the Writing Medium Shapes the Writing Process." *Research in the Teaching of English* 23(2):181–206.

Harris, Jeanette. (1985). "Student Writers and Word Processing: A Preliminary Evaluation." *College Composition and Communication* 36(3):323–330.

Harvey, T. Edward. (1986). "Computers and Composition in Hawaii." *CALICO Journal* 3(3):42–45.

Hawisher, Gail E. (1987). "The Effects of Word Processing on the Revision Strategies of College Freshmen." *Research in the Teaching of English* 21(2):145–159.

—— and Paul LeBlanc, (Eds.). (1992). *Re-imagining Computers and Composition*. Portsmouth, NH: Boynton/Cook.

Kellogg, Ronald T. (1989). "Idea Processors: Computer Aids for Planning and Composing Text." In B. K. Britton & S. M. Glynn, (Eds.), *Computer Writing Environments: Theory, Research, & Design*. Hillsdale, NJ: Lawrence Erlbaum Associates.

Kossuth, Karen, James S. Noblitt, and Willem J. A. Pet. (1996). **Quelle.** Boston, MA: Heinle & Heinle Publishers.

LeBlanc, Paul and Charles Moran. (1989). "Adapting to a New Environment: Word Processing and the Training of Writing Teachers at the University of Massachusetts at Amherst." In C. L. Selfe, D. Rodrigues & W. R. Oates, (Eds.), *Computers in English and the Language Arts: The Challenge of Teacher Education*. Urbana, IL: National Council of Teachers of English.

Montague, Marjorie. (1990). *Computers, Cognition, and Writing Instruction*. Albany, NY: State University of New York Press.

Neuwirth, Christine M. and David S. Kaufer. (1992). "Computers and Composition Studies: Articulating a Pattern of Discovery." In G. E. Hawisher and P. LeBlanc, (Eds.), *Re-imagining Computers and Composition*. Portsmouth, NH: Boynton/Cook.

Noblitt, James S., Willem J. A. Pet and Donald Solá. 1992. **Système-D.** Boston, MA: Heinle & Heinle Publishers.

Pennington, Martha C. (1993). "A Critical Examination of Word Processing Effects in Relation to L2 Writers." *Journal of Second Language Writing* 2(3):227–255.

Phinney, Marianne and Sandra Khouri. (1993). "Computers, Revision, and ESL Writers: The Role of Experience." *Journal of Second Language Writing* 2(3):257–277.

Rodrigues, Dawn and Raymond J. Rodrigues. (1984). "Computer-Based Creative Problem Solving." In W. Wresch, (Ed.), *The Computer in Composition Instruction*. Urbana, IL: National Council of Teachers of English.

Schwartz, Helen J. (1989). "Creating Writing Activities with the Word Processor." In C. L. Selfe, D. Rodrigues & W. R. Oates, (Eds.), *Computers in English and the Language Arts: The Challenge of Teacher Education*. Urbana, IL: National Council of Teachers of English.

Scott, Virginia M. and Robert M. Terry. (1992). *Teacher's Guide:* **Système-D** *Writing Assistant for French*. Boston, MA: Heinle & Heinle Publishers.

Selfe, Cynthia L. (1986). *Computer-Assisted Instruction in Composition*. Urbana, IL: National Council of Teachers of English.

——, Dawn Rodrigues and William R. Oates, (Eds.). (1989). *Computers in English and the Language Arts: The Challenge of Teacher Education*. Urbana, IL: National Council of Teachers of English.

Smith, John B. and Marcy Lansman. (1989). "A Cognitive Basis for a Computer Writing Environment." In B. K. Britton & S. M. Glynn, (Eds.), *Computer Writing Environments: Theory, Research, & Design*. Hillsdale, NJ: Lawrence Erlbaum.

Williamson, Michael M. and Penny Pence. (1989). "Word Processing and Student Writers." In B. K. Britton & S. M. Glynn, (Eds.), *Computer Writing Environments: Theory, Research, & Design*. Hillsdale, NJ: Lawrence Erlbaum.

Wresch, William, (Ed.). (1984). *The Computer in Composition Instruction*. Urbana, IL: National Council of Teachers of English.

Chapter 4

Correcting and Evaluating Foreign Language Writing

Hypothesis: *Correcting and evaluating FL writing are complex tasks that involve the entire writing process.*

Teacher response to student writing
        The role of the writing teacher
        Teacher expectations
        Research on teacher response to student writing
        Tolerance of grammatical errors
        Rater reliability

Student response to feedback
        Student expectations
        Research on student response to teacher feedback

Peer evaluation
        Research on peer evaluation

Self-evaluation

Scoring methods for evaluating student writing
        Holistic scoring
        Research on holistic scoring
        Analytic scoring
        Primary trait scoring
        T-unit analysis
        Research on T-unit analysis

Evaluating the process

Correcting and evaluating: the classroom implications

Case study 1

Case study 2

Case study 3

Conclusions

Topics for discussion and research

CORRECTING AND EVALUATING
FOREIGN LANGUAGE WRITING

Hypothesis
Correcting and evaluating foreign language writing are complex tasks
that involve the entire writing process.

For many teachers, correction and evaluation represent the most important strategies for teaching FL writing. Teachers often believe that students are motivated to become better writers when their papers are returned with corrections and a grade. However, rather than viewing correction and evaluation as a final step in teaching FL writing, they can be used as teaching strategies throughout the writing process. That is, during the stages of planning, generating ideas, editing, and revising, correction and evaluation can be important to students' success in learning how to write in the FL. The hypothesis for this chapter posits that both correction and evaluation represent essential components of teaching FL writing when these components involve the entire writing process.

Correcting errors in a written text has been studied extensively as it relates to improvement in writing. Much research is devoted to how, where, and when teachers should correct errors. Likewise, there is a significant amount of research on evaluation that explores the validity of different scoring methods for assessing the quality of writing. In order to understand the role that correction and evaluation play in teaching FL writing, this chapter explores theories and research in teacher response to student writing, student response to teacher feedback, peer review, and self-evaluation. In addition, this chapter discusses theories and research regarding evaluating both the written product and the writing process. Finally, because writing in a FL makes correction and evaluation of FL texts inherently different from L1 texts, this chapter will refer primarily to pertinent research in FL writing.

TEACHER RESPONSE TO STUDENT WRITING

Most teachers would agree that correcting and evaluating writing in a foreign language is a very difficult and time-consuming task. Generally, it is only after a good deal of experience reading student compositions that teachers have a sense of what represents good or poor writing in the target language. And, of course, for different levels of language proficiency there must be different criteria for assessing writing quality. The burden that teachers often feel when faced with evaluating student writing may, in fact, dissuade them from giving long or frequent writing assignments. A close examination of the many variables involved in responding to student writing may help put this challenging task into perspective.

□ THE ROLE OF THE WRITING TEACHER

Most FL teachers would not consider themselves writing teachers. In fact, most FL teachers have little or no training in teaching writing. However, given that writing is an essential part of language, civilization, and literature classes, FL teachers have an obligation to understand their role as writing teachers.

Typically the FL teacher serves as the sole audience and judge for student writing. However, the role of teacher-as-judge is a position of power that may be coming into question. Raimes points out that the teacher's role should be one of collaborator rather than judge:

> Remember that when you or any other reader responds to a student's piece of writing, your main job is not to pass judgment on its quality (unless you are an examiner and not a teacher), but to help the writer see what to do next. Ask yourself: What should the writer do now to improve this paper? What does this paper need most? (Raimes, 1983, 143).

The notion of teacher-as-collaborator is particularly valid in that it encourages a focus on the writing process rather than only on the final product, or text. Teachers who accept this role must work in collaboration with students during the different phases of the writing process. Leki (1990, 59) notes that the writing teacher is "split into three incompatible personas: teacher as real reader (i.e., audience), teacher as coach, and teacher as evaluator."

□ TEACHER EXPECTATIONS

The way teachers evaluate writing reflects their expectations. Every teacher has a concept of the perfect text, and the way a teacher responds to a text indicates the underlying notion of the perfect text (Knoblauch and Brannon, 1984). Comments such as "get rid of this sentence," or "awkward wording," or "don't use 'it' in formal essays" are all ways of suggesting what the teacher/reader expects. On the other hand, questions such as "How important are all these facts in your essay?" or "Do you believe this?" or "What does 'it' refer to here?" are facilitative, keeping the students' integrity intact and perhaps motivating them to seek clarity in a subsequent draft:

> The comments of the facilitative reader are designed to preserve the writer's control of the discourse, while also registering uncertainty about what the writer wishes to communicate. The questions posed suggest the possibility of negotiation between writer and reader, leading to richer insights and more meaningful communication. Negotiation assumes that the writer knows better than the reader the purposes involved, while the reader knows better than the writer the actual effects of authorial choices (Knoblauch and Brannon, 1984, 128).

Furthermore, a teacher's comments communicate expectations about the importance of grammatical accuracy, organization, and creative ideas. Regardless of whether teachers articulate their concept of good writing, students will interpret the teacher's expectations and attitudes based on the kinds of comments they find on their papers.

□ RESEARCH ON TEACHER RESPONSE TO STUDENT WRITING

Most research involving teacher response to FL writing centers on the degree to which feedback on grammar and/or content improves student writing. Semke's (1984) landmark study examined the effects of various methods of reacting to students' freewriting journal assignments. She analyzed four experimental groups, each one receiving a different kind of feedback: 1) comments only, 2) corrections only, 3) corrections with comments, and 4) errors signaled with a correction code for students to self-correct. All four groups were given pretests and posttests that involved one freewriting exercise (evaluated according to accuracy and fluency) and one cloze test exercise (evaluated according to general language proficiency). The results show that there was no significant difference among groups in terms of writing accuracy. However, the group that received comments only wrote significantly more than the other groups and made significantly more progress in general language ability. In addition, students in the group with comments only reacted more positively to the journal writing assignments, noting that it was enjoyable and helpful.

> . . . the results of this research . . . demonstrate that for this group of students, over a ten-week period of time, the absence of correction of free-writing assignments did not have a detrimental effect on progress in language learning. . . . The amount of practice, on the other hand, even without correction, did appear to have a positive effect on achievement (Semke, 1984, 201).

Semke concludes by pointing out that a positive and productive teacher-student relationship is fostered when teachers can get to know their students through their writing. She also notes that error correction is particularly effective when students ask for it.

In a similar study to determine what kind of error correction helps students improve their writing, Lalande (1984) found a significant difference between students whose errors were corrected by the teacher and students who were required to correct their own essays. In the control group, the teacher made corrections and required the students to rewrite their essays incorporating the corrections. The teacher in the experimental group, on the other hand, used an Error Correction Code (ECCO), and the students were charged with interpreting the codes, correcting their own mistakes, and rewriting their essays. Figure 1 shows a modified version of Lalande's ECCO.

Figure 1: Composition Correction Code

angl	anglicism (inappropriate translation from English)
art	article
aux	wrong auxiliary (*avoir* vs. *être*)
g	gender (masculine/feminine)
inf	infinitive needed here
m	mode (subjunctive vs. indicative)
n/a	noun/adjective agreement
pl	placement (adjective, adverb, negation, etc.)
pn	pronoun
prep	preposition
sp	spelling (accents, contractions, elisions, etc.)
s/v	subject/verb agreement
t	tense
v	vocabulary (wrong word)
X	delete, not necessary
?	not clear
^	something is missing
+	nicely done!

(Based on Lalande's ECCO as described in "Reducing Composition Errors: An Experiment," *Foreign Language Annals* 17(2):109–117, 1984.)

In addition to the ECCO, the students used an Error Awareness Sheet (EASE) where they recorded what kind of errors they made and how frequently they made them. Lalande found that the students in the experimental group made significant progress in their writing:

> The results of this study indicate that the combination of error-awareness and problem-solving techniques had a significant beneficial effect on the development of writing skills within the context of the experiment. Specifically, the techniques designed for, implemented, and tested in this investigation effectively prevented students from making more grammatical and orthographic errors (Lalande, 1984, 114).

Another interesting finding in this study is that the students in the control group actually demonstrated deterioration in grammatical accuracy. Lalande concluded that instructional feedback regarding grammatical and orthographic errors must invoke problem-solving/active-correction strategies in rewrite activities.

Like Lalande, Kepner (1991) conducted a study to determine what kind of feedback is related to improvement in foreign language writing. In one group, all sentence-level errors were corrected with a brief note of explanation. In the other group, the comments were strictly related to the message and included use of the students' names, a summary of the main point, the reader's reaction and evaluation based on the assignment, and a question or suggestion for improving upon the topic. The results show that consistently using message-related comments for discourse-level writing is effective for promoting the development of writing proficiency in intermediate-level college FL courses in terms of both the quality of ideas and grammatical accuracy. By the same token, the error correction model did not help students avoid surface-level errors or facilitate higher-level writing.

In a slightly different vein, Chastain's (1990) study shows that when students know that their written work will be graded, the compositions are longer and contain more complex sentences. However, the anticipated grade did not have a significant effect on the number or type of errors that students made. He concludes that while grades may foster enhanced effort on the part of many students to increase the length and complexity of their essays, it does not directly affect grammatical accuracy.

In general, studies on teacher response to student writing suggest that correcting student errors has little effect on improvement in the form or content of a text. Regardless of the feedback, it appears that rewriting is a good exercise and can do a great deal to help students improve their writing overall (Fathman and Whalley, 1990).

□ TOLERANCE OF GRAMMATICAL ERRORS

Teachers are frequently intolerant of grammatical errors. In fact, they spend a good deal of energy wondering what to do with errors. Should they be signaled, corrected, or ignored? Shakir's (1991) study analyzes the reactions of teachers to texts of Arabic students writing in English. Twenty-four secondary school teachers of English were asked to evaluate ten expository texts for coherence. The teachers were given no instructions about what features make a text coherent or incoherent. The results of this study clearly show that teachers consider the grammaticality of sentences to be the most important factor for establishing coherence. Shakir points out that a text linguist, by contrast, evaluated the same texts according to aspects of global coherence such as "interconnectivity of sentences, topic development, relevance of ideas to the rhetorical function of the writing task, the role of cohesive connectives and lexical items used in the text . . ." (1991, 400). The results of evaluating the texts according to more global criteria show that what "student writers seem to need, more than mastery of sentence structure and mechanics of writing, is an awareness-building process—a process through which they can become familiarized with what renders a text coherent and, consequently, complete and communicatively acceptable" (1991, 407). Moreover, with regard to the teachers, Shakir states:

The EFL teacher needs to be aware of the fact that textural coherence is a characteristic realized in not only appropriate use of grammatical structures, but also in interaction between contextual variables, such as the intention of the writer, the rhetorical function of the writing task, and the configuration of such variables in the surface structure of the text in hand. In such a view, grammaticality is sought not as an end, but as a means (Shakir, 1991, 410).

Given that grammatical accuracy is not necessarily the most important feature of a text, and given that teachers generally have a low tolerance for grammatical errors, they need to develop strategies for dealing with grammar errors. Raimes (1983) proposes that teachers not try to mark all errors, but rather try to decide which errors should be dealt with. She further suggests that teachers should point out what the student has done correctly so that concern for error does not dominate the writing class. Similarly, Leki (1992) suggests that all errors should not be corrected, but rather that certain errors can be selected for attention. For example, errors should be corrected if native speakers of English typically associate them with a lack of education. Stigmatizing errors such as subject/verb agreement or the use of "theirselves" should not be left to "fade out of a student's interlanguage at their own speed" (Leki, 1992, 130). Global errors that interfere with understanding should also be corrected. For example, incorrect lexical choices or errors that disturb the syntax are more serious than surface errors such as a missing or incorrect article.

Teachers are more likely to tolerate grammatical errors if they understand that they are quite normal as students progress through various stages of language proficiency. Selinker's (1972) interlanguage hypothesis posits that students of a second language move through interlanguage stages on a continuum between incompetence and proficiency. In these stages, errors are systematic and often predictable and should be considered as indications of progress rather than failure.[1]

□ RATER RELIABILITY

Given that every teacher has a set notion about what constitutes good writing, it would seem that no two teachers would rate a written text in the same way. However, teacher consensus is particularly important in settings where there are multiple sections and several teachers responsible for evaluating student writing. Equally important is a single teacher's consistency and reliability over time in evaluating student writing. The degree to which different raters would agree about the quality of a text is called *inter-rater reliability*. The term *intra-rater reliability* describes the degree to which the same rater would be consistent in assessing the quality of a text.

Several factors influence rater reliability. First, the raters' experience both with teaching and evaluating writing can affect the assessment. Teachers may be influenced by their past experience, the goals of the course, or their relationship with the students. Second, rater training can influence the evaluation. When there has been rigorous instruction and practice in assessing the quality of writing, there may be greater inter- and intra-rater reliability (Terry, 1992). Third, the rating scale may have an effect on reliability. A scale provides the criteria for assessment of quality and may reflect the biases of some raters.

In a study of rater reliability in an EFL program, Shohamy et al. (1992) compared four groups of raters: 1) professional teachers of English who received training in evaluating writing, 2) professional teachers of English who did not receive training, 3) lay English speakers who received training, and 4) lay English speakers who did not receive training. All raters used three rating scales: a holistic scale, a communicative scale, and an accuracy scale. The results show that the four groups of raters obtained relatively high inter-rater reliability. However, reliability was greater for the trained raters, regardless of background. This study provides significant data regarding the importance of intensive training:

> The practical implication of this finding is that decision makers, in selecting raters, should be less concerned about their background, since that variable seems not to increase reliability. More emphasis, however, should be put into intensive training sessions to prepare raters for their task (Shohamy et al., 1992, 31).

STUDENT RESPONSE TO FEEDBACK

For many students, the grade at the top of the paper is more important than any corrections or comments made by the teacher. Moreover, the paper may look like a battleground of red ink, and students may feel overwhelmed by the challenge of making sense of it all. Likewise, after spending time and energy reading, correcting, and evaluating student papers, teachers are often dismayed by the lack of attention that students give to their comments. This relationship between teacher and student writer merits close examination to avoid wasting teacher effort and potentially demoralizing students.

□ STUDENT EXPECTATIONS

Students writing in a foreign language often expect that their writing will be judged by its errors, both in kind and number. In a study of 100 students in beginning ESL freshman writing classes, Leki (1991) found that the students showed a great deal of interest in having their errors pointed out and did not approve of teacher comments that dealt only with organization and content. Generally speaking, the students were very concerned about surface-level errors and considered that it was the teacher's job to mark their errors. In fact, the students in this study were reluctant to rely on their nonnative peers for feedback or assistance. Leki points out that teachers who espouse a communicative approach to language teaching may tend to de-emphasize the role of error correction in writing and respond more to the content of the text. However, this tendency may stand in contrast to student expectations. Leki suggests that it is important to consult students about their expectations regarding feedback on their writing:

> It seems at best counter-productive, at worst high-handed and disrespectful of our students, to simply insist that they trust our preferences [with regard to error correction]. Language teachers might consider questioning their students on what the students feel has helped them most in their language studies, which teaching behaviors they find conducive to their progress, and which seem detrimental (Leki, 1991, 210).

In this study, the students had distinct expectations of their teachers and equated improvement in writing with error correction.

Clearly, if students want corrections and feedback, it is because they feel that they will be able to use the feedback in a subsequent paper and that it will help them become better writers. Therefore, as Leki (1992) points out, corrections and feedback are worthless on a "dead" paper, that is, a final draft that has been corrected and returned. Corrections and comments serve no purpose if the student never has the opportunity to rewrite the piece. The teacher's input is only valid if it can help students perform better, not just judge the finished product.

□ RESEARCH ON STUDENT RESPONSE TO TEACHER FEEDBACK

In a study of student writers in English courses, in English as a second language classes, and in several different foreign language courses, Cohen (1987) found that teacher feedback has a limited impact because students feel that teacher comments are often too short and uninformative. Students considered it difficult to interpret remarks such as "not clear," "needs transition," or "confusing." Cohen concludes that teachers need training with respect to providing effective feedback, just as students need training to develop effective strategies for handling teacher feedback.

In another study, Cohen and Cavalcanti (1990) examined how teachers and students in three kinds of language programs reacted to feedback on compositions. Teachers in an EFL institute program, a university EFL program, and a university L1 program generally pointed out weaknesses rather than strengths in students' work. Students in all three programs often considered their teachers to be judges of their work rather than interested readers. The importance of their findings is that there was not always a fit between the kinds of feedback that the teachers provided and what the students wanted.

In addition to assessing teacher and student attitudes and perceptions, the researchers analyzed eight strategies students used for handling feedback:

1. making a mental note
2. writing down points by type
3. identifying points to be explained
4. asking for teacher explanation
5. referring back to previous compositions
6. consulting a grammar book
7. rewriting
   a. only incorporating teacher's comments
   b. revising and expanding
8. not doing anything

(Cohen and Cavalcanti, 1990, 169).

They found that most students in all three settings either made a mental note or wanted additional teacher explanation. The researchers conclude that most students want feedback on what they are doing correctly and that there should be agreements between teachers and students on procedures and strategies for handling feedback.

Studies of students in L1, EFL, and ESL programs provide much insight about student response to teacher feedback. However, a study by Hedgcock and Lefkowitz (1994) indicates that FL students have very different experiences from ESL students with regard to teacher feedback on their writing. Generally speaking, ESL students reported that teachers assigned priority to content and organization, while FL students stated that teachers assigned priority to language accuracy and mechanical features, such as spelling and punctuation. Moreover, both groups of students expected and appreciated the kind of feedback that they got from their teachers because it was in line with course goals and expectations.

> FL and ESL practitioners will find some good news and some bad news in these findings. The good news seems to be the consistently high concern among ESL subjects for matters of content, rhetorical structure, and writing style. The very stable patterns suggest that aspects of process-oriented pedagogy have influenced the thinking of this category of L2 learner. FL subjects, on the other hand, displayed response norms which were distinctly form-focused; FL students further report that their teachers display feedback behaviors aimed largely at grammatical and lexical accuracy, as opposed to fluency, idea generation, and rhetorical organization. This finding may be attributable to a view among FL learners and practitioners that composing is primarily a form of language practice—a purpose rather different from that which drives most college-level ESL writing instruction (Hedgcock and Lefkowitz, 1994, 157).

While these findings indicate that students believe that they benefit from their teacher's feedback, it is clear that ESL and FL students get very different information from their teachers about their writing. However, it is important to bear in mind that ESL students are often learning to write in the target language in order to be able to succeed in other courses. In other words, their motivation is high because learning to write represents academic survival. For FL students, on the other hand, the writing exercise is often a goal in itself, and students believe they are writing to practice the target language.

PEER EVALUATION

Peer evaluation is an increasingly common practice in English and ESL composition classes. There are several reasons for having students engage in peer review sessions, including providing student writers with an audience other than the teacher, encouraging students to work together during the writing process, and helping student writers edit and revise their texts. While these reasons seem legitimate, teachers are beginning to explore how students actually evaluate their peers and whether peer evaluation helps student writers improve their writing.

□ RESEARCH ON PEER EVALUATION

One of the most important questions regarding peer evaluation centers on what students actually do when asked to review a peer's writing. In order to explore this question, Mangelsdorf and Schlumberger (1992) analyzed the peer review comments made by students in an advanced ESL composition class. The students in this study reviewed compositions written by students the previous semester and there was, therefore, no direct interaction between the student writers and peer reviewers. The researchers categorized the reviews according to the stance that the peer reviewers took when reading a composition. They found that students displayed three dominant stances:

1. **Prescriptive.** These peer reviewers expected the text to conform to a prescribed form, tended to put form before meaning, had a preconceived idea of what the essay should be, functioned as an editor, and identified faults and/or corrected them.

2. **Interpretive.** These peer reviewers imposed their own ideas about the topic onto the text, "rewrote" for personal understanding, distanced themselves from the author, reacted to perceived inaccuracies in content, and used the text as a prompt for personal elaboration.

3. **Collaborative.** These peer reviewers tried to see the text from the writer's viewpoint, positioned themselves with the author, pointed out problems the hypothesized reader would have, made suggestions to the author, and did not impose form.

Nearly half of the 60 peer reviewers in the study fell into the prescriptive category, taking a somewhat superior attitude toward the writer, and subordinating meaning to form; fewer peer reviewers fell in the interpretive category, often trying to provide more information on the topic and almost rewriting the composition in the process; the fewest peer reviewers fell into the collaborative category and did not try to change the text or dictate how the text should be modified, but rather were empathetic and gave reasons for their comments.

The researchers conclude that students often adopt a reviewing stance based upon the kind of feedback that they, themselves, have gotten from teachers in the past. According to the researchers, the collaborative stance is the most productive, and teachers should model this stance in their relationships with student writers so that peer reviewers will act collaboratively with each other.

In a similar study of ESL students involved in peer review, De Guerrero and Villamil (1994) examined the social-cognitive dimensions of interactive peer revision from a Vygotskyan perspective. With regard to cognitive stages of regulation during peer review sessions, they categorize students as *object-related* (the learner is controlled by the draft and does not respond to suggestions from a peer), *other-regulated* (the learner is guided by a peer), and *self-regulated* (the learner is capable of independent problem solving and responds quickly and efficiently to suggestions from a peer). As concerns social relationships, the researchers found two kinds of peer interaction: *symmetrical* and *asymmetrical*. In the former, both participants are either object-related, other-regulated, or self-regulated. In the latter, each participant has a different level of regulation. While the researchers did not investigate the number or type of revisions that students made, nor the kind of relationships between peers that were most likely to lead to revision, this study provides insight into the complexity of student relationships during peer review sessions. In addition, the researchers point out that the students were using L1 (in this case Spanish) during their peer review sessions. They argue that interacting in L1 can be very beneficial in that it is a practical and effective way to achieve goals during peer review.

Another question involves the degree to which student writers revise their texts when they participate in peer evaluation sessions. Hedgcock and Lefkowitz (1992) designed a study of FL students to compare revisions made after getting feedback from peers with revisions made after getting feedback from teachers. The experimental group engaged in oral/aural peer review sessions during which student writers read their papers aloud and their peers listened and followed along in the text, giving feedback according to very explicit guidelines. The control group received traditional written teacher feedback on their texts. The results show that the experimental group (oral/aural peer review) performed slightly lower overall than the control group (traditional teacher feedback), although the difference in performance was not statistically significant. The researchers further note that the experimental group showed greater improvement in the areas of content, organization, and vocabulary, while the control group showed improvement in the area of grammar. The fact that the two groups performed on a nearly equal level suggests that peer review does not result in inferior writing as many teachers might think.

A valuable aspect of Hedgcock and Lefkowitz's study is their peer revision guides. According to their model, both the student writer and the peer reviewers are provided with explicit guidelines for reviewing a composition. In stage one of the peer review session, the student writer distributes photocopies of the composition to the peer reviewers and then reads the text aloud while the others listen and note their reactions. The peer reviewers are directed to ignore the grammatical aspects of the text and to focus on the content and clarity of the message. In stage two of the peer review session photocopies of the revised composition are distributed and the same process is repeated, followed by a final reading aloud by the student writer during which peer reviewers identify grammatical errors.

Connor and Asenavage (1994) designed a similar study involving ESL students, however, their results point to very different conclusions about the effect of peer commentary. The researchers measured the type and number of revisions student writers made as a result of comments from peers, from the teacher, and as a result of self/other help. The overall results show that only 5 percent of the revisions resulted from peer comments, 35 percent resulted from teacher comments, and 60 percent occurred as a result of self/others. These findings clearly call into question the value of peer review as a means to engage student writers in both surface-level (form) and text-based (content) revisions.[2]

There is some disagreement about the effectiveness of peer evaluation. One view holds that peer evaluation can be beneficial by providing another kind of audience and less anxiety for student writers. Another point of view is that peers do not always provide helpful suggestions. However, some research shows that when students go through intensive training, they are able to react productively to peers' writing (Stanley, 1992). Peer evaluators can learn to identify strengths and weaknesses in the content as well as in the form of a text if there is a great deal of preparation and training to do so.

SELF-EVALUATION

FL teachers generally require students to correct the errors in their written work. In fact, this exercise is considered to be an essential part of learning how to write. Another important aspect of learning how to write involves learning how to assess the overall strengths or weaknesses of one's own work. Most students, however, have difficulty distancing themselves from their writing in order to engage in this kind of self-evaluation. Beach (1989) suggests that students may require help from the teacher in learning how to evaluate their work. First, the teacher can guide individual students in describing various aspects of their texts such as the goals for the content, what the audience is supposed to think, what rhetorical strategies are being used (i.e., supporting, contrasting, etc.), and the role that the writer wants to play (i.e., student, scientist, etc.). After describing these aspects of their texts, the students are more capable of judging them. Typically, students will see that the ideal goals that they envisioned during the describing stage of the conference are not actually realized in the paper. At this point, students can define how to reconcile the ideal with the real. Finally, students need some guidance in selecting the kinds of revision that will meet their needs. For example, they may want to add, modify, delete, reword, or reorganize. Beach contends that students can learn to describe, judge, and revise their texts on their own if they are initially guided through this process during a student-teacher conference.[3]

SCORING METHODS FOR EVALUATING STUDENT WRITING

Evaluating student writing and assigning a grade is a very difficult task for teachers. In fact, both teachers and students may regard grades on student writing as often subjective and arbitrary. There is no question that evaluating student writing involves some degree of subjectivity on the part of the teacher or evaluator. However, there are several scoring methods that define performance criteria in such a way that there is a high degree of objectivity.[4]

□ HOLISTIC SCORING

This method of scoring involves assigning a single grade to a whole text. Individual features of a text, such as grammar, spelling, and organization, should not be considered as separate entities:

> Since, in holistic scoring, the entire written text is evaluated as a whole, it is important to establish the specific criteria upon which the evaluation is to be based prior to undertaking the evaluation. This does not mean establishing a catalogue of precise individual errors that might appear, but rather deciding what impact the errors that are present have on the overall tone, structure, and comprehensibility of the writing sample (Terry, 1989, 49).

According to Terry (1989), the holistic scoring instrument used by the Educational Testing Service for evaluating the Advanced Placement Examination in foreign languages, shown in Figure 2, works well and can be altered to fit the level of students and the focus of instruction. The numerical scale ranks performance at levels described as "superior," "competent," and "incompetent." For each level, the descriptions can be changed to reflect the kind of performance that teachers expect at a given level of language ability. Furthermore, the reliability of this scoring method is considered good when the raters are trained to establish common standards based on practice with the kinds of writing samples that they will be evaluating (Cooper, 1977b).

Figure 2: Holistic Scoring Scale		
Demonstrates Superiority	9	*Strong* control of the language; proficiency and variety in grammatical usage with few significant errors; broad command of vocabulary and of idiomatic language.
Demonstrates Competence	8 7	*Good* general control of grammatical structures despite some errors and/or some awkwardness of style. Good use of idioms and vocabulary. Reads smoothly overall.
Suggests Competence	6 5	*Fair* ability to express ideas in target language; correct use of simple grammatical structures or use of more complex structures without numerous serious errors. Some apt vocabulary and idioms. Occasional signs of fluency and sense of style.
Suggests Incompetence	4 3	*Weak* use of language with little control of grammatical structures. Limited vocabulary. Frequent use of anglicisms, which force interpretations on the part of the reader. Occasional redeeming features.
Demonstrates Incompetence	2 1	*Clearly unacceptable* from most points of view. Almost total lack of vocabulary resources, little or no sense of idiom and/or style. Essentially translated from English.
Floating point		A one-point bonus should be awarded for a coherent and well-organized essay or for a particularly inventive one.

(Taken from Johnson's *Grading the Advanced Placement Examination in French Language*, Princeton, NJ: Advanced Placed Program of the College Board, 1983.)

□ RESEARCH ON HOLISTIC SCORING

Research shows that teachers who are not accustomed to using holistic scoring may inadvertently disadvantage certain groups of students. Sweedler-Brown (1993) and Ruetten (1994) point out that ESL students are more likely to do poorly on holistically scored writing exams than native English-speaking students. According to their separate findings, writing instructors with no specific training in teaching or evaluating ESL students tend to react negatively to sentence-level errors:

> In this study, sentence-level error was the only significant influence on holistic score and was, furthermore, the critical factor in pass/fail decisions in these ESL essays. It is discouraging to note that the quality of organization and paragraph development had no observable effect on the essays' holistic scores (Sweedler-Brown, 1993, 12).

The researchers conclude that holistic scoring may not be an effective means to assess ESL writing and that composition programs need to clarify their standards regarding acceptability of error for essays written by ESL students.

In a very different study of holistic scoring, Scott (1993) describes a collaborative effort among high school and college teachers to develop a clear set of assessment criteria for a proficiency-oriented writing contest in Spanish. The participating teachers chose a holistic scoring method based on a 20-point scale and 4 rubrics (*sobresaliente, notable, bien, mención honorifica*). For each level of language study (Spanish I, II, III, IV), the rubrics describe a set of criteria, including coherence, organization, grammar, vocabulary, and spelling. Scott points out that this exercise resulted in more than a successful writing contest, since the participating teachers came away with a clear sense that teaching and evaluating writing are important curricular considerations:

> As a part of the philosophy of teaching for communicative proficiency, the teaching and assessment of student writing become essential *from the very beginning*, not just at the advanced levels. This notion was new to many of the teachers involved in this project. The ability to assess writing in a way that is different from the "mark every error" approach can lead to a better understanding of a student's ability to communicate in the second language (Scott, 1993, 386).

For holistic scoring to accurately measure students' writing proficiency, teachers must consider more than linguistic accuracy. The task requirements, the level of language proficiency, the use of vocabulary, and sentence complexity are as important as accuracy in a holistic evaluation.[5]

□   ANALYTIC SCORING

This method of scoring involves evaluating various features of a text, such as grammatical accuracy, vocabulary, idiomatic expression, organization, relevance, and coherence (see Figures 3 and 4). For many classroom teachers, analytic scoring has more appeal than holistic scoring because the separation of features encourages a greater degree of objectivity. In addition, Terry notes that students are likely to benefit from seeing how the different components of their written work are being evaluated:

> Students should receive a copy of the analytic scoring criteria in advance. They will then know what is expected of them and how to interpret the evaluation of their written work. They can readily see where their strengths and weaknesses lie and can, over time, visualize their progress with subsequent evaluated samples of their writing (Terry, 1992, 247).

Like a holistic scale, an analytic scale may be adapted to the level of language proficiency of the student writers. However, a potential problem with

Figure 3: Analytic Scoring Scale		
Grammar		
Many errors	1	
Some errors	2	3
Few errors	4	5
Expression		
Many anglicisms	1	
Acceptable	2	3
Idiomatic	4	5
Organization of ideas		
Series of unrelated sentences	1	
Coherence between sentences	2	3
Good coherence between sentences and paragraphs	4	5
Global impression		
Incomprehensible	1	
Acceptable	2	3
Excellent	4	5
TOTAL _____ /20		

(Taken from pedagogical materials used by the author.)

analytic scoring involves defining exactly what is meant by each category. For example, the rating scale shown in Figure 3 describes grammatical accuracy according to "many errors," "some errors," or "few errors." An experienced teacher using this scale is likely to have a sense of how to evaluate a student essay according to these criteria. However, a novice teacher may be less capable of distinguishing between descriptions such as "acceptable" and "excellent." An analytic rating scale with more detailed descriptions for each feature, such as shown in Figure 4, is likely to increase inter-rater reliability.

□ PRIMARY TRAIT SCORING

This method of scoring is similar to holistic scoring in that the entire writing sample is rated as a whole. However, with primary trait scoring, the mode of discourse to be evaluated is defined precisely, and a holistic score is designed to reflect the specific criteria of the discourse mode. Lloyd-Jones (1977) describes a model that includes explanatory, persuasive, and expressive modes of discourse. His model considers explanatory writing to be subject-oriented, persuasive writing to be audience-oriented, and expressive writing to be discourser-oriented

Figure 4: Analytic Scoring Scale

SCORE CRITERIA

Content	27–30	*Excellent to very good:* knowledgeable; substantive, throrough development of thesis; relevant to topic assigned.
	22–26	*Good to average:* some knowledge of subject; adequate range; limited thematic development; mostly relevant to topic, but lacks detail.
	17–21	*Fair to poor:* limited knowledge of subject; minimal substance; poor thematic development.
	13–16	*Very poor:* shows little or no knowledge of subject; inadequate quantity; not relevant, or not enough to rate.
Organization	18–20	*Excellent to very good:* fluent expression; clear statement of ideas; solid support; clear organization; logical and cohesive sequencing.
	14–17	*Good to average:* adequate fluency; main ideas clear but loosely organized; supporting material limited; sequencing logical but incomplete.
	10–13	*Fair to poor:* low fluency; ideas not well connected; logical sequencing and development lacking.
	7–9	*Very poor:* ideas not communicated; organization lacking, or not enough to rate.
Grammar	22–25	*Excellent to very good:* accurate use of relatively complex structures; few errors in agreement, number, tense, word order, articles, pronouns, prepositions.
	18–21	*Good to average:* simple constructions used effectively; some problems in use of complex constructions; errors in agreement, number, tense, word order, articles, pronouns, prepositions.
	11–17	*Fair to poor:* significant defects in use of complex constructions; frequent errors in agreement, number, tense, negation, word order, articles, pronouns, prepositions; fragments and deletions; lack of accuracy interferes with meaning.
	5–10	*Very poor:* no mastery of simple sentence construction; text dominated by errors; does not communicate, or not enough to rate.
Vocabulary	18–20	*Excellent to very good:* complex range; accurate word/idiom choice; mastery of word forms; appropriate register.
	14–17	*Good to average:* adequate range; errors of word/idiom choice; effective transmission of meaning.
	10–13	*Fair to poor:* limited range; frequent word/idiom errors; inappropriate choice, usage; meaning not effectively communicated.
	7–9	*Very poor:* translation-based errors; little knowledge of target language vocabulary, or not enough to rate.
Mechanics	5	*Excellent to very good:* masters conventions of spelling, punctuation, capitalization, paragraph indentation, etc.
	4	*Good to average:* occasional errors in spelling, punctuation, capitalization, paragraph indentation, etc., which do not interfere with meaning.
	3	*Fair to poor:* frequent spelling, punctutation, capitalization, paragraphing errors; meaning disrupted by formal problems.
	2	*Very poor:* no mastery of conventions due to frequency of mechanical errors, or not enough to rate.
Total	____/100	

(Taken from Hedgcock and Lefkowitz, *Collaborative Oral/Aural Revision in Foreign Language Writing Instruction,* Journal of Second Language Writing 1(3):255–276, 1992.)

(self-oriented). He states that primary trait scoring guides include several features that are specific for each writing task:

> A scoring guide consists of (1) the exercise itself, (2) a statement of the primary rhetorical trait of the writing which should be elicited by the exercise (a kind of statement of the limited test objective), (3) an interpretation of the exercise indicating how each element of the stimulus is presumed to affect the respondent (a kind of hypothesis about performance), (4) an interpretation of how the situation of the exercise is related to the posited primary trait (a synthesis of #2 and #3), (5) a system for defining the shorthand which is to be used in reporting descriptions of the writing (the actual scoring guide), (6) samples of papers which have been scored (definition of the score points), and (7) discussions of why each sample paper was scored as it was (extensions of the definitions) (Lloyd-Jones, 1977, 45).

Lloyd-Jones further states that primary trait scoring is more difficult than other methods because it is heavily dependent on the task and the scoring guide. Moreover, primary trait scoring is labor intensive, since the teacher must identify the type of discourse to be evoked by the writing task and develop criteria for assessing the degree to which the writer performed the rhetorical task. Figures 5 and 6 show an example of a primary trait task and scoring guide for explanatory writing.

□   T-UNIT ANALYSIS

Very different from holistic, analytic, or primary trait scoring, T-unit analysis examines the length and complexity of sentences in a written text. While this

---

Figure 5: Primary Trait Task for Explanatory Writing

Writing task: Write an informative article for a German magazine, describing typical American high school students. Describe how typical students dress and what they do in school and during leisure time.

Student writer: Intermediate student of FL.

Primary trait: Explanatory—subject oriented.

Rationale:
1. To determine whether the writer uses an appropriate register of language for writing a magazine article on the topic.
2. To test whether the writer can take an objective stance in order to communicate interesting information to someone of a different culture.
3. To evaluate the writer's use of the present tense.
4. To evaluate the vocabulary used to describe clothing and leisure activities, especially nouns and adjectives.

(Taken from pedagogical materials used by the author.)

Figure 6: Primary Trait Evaluation Guide for Explanatory Text

Language register:

1 Writer uses a register commonly reserved for oral communication.
2 Writer uses a combination of oral and written registers.
3 Writer uses a register appropriate for written communication.

Writer's stance with regard to cultural aspects of the topic:

1 Writer seems unaware that German students might be different from American students.
2 Writer chooses to talk about aspects that suggest some awareness of cultural difference.
3 Writer seems very aware of aspects of American culture that may make American students different from German students.

Use of the present tense:

1 Three to five different verbs used, subject/verb agreement errors, spelling errors.
2 Five to seven different verbs used, occasional subject/verb errors, few spelling errors.
3 Seven to ten different verbs used, no subject/verb errors, no spelling errors.

Use of vocabulary:

1 Nouns frequently misspelled, articles often incorrect, little use of adjectives, consistent errors in noun/adjective agreement.
2 Some errors in spelling, occasional incorrect articles, acceptable number of adjectives used to create a visual image, some noun/adjective agreement errors.
3 Correct use of nouns to describe male and female students, no errors in use of articles, variety of adjectives creates vivid image for reader, no noun/adjective agreement errors.

FINAL PRIMARY TRAIT SCORING GUIDE

Inadequate		Acceptable		Highly competent
1	2	3	4	5

(Taken from pedagogical materials used by the author.)

type of textual analysis is rarely used by teachers, it merits mention since some composition researchers and applied linguists claim that the syntactic complexity of a text is a good predictor of its quality.

Hunt (1965) invented the term T-unit (minimal terminable unit) and defined it as one main clause plus the subordinate clauses attached to or embedded within it. He defined a clause as a structure with a subject and a finite verb (a verb with a tense marker), including any coordinated subjects and coordinated verb phrases. For example, the sentence "He said I ought to be more careful" includes two clauses and represents one T-unit. In determining syntactic complexity of a text, Hunt calculated the *mean sentence length*, the *mean clause length*, the *number of T-units*, and the *ratio of clauses per T-unit*. Mean sentence length is determined by dividing the number of words by the number of sentences in a text; mean clause length is calculated by dividing the total number of words in a T-unit by the total number of clauses (the sentence cited previously includes two clauses, "he said," with two words, and "I ought to be more careful," with six words, or a total of eight words divided by two clauses, giving a mean clause length of four); the ratio of clauses per T-unit is figured by comparing the sum of clauses and the sum of T-units (for example, a text with 40 clauses and 10 T-units will yield a T-unit ratio of 4:1).

□ RESEARCH ON T-UNIT ANALYSIS

By using this type of calculation in analyzing the native language writing of students in grades 4, 8, and 12, Hunt determined that sentence length, mean clause length, and the number of T-units generally increased with age. He further found that the mean length of T-units and the ratio of clauses per T-unit also increased with age, while the number of T-units per sentence decreased with age. Of the four measurements, a statistical calculation showed that the T-unit was the best indicator of a student's grade level, second best was mean clause length, third best was subordination ratio, and poorest was sentence length.

Hunt's finding that T-units were a good indicator of writing quality is corroborated by Mills's (1990) study of 177 exit exam essays of students from a college freshman English program. Mills used several methods to analyze the essays, including syntactic complexity (based on Hunt's mean length of T-unit), mean length of sentences, mean length of clauses, and overall length of essay. While Mills admits that the results of his study are not conclusive, he states that there is evidence that the mean length of T-unit (MLTU) is an indicator of the quality of a text. Finally, in order for T-unit assessment to have meaning, the MLTU must be calculated for an entire group. For example, with regard to FL writing, one might want to calculate the MLTU that corresponds to good, average, and poor writing for each level of language study.

EVALUATING THE PROCESS

While there is little or no research on evaluating the writing process, teachers are becoming increasingly aware of the importance of assessing the work that students do during the planning, idea generation, editing, and revising stages of the writing process. Moreover, learning how to write is viewed as a complex process, and teachers may tend to de-emphasize any single draft and focus instead on the overall progress that a student makes during the course of study.

One of the effects of the process movement has been to occlude the criteria used to evaluate writing. While most teachers of writing still assign grades to papers at some point in the course of instruction, the emphasis has shifted from summative to formative evaluation, or, in the language of process advocates, for a teacher's role as judge to one of coach (Faigley, 1992, 112–113).

CORRECTING AND EVALUATING: THE CLASSROOM IMPLICATIONS

If teachers want students to improve their FL writing, it is possible that they may have to change some preconceived notions about what it means to correct and evaluate student writing. The following suggestions may help teachers to rethink their approaches to judging FL writing.

1. *Clearly define expectations.*

Although the teacher generally designs the course goals, students are not always aware of those goals and may tend to interpret them according to how the teacher presents the material. If the focus of instruction is on grammar, then writing will be viewed as a grammar exercise. With this focus, students will perceive the teacher as a judge of grammaticality. If the focus of instruction is on communication, writing will be viewed as a skill that requires clarity of meaning. With this focus, the teacher will be viewed as a member of the classroom community whose role is primarily facilitative.

In any FL course, teachers must define the role that writing plays. That is, students should understand the distinction between writing and other skill development. Second, teachers must explain what kind of writing the students will be doing. A course may include some freewriting during class, journal writing, creative writing, or academic essay writing. Finally, it is important for students to understand the criteria that will be used to evaluate each kind of writing. Students need to be familiar with the criteria by which they will be judged and need to have an opportunity to discuss the scoring method with the teacher.

Since students vary a great deal in their writing ability, it can be helpful for teachers to collect examples of good student writing. Showing students what constitutes "good" writing at each level of language study can be very useful. Model texts are especially important at more advanced levels of study when students use more sophisticated words and more complex structures. Ultimately teachers must define what they want from their students and communicate those expectations clearly.

2. *Clearly define the teacher's role.*

Students automatically perceive the teacher's role as that of judge. This is not, in fact, a faulty perspective, since teachers generally give grades and **are** judges. Therefore, there is no point in denying that the teacher ultimately decides whether a student has performed adequately. However, teachers can alter their function as judge and take on a coaching role during the writing process. That is, during the planning, idea generation, editing, and revising stages of writing, teachers can work in collaboration with students. Thus, students who work seriously to incorporate teacher suggestions during the writing process will rarely be surprised by a grade that they get. It is important that students understand that teachers must play two roles: collaborator **and** judge.

3. *Have students work together collaboratively.*

There is no conclusive evidence that peer review helps students improve their writing. However, peer review has become an accepted feature of most L1 and ESL writing programs. With regard to FL writing, both teachers and students may perceive peer reviewers as not linguistically sophisticated enough to respond effectively to their peers' work. This perception is not entirely false. Students who are asked to proofread or evaluate a classmate's work may have no idea what to look for, or worse, may change something that was correct. Moreover, weak writers may be weak readers. How, then, can FL students work together productively when learning how to write?

The first and most important issue relates to the language that students are expected to speak during peer review sessions: Should they use L1 or L2? While it may seem like heresy to some teachers, the answer is both L1 and L2. During the planning and idea-generation stages of the writing process, students can be directed to use the FL. Communicating their ideas to peers and making notes on their responses can be an important part of the writing process. Depending on the level of language study, the teacher may need to guide students explicitly in their interaction. For example, if the composition task for intermediate-level students is "describe the person you admire most and explain why you admire this person," the teacher might provide the following sentence completion exercise in the FL:

The person I admire most is ___
This person lives ___ / works ___
I first saw/met this person ___
Physically, this person is ___
The personality traits of this person are ___
I admire this person because ___ (give 3 reasons)

With this kind of framework, two or more students are able to talk together about their topics, ask each other questions, and begin the process of organizing and generating ideas.

During the editing and revising stages of the writing process, students are no longer focused on "What am I going to write?" but rather on "Do you understand what I wrote?" With this focus, students are more likely to work effectively if they can be free to question and comment on their peer's work in L1. A classroom can come alive with productive discussion: "What is this word?" "Are you sure it's spelled correctly?" "I can't figure out what you mean in this sentence." If the teacher is careful to define the parameters for speaking in the native language in class, students and teachers will see the benefits of using both L1 and FL during peer review sessions.

In addition to concerns about the language of expression, it is important to provide students with clear directions during peer review sessions. If they are asked to read a peer's text for grammatical accuracy, they may need checklists or tasks that focus their attention on specific linguistic features. For example, they may be told to underline all adjectives and to verify that they agree with the noun they modify. Or, they may be asked to note the tense of verbs in the margins and analyze whether they are used correctly. Students are generally unable to attend to the overall accuracy of a text without explicit tasks and directions.

The most helpful activity during peer review sessions is for students to read their own texts aloud while their peer(s) follow along on a copy. Research has shown that this kind of exercise may help both the student writer and the peer reviewer identify grammar errors as well as awkward, confusing, or incomplete sentences (Raimes, 1983; Hedgcock and Lefkowitz, 1992).

4. *Make sure that the scoring method fits the task.*

Teachers will often adopt one kind of scoring method and use it for all writing assignments. However, it is important to recognize that this is not always appropriate. Holistic scoring evaluates the overall quality of a text and is typically generic enough to be used for any kind of text. Analytic scoring, on the other hand, evaluates different features of the text and may require careful weighting of each feature. For example, Figure 4 shows an analytic scoring scale that assigns 30 points to content, 20 points to organization, 25 points to grammar, 20 points to vocabulary, and 5 points to mechanics, for a total of 100 points. Depending on the nature of the composition task, the importance of each feature will vary. For a composition task that requires students to express their ideas on a topic, content would be heavily weighted; for a composition task that requires students to write a postcard recounting what they did on vacation, grammar and vocabulary might be weighted more heavily than content or organization.

The analytic scoring scale shown in Figure 3 assigns the same weight to the four categories—grammar, expression, organization of ideas, and global impression. However, this scale can also be modified to reflect the goals of the composition task. Figure 7 shows a modified scale with varied weighting in which grammar and expression, each worth 6 points, are weighted more heavily than organization of ideas, 3 points, and global impression, 5 points. Furthermore, if a teacher is not comfortable with a 20-point scale, this can also be modified.

Figure 7: Analytic Scoring Scale with Varied Weighting

Grammar

Many errors	1		1	2
Some errors	2	3	3	4
Few errors	4	5	5	6

Expression

Many anglicisms	1		1	2
Acceptable	2	3	3	4
Idiomatic	4	5	5	6

Organization of ideas

Series of unrelated sentences	1		1
Coherence between sentences	2	3	2
Good coherence between sentences and paragraphs	4	5	3

Global impression

Incomprehensible	1		1	
Acceptable	2	3	2	3
Excellent	4	5	4	5

TOTAL _____ /20

(Taken from pedagogical materials used by the author.)

Primary trait and T-unit scoring are rarely used in FL teaching, however, they each represent very interesting ways to evaluate writing. Primary trait scoring forces the teacher to analyze the goals of the composition task closely and define the desired student performance. T-unit scoring, while extremely time consuming, can provide interesting information about the syntactic complexity in writing of individual students as well as of an entire class or level.

5. *Carefully consider how to correct errors.*

Many teachers feel compelled to write the correct form by an error on a student paper. This practice can be appropriate, especially if a student can benefit from seeing how a sentence could be rephrased to communicate the idea more clearly. Nevertheless, most studies suggest that students rarely pay attention to these kinds of corrections and often make the same errors again. Some researchers suggest that teachers should focus more on the content of the message than on the grammatical errors, however, this suggestion is not always practical in the classroom setting.

There are basically two kinds of error correction that have been shown to benefit students: *indirect* and *direct* correction (Hendrickson, 1980). Indirect correction indicates the location of an error by underlining, circling, making marks where something is missing, or putting a question mark where something is unclear. Direct correction indicates the location of an error and provides clues on how to correct it, such as writing "tense" or "agreement" near the error. A correction code, such as the one shown in Figure 1, has also proven to be helpful (Lalande, 1984). Both direct and indirect correction can be used together. Moreover, students can benefit from identifying and listing of errors that occur frequently in their writing (Hendrickson, 1980).

   6. *Give feedback that encourages students to improve their writing.*

There are some teachers who would argue that using a red pen to correct written work can have a negative effect on students. They point out that a paper covered in red marks may discourage rather than motivate students. In fact, it may not be the color of the ink that disheartens students but the way that feedback is presented.

First, it is not always productive to write everything directly on the students' papers. Using a separate sheet of paper for corrections, questions, and comments can give students a sense that their papers have been analyzed rather than mutilated. Second, students may feel a sense of accomplishment when everything that is **correct** is highlighted on their papers. This approach provides a visible reinforcement for work that is acceptable and comprehensible. Finally, when the comments are personalized, students are more likely to react positively than when they feel the remarks are generic.

   7. *Teach students how to respond to feedback on their writing.*

All writers, regardless of the language of expression, have difficulty being objective about their own work. When FL students are asked to reread their work before handing it in, they often make no corrections or changes. Once the paper is written, students seem overwhelmed when asked to check for grammatical errors, unclear wording, or problems with coherence and organization. However, when students get a paper back from the teacher with marks drawing their attention to problems in the text, it is important to help them make productive use of the feedback. Figure 8 shows a worksheet that may help students focus on how to proceed with revisions.

   8. *Evaluate the writing process.*

If we subscribe to the notion that FL writing is a particularly complex process, and that students should be explicitly guided to engage in the process,

---

Figure 8: Revision Worksheet

After carefully reviewing the comments that the teacher has written, do the exercises below:

GRAMMAR:
Make a list of corrections.

EXPRESSION:
A) Reformulate sentences that are marked as unclear.

B) Reread your composition, checking for repeated subjects at the beginning of sentences. Then, link sentences with appropriate conjunctions and rewrite them.

ORGANIZATION:
Make a brief outline of your paper **as it is currently written**.

REORGANIZATION:
Put your paper aside and rework the outline above.

(Taken from pedagogical materials used by the author.)

---

it stands to reason that the writing process should be evaluated. That is, students should be held accountable for the work they do during the planning, idea generation, writing, editing, and revising stages of the writing process.

The most effective way to hold students accountable for planning and generating ideas is to require them to make informal notes of their ideas. A prewriting worksheet with specific tasks, such as the one shown in Figure 9, provides students with clear guidelines. Then, using the prewriting evaluation sheet in Figure 10, teachers can give students a grade for their work.

In addition to evaluating the planning and idea-generation stages of the writing process, it is important to evaluate how students edit and revise. (See suggestion 7.) Teachers need to monitor students and reinforce good work during these stages of the writing process also. Finally, rewriting is the most important work that students do in the composition class. In fact, some researchers suggest that students should have the opportunity to rewrite twice, with the third draft being the final one (Hedgcock and Lefkowitz, 1992; Raimes, 1983). However, when students are required to do pre-writing exercises, such as

Figure 9: Prewriting Worksheet

(Writing a description of someone)

NAME:

Subject:

Background: (Describe **where** your subject is.)

12 adjectives:

1.	7.
2.	8.
3.	9.
4.	10.
5.	11.
6.	12.

Synonyms for 5 of the adjectives:
1.
2.
3.
4.
5.

Antonyms for 5 of the adjectives:
1.
2.
3.
4.
5.

Figures of speech:

Write one antithesis:

Write one simile:

Write one metaphor:

(Taken from pedagogical materials used by the author.)

Figure 10: Prewriting Worksheet Evaluation

Composition: _____

5   All tasks are complete. There is clear evidence of serious creative work.

4   Most tasks are complete. There is some evidence of creative work.

3   Some tasks are complete. There is evidence that the work was done without sufficient thought.

2   Few tasks are complete. The work is insufficient.

1   No tasks were completed.

TOTAL _____/5

(Taken from pedagogical materials used by the author.)

the composition worksheet shown in suggestion 8, one rewrite and a final draft are generally sufficient.

    9. *Work with colleagues.*

    Since writing plays a relatively important role in language, civilization, and literature courses, teachers should work together to establish criteria for correcting and evaluating writing. It is often very difficult for students when the criteria for evaluating writing change as they advance from language to literature and civilization courses.[6]

CASE STUDY 1

A college French professor with 15 years teaching experience decided to compare four different scoring methods: holistic, analytic, primary trait, and T-unit assessment. She had always used an analytic scoring scale when teaching advanced grammar and composition but wanted to explore the validity of other methods. By analyzing one composition according to criteria for each of the four scoring methods, she hoped to gain insight into the strengths and weaknesses of each method. The composition she used for this informal experiment was written by a student enrolled her third-year college French grammar and composition course who consistently did above-average work.

    Composition assignment:
    Décrivez quelqu'un et faites "vivre" cette personne pour le lecteur.
    [Describe someone and make this person "come alive" for the reader.]

Le Portrait

Une seule figure est assis à une table dans les ombres noires du coin de la salle penché au-dessus d'un papier sur laquelle il écrit lentement. Ses cheveux longs mettent collé au mélange de sueur et larmes qui couvre sa visage maussade. Il ne tente pas d'essuyer les cheveux insouciant de ses yeux, mais plutôt, il atteint pour une autre cigarette. Puisqu'il allume la cigarette, sa figure est calme. Il regarde la fumée qui rampe au loin de la cigarette et le long du mur, et se replie au plafond. Ensuite ses yeux vides se fixe sur la main qui écrit — à qui il concerne. Ce jeune homme écrit comme un étudiant qui est résolu à finir un examen, mais il sait que le travaille est désespéré. A la fin, il donne sa signature à la page sans hésitation, décroche le fusil qui reste à son côté, et se repose dans sa chaise. Pendant que ses yeux mornes sont fixé sur le plafond qui est rempli de la fumée, il crie les mots . . . à Dieu . . . [7]

[A lone figure is sitting at a table in the black shadows of the corner of the room leaning over a paper on which he is writing slowly. His long hair stuck to the mixture of sweat and tears that cover his somber face. He does not try to wipe the indifferent hair from his eyes, but rather, he reaches for another cigarette. Since he lights the cigarette, his face is calm. He watches the smoke that crawls far from the cigarette and along the wall, and folds itself on the ceiling. Then his vacant eyes fixate on the hand that writes — on which he is concerned. This young man writes like a student who is resolute to finish an exam, but he knows that the work is in vain. At the end, he gives his signature to the page without hesitation, cocks the gun that rests at his side, and rests in his chair. While his sad eyes are fixated on the ceiling that is filled with the smoke, he cries the words . . . to God . . .]

HOLISTIC SCORING using the scale shown in Figure 2:

Demonstrates competence: 8 points
The writer shows overall control of the structure of the language. There is also creative use of vocabulary, and the sentences are linked in a logical and coherent fashion. The grammatical errors and awkwardness of style do not interfere with the essence of the message.

Floating point: 1 point
The writer is especially inventive, leading the reader skillfully to a climactic ending.

Commentary:
The total score is 9/10 and represents excellent work.

ANALYTIC SCORING using the scale shown in Figure 4:

Content: 28
The writer did a good job of carrying out the assignment. The only weakness is that, compared to other compositions in the class, this one is quite short.

Organization: 20

The writer's sense of narrative and timing make this description exceptionally engaging. The composition is organized to the degree that the reader is taken by surprise at the end.

Grammar: 22

The use of complex sentences is quite impressive. There are several noun/adjective agreement errors (*assis, insouciant, fixé*), the use of *puisque* when the writer meant *pendant que*, and an incorrect relative pronoun (*à qui*).

Vocabulary: 17

The writer clearly tried to use rich imagery, unusual descriptive adjectives (*maussade, insouciant, désespéré, morne*) and distinct verbs (*tenter, ramper, replier*). There are some word-choice errors that interfere with comprehension, such as *ses cheveux longs **mettent collé**, les cheveux **insouciant**,* and *il **atteint** pour une autre cigarette.* **Mechanics:** 5

Commentary:

The total score is 92/100, which represents excellent work.

PRIMARY TRAIT SCORING:

Primary trait: Expressive—discourser-oriented

Rationale:

1. To determine whether the writer can describe a person in such a way that the reader can "see" the subject in a particular setting. The writer will have read three texts from French literature that provide vivid descriptions of a person in a setting.
2. To evaluate the writer's use of unusual adjectives as well as to incorporate figures of speech, such as antithesis, comparison, metaphor, and metonymie.

Preliminary scoring guide:

Description of setting:

1 There is no setting.

2 The setting is suggested, but is not clear.

3 The setting is vivid and provides a good background for the subject to be described.

Description of person:

1 The writer provides a series of vague qualities to describe the person, such as "she is generous", and the reader has no sense of the person in question.

2 The writer elicits some aspects of the person, but the character is not "visible" to the reader.

3   The writer describes the person vividly and engages the reader in the description.

Use of adjectives:

1   Three to five different adjectives used; agreement and spelling errors.

2   Five to seven different adjectives used, occasional agreement errors, few spelling errors.

3   Seven to ten different adjectives used, no agreement errors, no spelling errors.

Commentary on preliminary scoring:

The writer receives a 3 for description of setting, a 3 for description of person, and a 3 for use of adjectives.

Final Scoring Guide:

Inadequate		Acceptable		Highly competent
1	2	3	4	**5**

Commentary:

The writer has demonstrated a high level of competence on preliminary scoring and therefore receives a score of 5 on the final scoring. This score represents excellent work.

T-UNIT SCORING:

T-unit 1 (27 words):

Une seule figure est assis à une table dans les ombres noires du coin de la salle penché au-dessus d'un papier sur laquelle il écrit lentement.

T-unit 2 (16 words):

Ses cheveux longs mettent collé au mélange de sueur et larmes qui couvre sa visage maussade.

T-unit 3 (12 words):

Il ne tente pas d'essuyer les cheveux insouciant de ses yeux,

T-unit 4 (8 words):

mais plutôt, il atteint pour une autre cigarette.

T-unit 5 (9 words):

Puisqu'il allume la cigarette, sa figure est calme.

T-unit 6 (21 words):

Il regarde la fumée qui rampe au loin de la cigarette et le long du mur, et se replie au plafond.

T-unit 7 (15 words):

Ensuite ses yeux vides se fixe sur la main qui écrit — à qui il concerne.

T-unit 8 (14 words):

Ce jeune homme écrit comme un étudiant qui est résolu à finir un examen,

T-unit 9 (8 words):

mais il sait que le travaille est désespéré.

T-unit 10 (12 words):

A la fin, il donne sa signature à la page sans hésitation,

T-unit 11 (8 words):

décroche le fusil qui reste à son côté,

T-unit 12 (6 words):

et se repose dans sa chaise.

T-unit 13 (22 words):

Pendant que ses yeux mornes sont fixé sur le plafond qui est rempli de la fumée, il crie les mots . . . à Dieu . . .

Total number of words = 178

Total number of T-units = 13

MLTU = 13.7

Commentary:

The MLTU for most compositions in this class was 8; this score of 13.7 was the highest in the class and represents excellent work.

The results of this analysis surprised the professor. All four scoring methods used to evaluate this essay indicate excellence, which suggests that the scoring method is unlikely to alter the final evaluation. Holistic and analytic scoring methods were far less time consuming than primary trait and T-unit scoring. However, the kind of insight that teachers can gain from writing primary trait scoring guides and from calculating the MLTU are very beneficial. Ultimately the professor concluded that, while each scoring method differs in its general focus, the selection of a scoring method should reflect the goals of the course and the evaluation criteria upon which the teacher and students agree.

CASE STUDY 2

Students in a high school Advanced Placement French class were working on their writing skills. The teacher noted that students who worked seriously on pre-writing exercises wrote better than those who did not. In order to encourage all the students to write better, she decided to give them grades on the prewriting exercises. The following prewriting worksheet was filled out by a student in her class and then evaluated according to the criteria in Figure 10. The words in italics represent student work.

COMPOSITION WORKSHEET

Nom: *Missy*

Rédaction 3: Le portrait

Sujet: *une personne qui habite sur la rue*

Fond: *un seuil de la porte [door-step] devant une boutique qui vend les choses élégant et cher*

12 adjectifs:

ridé (wrinkled)	*bombé (bulging)*
lourd et gauche (slouching)	*grand (large)*
gros (coarse)	*dodu (plump)*
déguenillé (tattered)	*indigent (poverty-stricken)*
râpé (threadbare)	*affligé (sorrowful)*
morne (gloomy)	*solonnel (solemn)*
isolé (lonely)	*débraillé (untidy)*

Synonymes pour 5 adjectifs:

potelé (dodu)	*sombre (morne)*
étendu (grand)	*délaissé (isolé)*
réduit à la misère (indigent)	

Antonymes pour 5 adjectifs:

lisse (ridé)	*illustre (morne)*
mince (dodu)	*menu (grand)*
enfoncé (bulging)	

Images:

antithèse - *"not this but that"*
elle attends [outside] la boutique, mais elle n'est pas [a customer]

comparaison - *"comme"*
salt & peppery hair

métaphore -
scavenger - uses what she can find

This student received 5 points, or the maximum number of points possible. Although there are errors in French and an occasional use of English, this sheet represents very good work. The corresponding composition shows how the student used the words and ideas from the worksheet to complete the assignment:

Sa figure est rideé et la poussière avait recueilli dans chaque ride comme il recueille sur un rayon de bibliothèque. Sa figure est encadrée par une masse de cheveux gros, ce qui ressemble le sel et le poivre. Elle a les yeux bombés qui cherchent un refuge dans un temps de besoin. Sa bouche est presque invisible parce qu'elle ne sourit jamais et ne parle jamais à quelqu'un.

Elle s'adosse au seuil de la porte où elle reste souvent ses ossements fatigués. Elle est devant une boutique qui vend les choses élégantes et chères, mais elle n'est pas un chaland, ni un marchand. Elle est habillée en vêtements déguenillés et râpés, qui sont en contraste aux vêtements qui sont montrés dans la vitrine de la boutique.

Elle est un peu potelée et des boutons sur son pull-over sont près de se fendre, aussi parce qu'il est deux tailles trop petit. Ses épaules sont lourdes et gauches, qui se fait avoir l'air des ténèbres. Elle est une saule pleurer qui porte tous ses problèmes sur ces épaules affligées.

Elle est indigente, isolée et délaissée. Elle a une exhalaison morne qui touche même le passant le plus content et lui donne un goût de l'âpreté de la vie. Alors, elle rôde toujours et habite sur la rue. Elle vit sans luxe, sans amis et sans place à appeler chez elle.⁸

*[Her face is wrinkled and the dust had picked (**collected**) in each wrinkle like it picks (**collects**) on a library shelf. Her face is framed by a mass of big hair that looks salt and pepper. She has bulging eyes that look for a refuge in a time of need. Her mouth is nearly invisible because she never smiles and never talks to someone.*

*She leans on the threshold of the door where she stays (**rests**) her tired bones. She is in front of a store that sells elegant and expensive things, but she is not a buyer, nor a merchant. She is dressed in tattered and threadbare clothes, which are in contrast to the clothes which are shown in the window of the shop.*

She is a bit round and some buttons on her sweater are near to split, also because it is two sizes too small. Her shoulders are heavy and uneven, which ? the air of the shadows. She is a weeping willow who carries all her problems on these sorrowful shoulders.

She is indigent, isolated and abandoned. She has a gloomy breath which touches even the most happy by-passer and gives him a taste of the bitterness of life. So, she always wanders and lives in the street. She lives without luxury, without friends and without a place to name her home.]

The teacher found that evaluating prewriting exercises had several advantages. First, students worked harder on the prewriting exercises. Second, they were more motivated to write since their worksheets had helped them plan and generate ideas. In other words, they knew what they were going to write. Third, it was easier to evaluate their compositions because the teacher was already somewhat familiar with each student's topic.

CASE STUDY 3

A graduate teaching assistant in Spanish at Vanderbilt University used *Atajo,* the Spanish computer writing assistant, to evaluate students' planning and generating ideas. (See chapter 3 for a detailed description of *Atajo.*) The students had been studying Spanish for ten weeks and were assigned to write their first composition with *Atajo.* The task-oriented assignment required students to look at information in several of the databases, type the information of their choice, and bring it to class for discussion and evaluation:

> **Situation:** You are writing a letter to a Spanish friend.

> **Brainstorming and writing down ideas:** Look at the following categories in the indexes and type the words and expressions that you want to use in your composition. Also take the time to browse through the information screens that interest you. Save what you have typed on your data disk, print your notes, and bring them for discussion on (date).

> **PHRASES:** writing a letter (informal)

> **VOCABULARY:** leisure, sports, musical instruments

> **GRAMMAR:** present tense, negation, interrogative

Most of the notes that students made were taken directly from the information screens in *Atajo,* however each student had selected different structures. The following notes, written by a male student, were typical of the kind of work that students brought to class:

> *Querida Juana*
> *Como estás   espero que se encuentren bien*
> *estudio cada día*
> *no tengo*
> *el cine*
> *la natación   nadar   nado*
> *jugar al tenis jugo*
> *hacer alpinismo (no)   hago camping*
> *cuándo es tu cumpleaños*
> *nací el 18 de marzo de 1978*
> *(quiero) salir para España*
> *Espero que nos volvamos a ver pronto*
> *Quiero que vengas a verme*
> *Saludo ? / Un abrazo*

[Dear Juana
How are you   I hope that you are fine
I study every day
I don't have
the movies
swimming   to swim   I swim
to play tennis   I play
to go mountain climbing (no)   I go camping
when is your birthday
I was born the 18th of March, 1978
(I want)   to go to Spain
I hope that we will see each other soon
I want you to come see me
Sincerely ? / Love]

During class, students worked in groups of three or four, reading their notes aloud and hearing what other students had written. The TA encouraged the students to borrow ideas from their peers and to add to their own notes. Then the TA collected the notes and evaluated each student's work by recording a (**0**) for poor work, a (**#**) for acceptable work, or a (**+**) for good work.

CONCLUSIONS

The hypothesis upon which this chapter is founded states that correcting and evaluating FL writing involves the entire writing process. The theories, research, and pedagogical suggestions in this chapter point to the fact that correction and evaluation involve much more than the comments a teacher makes on a final draft. Correction and evaluation during the planning, idea generation, editing, and revising stages of the FL writing process provide systematic and consistent reinforcement as students learn to write in the FL. Furthermore, a sound approach to correction and evaluation involves the careful selection and/or design of a scoring instrument. Finally, when correction and evaluation are an integral part of the FL writing process, there is ample guidance as well as high expectations. Successful writing teachers "give students sufficient help during the writing process to allow them to write better than the students themselves thought was possible" (Freedman, 1987, 161).

TOPICS FOR DISCUSSION AND RESEARCH

1. Compare the quantity of writing in student journals in which the teacher has responded to the content and those in which peers have responded to the content.

2. Compare the results of holistic and analytic scoring on narrative, descriptive, expository, and argumentative writing tasks.

3. Determine the mean length of T-units (MLTU) for student writing at different levels of language study.

4. Analyze the impact of using L1 during peer review sessions.

5. Analyze the effect of different prewriting exercises on the quality and quantity of ideas generated.

Notes

1. In her book entitled *Teaching Writing as a Second Language* (Carbondale and Edwardsville, IL: Southern Illinois University Press, 1987), Horning proposes that written discourse is like a foreign language and that teaching writing in the native language is very much like teaching a second language. In addition, she suggests that students learning to write in their native language go through stages of interlanguage.

2. In "Analyzing Revision" (*College Composition and Communication* 32, 401–414, 1981), Faigley and Witte devised a taxonomy of two kinds of revisions: 1) surface changes that are meaning preserving and 2) text-based changes that alter the meaning, or the summary, of the text.

3. In a discussion of native language writing entitled "Individualized Goal Setting, Self Evaluation, and Peer Evaluation" (Cooper and Odell, (Eds.), *Evaluating Writing*, Urbana, IL: National Council of Teachers of English, 135–156, 1977), Beaven suggests that in student-centered approaches in which the teacher plays a collaborative role, individualized goal setting and self-evaluation can help students improve. Setting goals includes deciding what kind of writing a student wants or needs to do, prescribing the tasks, and discussing the criteria for evaluation. In the early stages of writing, teachers should be involved in helping students set goals that are compatible with the course curriculum. In self-evaluation, students might discuss how much time was spent on the paper, what the special strengths and weaknesses of their work are, how they might improve it, and what grade they would assign themselves.

4. Cooper and Odell's *Evaluating Writing* (Urbana, IL: National Council of Teachers of English, 1977) is a collection of essays that provides an overview of the ways that writing is evaluated in L1 composition.

5. Koda's study ("Task-Induced Variability in FL Composition: Language-Specific Perspectives," *Foreign Language Annals* 26(3):332–346, 1993) sheds light on several aspects of FL writing evaluation. Twenty-five American college students who were studying first- and second-year Japanese were each given grammar and vocabulary tests to determine their linguistic knowledge. They were then each given two writing tasks, a descriptive task and a narrative task. The writing samples were evaluated according to linguistic feature analysis

(word count, diversity of words, sentence length, and number of subordinate clauses), topical structure analysis (comparison of discourse coherence between writers as well as a comparison of discourse coherence between the two writing tasks for each writer), and a quality rating by three native speakers. These three types of analyses (linguistic feature, topical structure, and perceived composition quality) point to several pertinent findings: 1) Writing tasks pose varying linguistic and rhetorical findings; 2) There is a high correlation between linguistic knowledge and quality ratings for both composition tasks; and 3) Vocabulary knowledge contributes more to the quality of the text than sentence complexity.

6. I offer special thanks to my colleague Margaret Miner for her eagerness to talk with me at length about the problems she encounters in evaluating writing in her literature courses.

7. Thanks to Denise Scruggs for allowing her composition to be published in this study.

8. Thanks to Melissa Gilleland for allowing her composition to be published in this study.

REFERENCES

Beach, Richard. (1989). "Showing Students How to Assess: Demonstrating Techniques for Response in the Writing Conference." In C. Anson, (Ed.), *Writing and Response*. Urbana, IL: National Council of Teachers of English, 127–148.

Beaven, Mary H. (1977). "Individualized Goal Setting, Self-Evaluation, and Peer Evaluation." In C. R. Cooper and L. Odell, (Eds.), *Evaluating Writing*. Urbana, IL: National Council of Teachers of English, 135–156.

Chastain, Kenneth. (1990). "Characteristics of Graded and Ungraded Compositions." *The Modern Language Journal* 74(1):10–14.

Cohen, Andrew. (1987). "Student Processing of Feedback on Their Compositions." In A. Wenden and J. Rubin, (Eds.), *Learner Strategies in Language Learning*. Englewood Cliffs, NJ: Prentice/Hall.

———— and Marilda C. Cavalcanti. (1990). "Feedback on Compositions: Teacher and Student Verbal Reports." In B. Kroll, (Ed.), *Second Language Writing: Research Insights for the Classroom*. New York: Cambridge University Press.

Connor, Ulla and Karen Asenavage. (1994). "Peer Response Groups in ESL Writing Classes: How Much Impact on Revision?" *Journal of Second Language Writing* 3(3):257–276.

Cooper, Charles R. and Lee Odell, (Eds.). (1977a). *Evaluating Writing*. Urbana, IL: National Council of Teachers of English.

————. (1977b). "Holistic Evaluation of Writing". In C. R. Cooper and L. Odell, (Eds.), *Evaluating Writing*. Urbana, IL: National Council of Teachers of English, 3–31.

De Guerrero, Maria C. M. and Olga S. Villamil. (1994). "Social-Cognitive Dimensions of Interaction in L2 Peer Revision." *Modern Language Journal* 78(4):484–496.

Fathman, Ann K. and Elizabeth Whalley. (1990). "Teacher Response to Student Writing: Focus on Form versus Content." In B. Kroll, (Ed.), *Second Language Writing: Research Insights for the Classroom.* New York: Cambridge University Press.

Faigley, Lester. (1992). *Fragments of Rationality.* Pittsburgh: University of Pittsburgh Press.

Frantzen, Diana and Dorothy Rissell. (1987). "Learner Self-Correction of Written Compositions: What Does It Show Us?" In B. Van Patten, T. R. Dvorak, J. Lee, (Eds.), *Foreign Language Learning: A Research Perspective.* Cambridge, MA: Newbury House Publishers.

Freedman, Sarah Warshauer. (1987). *Response to Student Writing.* Urbana, IL: National Council of Teachers of English, Research Report No. 23.

Hamp-Lyons, Liz, (Ed.). (1990). *Assessing Second Language Writing in Academic Contexts.* Norwood, NJ: Ablex Publishing Corporation.

Hedgcock, John and Natalie Lefkowitz. (1992). "Collaborative Oral/Aural Revision in Foreign Language Writing Instruction." *Journal of Second Language Writing* 1(3):255–276.

———. (1994). "Feedback on Feedback: Assessing Learner Receptivity to Teacher Response in L2 Composing." *Journal of Second Language Writing* 3(2):141–163.

Hendrickson, James M. (1980). "The Treatment of Error in Written Work." *The Modern Language Journal* 64(2):216–221.

Horning, Alice S. (1987). *Teaching Writing as a Second Language.* Carbondale and Edwardsville, IL: Southern Illinois University Press.

Hunt, Kellogg W. (1965). *Grammatical Structures Written at Three Grade Levels.* Champaign, IL: National Council of Teachers of English, Research Report No. 3.

Johnson, Leonard W. (1983). "Grading the Advanced Placement Examination in French Language." Princeton, NJ: Advanced Placement Program of the College Board.

Kepner, Christine Goring. (1991). "An Experiment in the Relationship of Types of Written Feedback to the Development of Second Language Writing Skills." *The Modern Language Journal* 75(3):305–313.

Koda, Keiko. (1993). "Task-Induced Variability in FL Composition: Language-Specific Perspectives." *Foreign Language Annals* 26(3):332–346.

Kroll, Barbara, (Ed.). (1990). *Second Language Writing: Research Insights for the Classroom.* New York: Cambridge University Press.

Lalande, John F. II. (1984). "Reducing Composition Errors: An Experiment." *Foreign Language Annals* 17(2):109–117.

Leki, Ilona. (1990). "Coaching From the Margins: Issues in Written Response." In B. Kroll, (Ed.), *Second Language Writing: Research Insights for the Classroom.* New York: Cambridge University Press.

———.(1991). "The Preferences of ESL Sudents for Error Correction in College-Level Writing Classes." *Foreign Language Annals* 24(3):203–218.

———. (1992). *Understanding ESL Writers.* Portsmouth, NH: Boynton/Cook Publishers.

Lloyd-Jones, Richard. (1977). "Primary Trait Scoring." In C. R. Cooper and L. Odell, (Eds.), *Evaluating Writing.* Urbana, IL: National Council of Teachers of English, 33–66.

Mangelsdorf, Kate and Ann Schlumberger. (1992). "ESL Student Response Stances in a Peer-Review Task." *Journal of Second Language Writing* 1(3):235–254.

Mills, Carl. (1990). "Syntax and the Evaluation of College Writing: A Blind Alley." In L. Arena, (Ed.), *Language Proficiency: Defining, Teaching and Testing*. New York: Plenum Press.

Raimes, Ann. (1983). *Techniques in Teaching Writing*. New York: Oxford University Press.

Ruetten, Mary K. (1994). "Evaluating ESL Students' Performance on Proficiency Exams." *Journal of Second Language Writing* 3(2):85–96.

Selinker, Larry. (1972). "Interlanguage." *International Review of Applied Linguistics* 10:201–231.

Semke, Harriet D. (1984). "Effects of the Red Pen." *Foreign Language Annals* 17(3):195–202.

Scott, Renee S. (1993). "Assessing Communication in Writing: The Development of a Spanish Writing Contest." *Foreign Language Annals* 26(3):383–392.

Shakir, Abdullah. (1991). "Coherence in EFL Student-Written Texts: Two Perspectives." *Foreign Language Annals* 24(5):399–411.

Shohamy, Elana, Claire M. Gordon, and Roberta Kraemer. (1992). "The Effect of Raters' Background and Training on the Reliability of Direct Writing Tests." *The Modern Language Journal* 76(1):27–33.

Stanley, Jane. (1992). "Coaching Student Writers to Be Effective Peer Evaluators." *Journal of Second Language Writing* 1(3):217–233.

Sweedler-Brown, Carol O. (1993). "ESL Essay Evaluation: The Influence of Sentence-Level and Rhetorical Features." *Journal of Second Language Writing* 2(1):3–17.

Terry, Robert M. (1989). "Teaching and Evaluating Writing as a Communicative Skill." *Foreign Language Annals* 22(1):43–54.

——. (1992). "Improving Inter-rater Reliability in Scoring Tests in Multisection Courses." *AAUSC Issues in Language Program Direction: Development and Supervision of Teaching Assistants in Foreign Languages*. Boston, MA: Heinle & Heinle Publishers.

Van Patten, Bill, Trisha R. Dvorak, and James F. Lee, (Eds.). (1987). *Foreign Language Learning: A Research Perspective*. Cambridge, MA: Newbury House Publishers.

Wenden, Anita and Joan Rubin (Eds.). (1987). *Learner Strategies in Language Learning*. Englewood Cliffs, NJ: Prentice/Hall.

Chapter 5
Teaching Foreign Language Writing

Hypothesis: *Teaching FL writing is essential at all levels of language study.*

Approaches to teaching L1 writing
       The process approach
       The prose model approach
       The experiential approach
       The rhetorical approach
       The epistemic approach
       A linguistic system approach

Approaches to teaching ESL writing
       The controlled-to-free approach
       The freewriting approach
       The pattern-paragraph approach
       The grammar-syntax-organization approach
       The communicative approach
       The process approach

Approaches to teaching FL writing

Research on teaching writing

The writing task
       Research on writing task difficulty

Teaching writing from the start: classroom implications

Case study

Conclusions

Topics for discussion and research

TEACHING FOREIGN LANGUAGE WRITING

Hypothesis
Teaching foreign language writing is essential at all levels of language study.

The focus of instruction at the elementary and intermediate levels of language study is typically on listening and speaking.[1] Students are encouraged primarily to develop skills that will help them communicate interactively in the target culture. Writing, or composition, is often reserved for advanced-level grammar, literature, and civilization courses. However, teachers in advanced courses are frequently dismayed by the quality of students' writing. They complain that students are ill prepared for the kinds of writing assignments that are required in their courses. And, very often this assessment is true.

If one of the goals of FL instruction is to prepare students to write in upper-level courses, teachers must reexamine their approaches to teaching FL writing at the beginning stages of language study. The hypothesis governing the final chapter of this book states that teaching writing is crucial at all levels of language study. While the preceding four chapters describe many considerations with regard to teaching FL writing, this chapter will review different approaches to teaching L1, ESL, and FL writing, the research in teaching writing, and the design of writing tasks in order to propose a sound approach to teaching writing from the beginning levels of FL study.

APPROACHES TO TEACHING L1 WRITING

Prior to World War II, L1 writing instruction in the United States involved primarily responding to the reading of great literature. Since that time, the teaching of canonical literature has become much less relevant and there has been no single model of writing instruction (Faigley, 1992). However, until quite recently, the *classical rhetorical tradition* dominated theories of writing instruction. This tradition views writing as a kind of performance with a specific textual shape and a fixed way of achieving it. For example, a mode, such as persuasion, is considered to have a formulaic pattern consisting basically of an introduction, a body, and a conclusion. This kind of regimented structure presupposes that form is the key to good expression. Modern rhetoric, however, which emphasizes the writing process more than the features of finished texts, is gaining in acceptance.

> It [modern rhetoric] is preoccupied with the writer's choice-making in the development of texts, the exploratory movement of mind, the discovery of connections among ideas, the progressive testing and reformulating of statements. Having had little preparation in the history of discourse theory,

teachers tend to be unfamiliar with the richer concepts of modern rhetoric—"composing process," "writing-as-learning," "coherence," "revision," . . . (Knoblauch and Brannon (1984, 4–5).

Current thinking in L1 composition instruction holds that teachers have a responsibility to teach the conventions of writing, the form, and the discourse modes, while not ignoring the highly individualized cognitive processes of writers. This thinking reflects a subtle shift in the instructional paradigm from the notion that writing can be taught to the notion that writing is a competence that is nurtured and develops with application (Knoblauch and Brannon, 1984, 4).

There are many approaches to teaching writing in English composition. While the approaches differ, there is a sense among most teachers today that attention to the writing process is as important as attention to the final product. Donovan and McClelland's *Eight Approaches to Teaching Composition* (1980) reviews the most common approaches practiced today: the process approach, the prose model approach, the experiential approach, the rhetorical approach, and the epistemic approach.

□ THE PROCESS APPROACH

According to this approach, teachers focus on what students need to experience rather than what they need to know. Moreover, teachers and students work together in a collaborative fashion to make meaning. (See chapter 2 for more information regarding writing as a process.)

□ THE PROSE MODEL APPROACH

In this approach, students read and analyze a text and then model their writing after the example text. The focus of instruction lies in identifying and imitating various rhetorical modes. The prose model approach is often criticized because it can intimidate students, since it places an emphasis on form, rather than on content. Eschholz (1980) discusses an approach that combines the prose model approach with the process approach to teaching writing by requiring students to write a great deal, by having individual conferences with students, and by introducing prose models when students need them.

□ THE EXPERIENTIAL APPROACH

This approach is based on four premises: 1) the best student writing is motivated by personal feelings and experience, 2) writing from experience can be done in many modes of discourse, including expository and academic modes, 3) writing from experience generally requires that students write for a readership that is often someone other than the teacher, and 4) the structure of writing is learned as one shapes ideas for oneself and for an audience. This approach commonly integrates the process approach in that it focuses on learning by doing (rather than studying rules), peer editing, and self-assessment (Stephen, 1980).

□ THE RHETORICAL APPROACH

According to this approach, writing is not a mysterious process but rather an art that can be taught. Lauer's (1980) approach is novel in that she contends that students need to begin with questions, not answers, as they organize and develop their thoughts. She further maintains that teaching writing as a rhetorical art involves showing students how description, narration, classification, and evaluation can be used to structure any paper. The example she uses is of a freshman assigned to write about the private world of relationships. The student chose to write about a relationship with a high school friend who ultimately committed suicide. While engaging in this expressive writing, the student was guided in her exploration of the topic, working through several stages of recalling the relationship in order to clarify it and discover new dimensions. The teacher directed her to first define the relationship, state her own values, and put into words the question she had often asked herself with reference to why her friend had killed herself. She then wrote a *static view,* or a description, of her friend, and a *dynamic view,* or a narration of the events, in their relationship. In the *relative view,* she compared herself with her friend, classified the type of person her friend was, and wrote an analogy comparing her friend to a coconut—rough on the outside and sweet on the inside. At this point, Lauer suggests that the teacher may interact with the student, pointing to avenues of further inquiry. Finally, Lauer suggests that the student choose the audience for the paper.

□ THE EPISTEMIC APPROACH

According to Dowst (1980), the epistemic approach begins by reviewing the fundamental aspects of each approach to writing:

> . . . formalistic (emphasizing *language*), referential (emphasizing *language* and *reality*), expressive (emphasizing *writer* and *language*), and rhetorical (emphasizing (*writer, language,* and *reader*) (Dowst, 1980, 68).

He further says that the epistemic approach includes *writer, language,* and *reality* and connects writing and knowledge. The students spend time not only exploring what they know about the world but also exploring what they know about language and prose. That is, they may describe the facade of a church and then later work on what they know about describing.

□ A LINGUISTIC SYSTEM APPROACH

In a very different vein, Horning (1987) proposes that the development of writing proficiency in formal, academic English involves learning a new linguistic system in much the same way adults learn a second language:

> Basic writers develop writing skills and achieve proficiency in the same way that other adults develop second language skills, principally because, for basic writers, academic, formal written English is a new and distinct linguistic system (Horning, 1987, 2).

In supporting her view, Horning cites Krashen's Monitor Theory of second language acquisition,[2] stating that it can be applied to teaching native language writing as well. The Monitor Theory is founded on five hypotheses: 1) that learning and acquisition are two distinct processes, 2) that there is a natural order in acquisition of grammatical structures, 3) that learning (as opposed to acquisition) functions only as a monitor for output, 4) that language is best acquired when the input is comprehensible yet challenging, and 5) that acquisition takes place when the acquirer is motivated, self-confident, and has a low level of anxiety. In line with Krashen's Monitor Theory, Horning proposes six corollaries regarding native language writing:

1) The written form of language constitutes a second language.
2) Much like skill in a second language, writing skill develops through processes of acquisition and learning.
3) The acquisition of writing skills comes about in an ordered fashion.
4) What students learn in the basic writing classroom functions only as a monitor on the output of the writing skills they have acquired.
5) Comprehensible input is essential if language acquisition is going to take place.
6) The affective filter must be down (not operating) in order for students to acquire writing skills.
(Horning, 1987, 2–5).

She further points out that written language is acquired through reading, internalizing patterns and principles of redundancy, and through a process of hypothesis testing:

> Writers formulate hypotheses about written forms and then test and revise their production in order to develop their own system of written language use. Writers must have an opportunity to test their writing out on readers and get feedback, particularly if they are basic writers (Horning, 1987, 25).

The approaches to teaching L1 writing are different yet they intersect and overlap in many ways. However, teachers and researchers who favor one approach over another can be aggressive about their choices, and the underlying principles of each approach are often a source of debate. Although teachers might argue about the best approach to teaching writing, most would agree that writing is an important skill, critical for ensuring academic success.

APPROACHES TO TEACHING ESL WRITING

The most important difference between teaching L1 writing and L2 writing is mastery of the language of expression. In native language writing instruction, the teacher assumes that the students have fundamental control of the language. In second-language writing instruction, on the other hand, students' command of the language plays a critical role. Raimes (1983) points out that there are many features that writers have to deal with when writing in a second language. Mechanics, word choice, grammar, and syntax are added to features such as content, organization, the writing process, and the audience. Given the constraint of the second language, most approaches to teaching ESL writing include a focus on both form and content.

In her book *Techniques in Teaching Writing*, Raimes (1983) discusses six different approaches to teaching ESL writing: 1) the controlled-to-free approach, 2) the freewriting approach, 3) the pattern-paragraph approach, 4) the grammar-syntax-organization approach, 5) the communicative approach, and 6) the process approach. While some of these approaches are similar to those used for L1 writing instruction, they all include some degree of concentration on L2 language development.

□   THE CONTROLLED-TO-FREE APPROACH

This approach stresses the importance of grammar, syntax, and mechanics. Generally taught sequentially, teaching writing first involves sentence exercises and then paragraph manipulations. Most of the writing is strictly controlled by having students change words or clauses or combine sentences. When students achieve mastery of these kinds of exercises, typically at an advanced level of proficiency, they are permitted to engage in autonomous writing.

□   THE FREEWRITING APPROACH

In this approach, teachers value quantity over quality in writing and do minimal error correction. The focus of instruction is on content and audience. Students are encouraged to be concerned about fluency and content and give cursory attention to form. Proponents of this approach consider that grammatical accuracy will develop over time.

☐ THE PATTERN-PARAGRAPH APPROACH

This approach involves the analysis and imitation of model texts and stresses organization above all. By imitating model paragraphs, putting scrambled sentences in order, identifying or writing topic sentences, and inserting or deleting sentences, students are taught to develop an awareness of the English features of writing.

☐ THE GRAMMAR-SYNTAX-ORGANIZATION APPROACH

This approach requires students to focus on several features of writing at once. The writing tasks are designed to make students pay attention to grammar and syntax while also giving them words such as *first*, *then*, and *finally* to organize their text.

☐ THE COMMUNICATIVE APPROACH

The purpose and audience are the focal points in this approach to writing. Students engage in real-life tasks, such as writing informal and formal letters.

☐ THE PROCESS APPROACH

Like in L1 writing instruction, there has been a shift in focus in ESL writing instruction from product to process. That is, rather than concentrating only on the final product, teachers are facilitative in helping students discover ideas, plan, draft, revise, and edit. The first draft is not expected to be error-free, and teacher feedback is designed to help students discover new ideas, words, and sentences to use on future drafts.

While the process approach in ESL has gained in favor, some teachers question the validity of this approach for developing writing skills necessary to survive in the academic community. In reaction to the process approach, many ESL writing teachers have adopted an approach called "English for academic or special purposes," in which the focus is on academic writing tasks designed to teach students to write prose that will be acceptable in the American academic setting (Silva, 1990; Leki, 1992).

APPROACHES TO TEACHING FL WRITING

There are no clearly defined approaches to teaching FL writing **per se**. When writing is taught in the FL classroom, it is usually incorporated into the overall goals of a lesson. For example, if the focus of instruction is narrating past events, students may study past tenses, and the writing assignment might require them to tell about something they did in the past. Therefore, an examination of approaches to FL teaching in general provides the best insight into how FL writing is taught.

After World War II, during the 1950s and 1960s, the *Audiolingual Method* was the dominant approach in FL teaching. This approach, which owed its beginnings to the Army Specialized Training Method,[3] was founded on behaviorist psychology and stressed the notion that language was speech, not writing. Oral language was learned through pattern practice and reinforcement; writing served only as a support skill for speaking activities. The 1970s gave rise to the notion of communicative competence, which stressed the view that language involves the negotiation of meaning and applies to both speech and writing. Writing instruction focused primarily on real-life tasks such as taking notes, making lists, and writing letters.

The publication of the *ACTFL Proficiency Guidelines* in 1986 marked the beginning of proficiency-oriented approaches to FL teaching.[4] The guidelines define proficiency in speaking, listening, reading, and writing at four basic levels: Novice, Intermediate, Advanced, and Superior. This document has had a profound impact on the FL teaching profession, primarily since it serves both as assessment criteria and instructional guidelines. That is, the generic descriptions give FL teachers both explicit ways to evaluate students' proficiency and guiding principles for improving proficiency in each skill.

With regard to teaching writing, a proficiency-oriented approach involves designing activities that help students perform at a given level of proficiency as described in the *ACTFL Proficiency Guidelines*. (Appendix A shows the *ACTFL Proficiency Guidelines* generic descriptions for writing.) In general, proficiency-oriented approaches to teaching writing are quite eclectic. Some teachers may focus on developing students' command of grammar and syntax, while others may stress practice of language functions, such as describing or expressing an opinion. In her book *Teaching Language in Context*, Hadley (1993) discusses activities that range from making lists and completing open-ended sentences for novice-level students, to writing simple descriptions and narrations for intermediate-level students, to sentence combining and guided compositions for advanced-level students. Most proficiency-oriented approaches incorporate the notion that writing must be taught as a process with activities for planning, editing, and revising.

Some FL teachers argue that the *ACTFL Proficiency Guidelines* do not accurately describe what students are capable of writing at each level of proficiency. For example, at the Novice-Mid level, the guidelines give the following description of ability: "Able to copy or transcribe familiar words or phrases and reproduce some from memory. No practical communicative writing skills." At the Intermediate-High level of writing proficiency, the guidelines state that "an ability to describe and narrate in paragraphs is emerging," but that students "rarely use basic cohesive elements, such as pronominal substitutions or synonyms." Given the research that supports the notion that writing competence is transferred from L1 to L2 (as discussed in chapter 1), some researchers argue that students do not necessarily begin writing in the FL with no practical communicative writing skills or little understanding of organization.

Regardless of the approach to FL teaching, writing is generally taught after students have studied the target language for two or more years. A typical third-year course focuses on grammar and composition, and teachers often rely on writing topics provided in the text. Some texts use a prose-model approach, while others suggest writing topics that are related to grammar, content, or a reading selection. Ultimately, teaching FL writing has been given relatively little attention, and teachers design instruction based on their individual sense of how students learn to write in a FL.

RESEARCH ON TEACHING WRITING

There is very little research on what teachers actually do when they teach writing. Cumming's (1992) study is unique in that it provides information about the characteristics of successful writing teachers. By analyzing the behavior of three successful ESL writing teachers, he found that there are certain types of teaching routines that can be observed. He lists six fundamental routines: 1) attracting students' attention, 2) assigning tasks, 3) collectively constructing interpretations, 4) establishing criteria, 5) providing individual feedback, and 6) guiding individual development.

THE WRITING TASK

The fundamental concern when teaching writing involves assigning topics that are relevant to students' lives in order to engage their interest and motivate them to communicate their thoughts and feelings. However, just because the topic is important to students, does not necessarily mean that they will want to write about it:

> Whether the topic is "summer vacation," "abortion," "women's rights," "violence on TV," or "premarital sex," it's equally inert and undynamic, even if names a potentially significant range of student experience, as long as it's unaccompanied by incentives to personal engagement beyond the requirement to produce a certain number of pages for a teacher's scrutiny (Knoblauch and Brannon, 1984, 106).

Motivating students to write can be elusive because the assigned topic is often arbitrary and artificial. However, Knoblauch and Brannon (1984) contend that when the teachers play collaborative roles, never dominating nor insisting on their personal views, students will be more likely to engage in the scholarly activity of exchanging ideas regardless of the topic. Also, given that the teacher is usually the sole audience, it is imperative that students sense that the teacher is genuinely interested in what is being said and not only on how it is being said.

While teacher attitude can be critical in motivating students to write, the writing task itself plays an equally important role in determining the success of the writing experience. Above all, the writing task must serve as a *prompt* to activate students' background knowledge and personal experiences. According to Kroll and Reid (1994), there are three basic kinds of writing prompts. A *bare prompt* is simple and direct and states the entire task. For example: "Do you favor or oppose the death penalty? Why?" A *framed prompt* presents a set of circumstances. For example: "The issue of obesity in America is gaining in importance. Recent statistics suggest that at least 30 percent of all American adults are substantially overweight. Most European adults, however, are not obese. What is your view of this issue? You may use personal experience in your answer." A *reading-based prompt* provides a text of varying length, and the student writer is asked to summarize, explain, or interpret the text.

Kroll and Reid (1994) stress the importance of designing prompts that will allow student writers to demonstrate their ability to write rather than to decipher a writing prompt. They cite the research of Hamp-Lyons, Johns, and Tedick in proposing the following variables that should be carefully considered in designing a writing prompt:

1) the writing situation (contextual variables), or the context in which the writing will occur, such as an entrance or exit exam, etc.;
2) the subject matter (content variable), or content based on a body of knowledge to which all writers have access;
3) the wording of both the prompt and the instructions (linguistic variables), or precise and unambiguous directions;
4) the task(s) (task variables), or the number of tasks that students are asked to perform, such as "choose," "identify," "give examples," etc.;
5) the rhetorical specifications (rhetorical variables), or the way a student is instructed to approach the content, such as "compare," "contrast," "illustrate," etc.; and
6) the scoring criteria (evaluation variables), or a clear definition of how the writing will be judged (Kroll and Reid, 1994).

Careful consideration of the various features of the writing task is not necessarily simple. Figure 1 shows a checklist for preparing writing tasks that takes into account many features, including purpose, the language used, the nature of the instructions, and the time allotted.

The most common writing tasks for FL students at the elementary and intermediate levels are *narrative* or *descriptive*. These kinds of tasks require students to tell a story by organizing events in space and time or to evoke an image of people, things, or places. For example, teachers often design communicative

Figure 1: Checklist for Preparing Writing Tasks

Does the task:

[　] require writers to **compose** a piece of connected discourse?

[　] establish a clear purpose for communicating, especially by indicating the intended reader and a context for the task?

[　] motivate writers to communicate their knowledge and perception of the topic?

[　] reflect the kind of writing students will normally be expected to do in their academic programs or the real world?

[　] provide a subject that will interest students of this age, sex, educational level, field of study, and cultural background?

[　] present a topic about which these students will have knowledge?

[　] appear to be the right level of difficulty for students of this proficiency range?

[　] provide a topic that is free of hidden elements of bias?

[　] present a clearly defined task that cannot easily be misinterpreted?

[　] provide a topic that is broad enough for every writer to approach from some angle?

[　] use as few words as possible, and definitions if necessary?

[　] give clear and concise instructions that indicate also the time allowed for writing and the approximate number of words or length of composition expected?

[　] present a writable and readable topic, pretested with students similar to the test group?

[　] include as many modes of discourse as are appropriate to the purpose of the test and to the actual writing needs of the students?

[　] provide at least two writing occasions, in order to produce an adequate sample of a student's ability?

[　] require all students to write on the same topic, unless skill at choosing a topic is a part of the abilities being tested?

[　] allow enough writing time for a reasonable performance?

[　] provide ruled paper for writing?

[　] use a coding system for identifying writers so that authorship will be anonymous during the evaluation?

[　] Is the writing task appropriate to the specific purpose(s) of this test?

(Taken from Hadley (1993, 332) with source from Jacobs et al. (1981, 22).)

tasks that require students to write postcards or letters to an imaginary friend in the target culture and that elicit certain grammatical structures or vocabulary. The following writing prompts elicit use of the present tense of the indicative, including affirmative, negative, interrogative, or reflexive forms, as well as vocabulary associated with letter writing and vacations:

> Imagine you are on vacation at your favorite resort. Write a postcard or short letter explaining what you are doing, what you like about the place, who you are meeting, and similar details.

> Your best friend at another school has a new roommate who comes from (country where target language is spoken). Write a letter to your friend, including a list of questions you would like him or her to ask this exchange student about life in his or her country. (Hadley, 1993, 313–314).

While narrative and descriptive tasks can be valuable for developing communicative language skills, they do not necessarily involve complex cognitive functioning. That is, students do not have to grapple with ideas or concepts. *Expository* or *argumentative* tasks, on the other hand, are more cognitively demanding. Expository tasks consist of collecting information and understanding it well enough to explain cause and effect, likeness and contrast, problems and solutions. Argumentative tasks involve similar demands, but include convincing, persuading, supporting, and refuting. According to Schultz (1991a, 1991b), and Kern and Schultz (1992), students should practice argumentative tasks, since they most closely reflect the kind of writing that is required in upper-level FL courses.

Challenging FL students to write expository and argumentative essays is certainly important, however, the task may become overwhelming given both the cognitive and the linguistic demands. By designing tasks that specify the linguistic structures required by the task, the linguistic demands can, to some degree, be alleviated. Scott (1990; 1992) proposes task-oriented writing guidelines that refer specifically to the language functions, vocabulary, and grammar necessary to complete the writing assignment. Figures 2, 3, and 4 show examples of task-oriented writing assignments that combine expository and argumentative modes of discourse, for students in first-, second-, and third-year FL courses.

□ RESEARCH ON WRITING TASK DIFFICULTY

Determining the difficulty of a writing task is important when designing assignments, however, it may not be easy. In fact, what may be an easy task for one student, may be a difficult task for another. Koda's (1993) research supports the notion that the difficulty of a writing task is related to learner differences. Her study indicates that FL writers employ different strategies to achieve discourse coherence in varying text types. That is, a narrative text invokes the use of different strategies and different linguistic skills than a descriptive text.

Figure 2: Task-Oriented Writing Guide for First-Year Students

Situation: You have heard that American and French/German/Spanish students are different. In order to promote cultural understanding, you are writing an article about American students for a French/German/Spanish magazine.

1. Begin with a general remark about American students.
   > FUNCTION: Generalizing
   > GRAMMAR: Present tense

2. State three things about the way that female students often dress and three things about the way that male students often dress.
   > FUNCTION: Describing people
   > VOCABULARY: Clothing

3. Indicate three things that American students often like to do.
   > FUNCTION: Expressing likes/preferences
   > VOCABULARY: Sports, leisure activities

4. Conclude with a personal opinion about American students.
   > FUNCTION: Expressing an opinion

(Taken from pedagogical materials used by the author.)

Figure 3: Task-Oriented Writing Guide for Second-Year Students

Situation: You have heard that American and French/German/Spanish students are different. In order to promote cultural understanding, you are writing an article about American students for a French/German/Spanish magazine.

1. Begin with two general remarks about American students.
   > FUNCTION: Generalizing; linking ideas
   > GRAMMAR: Present tense

2. State five things about the way that female students often look and five things about the way that male students often look.
   > FUNCTION: Describing people
   > VOCABULARY: Clothing; hair; personal possessions

3. Indicate five things that American students often like to do and three things that they often do not like to do.
   > FUNCTION: Expressing likes/preferences
   > VOCABULARY: Sports, leisure activities; studies
   > GRAMMAR: Negation(s)

4. Conclude with two personal opinions about the individuality or conformity of American students.
   > FUNCTION: Expressing an opinion

(Taken from pedagogical materials used by the author.)

Figure 4: Task-Oriented Writing Guide for Third-Year Students

Situation: You have heard that American and French/German/Spanish students are different. In order to promote cultural understanding, you are writing an article about American students for a French/German/Spanish magazine.

1. You will argue for or against the idea that all American students are alike. Begin with a thesis statement.

    FUNCTION: Writing an essay; generalizing; linking ideas

    GRAMMAR: Present tense

2. Describe American students.

    FUNCTION: Describing people

    VOCABULARY: Clothing; hair; studies; leisure; personal possessions

    GRAMMAR: Negation(s); relative pronouns; adjectives

3. Define the concept of stereotypes.

    FUNCTION: Explaining; comparing; contrasting

    GRAMMAR: Impersonal expressions

       (EX: It is evident/interesting/important)

4. Support or reject the validity of stereotypes.

    FUNCTION: Expressing an opinion

    GRAMMAR: Subjunctive

5. Conclude by showing how your argument supports your thesis statement.

    FUNCTION: Concluding

(Taken from pedagogical materials used by the author.)

> . . . the analyses consistently demonstrate that the two writing tasks [narrative and descriptive] pose varying levels of linguistic and rhetorical demands, and suggest that different linguistic competencies are required for successful performance. It is essential, therefore, that a simple task analysis be used to assess the information processing load before a task is assigned. While topics should be selected for the motivational value in stimulating FL learners to write, once chosen, the writing task should be adjusted to the learner's proficiency level. Describing a holiday on the basis of personal experience, for example, entails a set of processing procedures quite different from those used to describe the same holiday as an aspect of one's culture (Koda, 1993, 343).

Since each learner demonstrates different degrees of linguistic and rhetorical mastery, evaluating the difficulty of a task can be difficult.

A study by Hamp-Lyons and Mathias (1994) provides further confirmation of the fact that task difficulty is not easy to assess. In their study, they postulated that a difficult writing task would have a direct effect on the quality of student writing. That is, a difficult writing prompt would produce low scores, whereas a simple writing prompt would produce high scores. In determining the relationship between writing prompt difficulty and student scores, the researchers found that there was no clear answer. In fact, prompts that were judged to be difficult often produced high scores. The researchers speculate that the reasons for this result might include the possibility that raters were more lenient in their scoring when the prompt was difficult or that students performed better when the writing prompt was particularly challenging. However, the researchers point out that because their findings are not clear, a great deal more research is needed to understand what makes a writing prompt difficult.

TEACHING WRITING FROM THE START: THE CLASSROOM IMPLICATIONS

As stated previously, the kind of writing that students typically do in lower-level language courses does not prepare them for the kind of writing that is expected of them in upper-level literature and civilization courses:

> Often serving mainly as an extended form of grammar practice, writing in lower-division language courses traditionally consists of fill-in-the-blank workbook exercises and occasional descriptive essays about personal topics such as friends, family, and vacation. In these writing tasks, the focus is usually on surface feature accuracy rather than on the development, organization, and effective expression of the students' own thoughts or ideas. As a consequence, students often find themselves ill-prepared to write essays in upper-division courses in which they are held responsible not only for grammatical precision but also for their ideas, their style, and their ability to develop a lucid argument. Indeed, although conventional wisdom has it that the well-formed sentence is at the root of good writing, the ability to produce a good sentence does not automatically result in good paragraph writing . . . (Kern and Schultz, 1992, 1–2).

In order to bridge the gap between lower- and upper-level FL courses, teachers must design strategies for teaching writing from the beginning stages of language study. The following suggestions can help students write from the start:

1. *Distinguish between writing for communication and writing as an academic exercise.*

The kind of writing that teaches students real-life communication is a vital part of any FL course. Students gain a great deal from learning how to take notes and write messages and letters. However, teachers need to explain that writing can also be an academic exercise. That is, students can write to learn at the same time that they learn to write. Shrum and Glisan (1994, p. 182) suggest that ". . . language is a tool for building and shaping our thoughts rather than simply a means for conveying them. The writing process can help push students to the next developmental level." When students must organize and express their thoughts in the target language, they are developing critical-thinking skills such as analyzing, synthesizing, and decision-making. Figure 5 gives an example of a writing assignment designed for elementary-level students that has no real communicative purpose. The objective of the exercise is to practice analyzing an idea and then express it in the target language.

2. Combine reading and writing.

Because written discourse is culturally determined, reading should be linked to writing. Extensive reading, or reading texts for the gist, can help students internalize patterns of discourse, levels of register, and links between language and culture. Intensive reading, or close textual analysis, can provide students with models to follow.

> When our students read, they engage actively with the new language and culture . . . The more our students read, the more they become familiar with the vocabulary, idiom, sentence patterns, organizational flow, and cultural assumptions of native speakers of the language (Raimes, 1983, 50).

Figure 5: Academic Writing Task for Elementary-Level Students

Writing assignment: write a paragraph explaining the word *American*.

1) Prewriting exercise:
  □ Write the name of a person who symbolizes your notion of "American."
  □ Write a list of words that describe this person.
  □ Write a list of activities that this person does.
  □ Write several possible titles for your essay.

2) First draft:
  □ Write a title for your essay.
  □ Write two sentences describing this person physically.
  □ Write one sentence describing this person's personality.
  □ Write two sentences stating what this person does.
  □ Write a concluding sentence explaining why, in your opinion, this person is "American."
  (The teacher reads the first draft, commenting only on content; teacher can signal areas where errors interfere with comprehension.)

3) Final draft:
  □ Analyze the suggestions made by your teacher and rewrite your paragraph.
  (This short essay might be filed in a writing portfolio and could be corrected or rewritten any time during the course. Each revised version should be appended to the preceding versions and turned in at the end of the course for final evaluation and a grade.)

(Taken from pedagogical materials used by the author.)

As students read, they need guidance in identifying the aspects of written discourse that will help them in their own written expression. For example, students can identify and examine the use of tense and mode, the choice of nouns, verbs, adjectives, and adverbs, the syntax (simple, complex), the use of conjunctions, the punctuation, or the point of view (first person narration, third person/omniscient narration).[5]

Another important feature of written language that students can examine is *redundancy*. According to Horning (1987) "redundancy is information overlap in language" (p. 18). To show redundancy in grammatical forms, she gives the example "the teachers were grading their papers" where the subject, verb, and direct object all point to the plurality of the sentence. Redundancy also occurs in semantic form, with the same idea presented more than once in different words, and in discourse, with restatements of the main point of the essay. She points out that redundancy ensures comprehension even if one element is missed.

In a similar vein, Shakir (1991) contends that students need to be taught explicitly how to write coherent, communicatively acceptable texts through *exploration* prior to the stage of actual writing and *building relations via developing a core sentence* (407–409). By exploration, Shakir means using exploratory questions to identify the relationships among clauses and sentences written by experienced writers so that "student writers discover for themselves how the content of a text is structured and how general statements generate supportive ones" (p. 408). With regard to building relations via developing a core sentence, Shakir makes the following suggestion:

> The teacher can set the pace by putting forward a lead (core) sentence. Key words/phrases in this sentence should be identified by the students in order to anticipate concepts that key words/phrases can trigger. In other words, students should realize that key words/phrases in the lead sentence signal commitments on the part of the writers; such commitments must be fulfilled in sentences that follow.
>
> Having identified key words/phrases in the lead sentence, the students can write one more sentence in fulfillment of the anticipations triggered off by the key words. Another key word/phrase is identified in the second sentence and anticipations aroused by it are then marked, and a third sentence is generated accordingly. The process goes on until a paragraph organized around a developed idea is formed (Shakir, 1991, 408–409).

Shakir maintains that students must practice this kind of exercise, involving the notions of commitment and fulfillment, in order to develop an understanding of coherence in writing.

In addition to analyzing reading texts in order to improve students' understanding of written discourse, reading can serve as a good writing prompt. Summarizing and reacting to texts are traditional kinds of exercises, but they can be done at any stage of language learning.

3. *Work on sentence-combining exercises.*

There is some doubt about the effectiveness of sentence combining in teaching FL writing, given the fact that sentence combining and real writing are said to require different cognitive and linguistic processes. However, in a study of advanced-level ESL students Johnson (1992) found that the cognitive demands of sentence combining suggests that this kind of exercise may be beneficial in teaching second-language writing. Using both controlled sentence-combining tasks (paired sentences with cued responses) and open sentence-combining tasks (ten sentences without cued responses), the researchers found that students generally used similar cognitive strategies regardless of the type of sentence-combining task:

> The results revealed that these second language writers most frequently engaged in restating content, constructing meaning, and planning as they completed both controlled and open sentence-combining tasks. This suggests that sentence-combining tasks required these second language writers to think through content, formulate ideas in their own words, and plan their sentence constructions according to local and global discourse constraints (Johnson, 1992, 70).

The researchers identified ten types of cognitive strategies used by the students, including questions about the task and about ideas, local and global planning, restating the content both by reading the text and by writing their own text, constructing meaning, constructing cohesion, and evaluating.

4) *Work on reformulation exercises.*

Syntactic complexity in writing is often considered to be an indicator of the quality of writing. Moreover, according to Schultz (1994), "syntactic complexity serves not only as a tool for clear communication, but also as a tool for generating thought itself" (p. 171). In describing how to teach students about syntactic complexity, Schultz (1994) cites Cohen's *reformulation* technique, which involves having a native speaker or teacher rewrite a student's text so that the student can compare the original version with the reformulated version. The theory behind this approach is that students benefit from being able to analyze how a native speaker would have written it. Schultz contends that reformulation, even at the sentence level, can be an excellent exercise in teaching students about cohesive devices, overall coherence, and lexical as well as structural choices. She describes a practical classroom application of this technique that includes several steps. First, students are given a poorly written text, which may consist of only three or four sentences. Next, students working either individually or in groups rewrite the short text. Then, a native speaker rewrites what the students wrote. Finally, students compare their reformulated version with the one written by the native speaker:

All of this elaboration represents a significant amount of intellectual work on the part of the students, who must make interpretative choices about the content of the text in order to reformulate the passages. That is, learning how to use the foreign language more effectively by putting into practice the multiple aspects of that language (grammar, vocabulary, syntax) would seem to contribute to the development of students' critical thinking skills, particularly as they pertain to interpretative reading and analytical writing (Schultz, 1994, 176).

5. Work on vocabulary exercises.

Koda's (1993) research suggests that there is a strong correlation between vocabulary knowledge and text quality. In fact, her findings show that "vocabulary knowledge contributes substantially to FL composition, [while] sentence complexity has relatively little independent influence on native speakers' judgments regarding FL composition quality" (p. 337). Given this strong relationship between vocabulary knowledge and quality rating, she believes that teaching writing should include vocabulary exercises to provide a "linguistic scaffolding" for a given task.

6. Design prewriting exercises.

When students are first learning to write, it is important to provide adequate support in the prewriting phase. Students should have the opportunity to work with words and structures before they actually begin writing; this activity will help them generate more ideas on the topic as well as organize their ideas. Moreover, the composition will take shape early in the writing process. Figure 6 shows an example of a prewriting exercise for a narrative composition. Figure 7 shows an example of a prewriting exercise for a textual analysis, or an expository composition. These kinds of exercises can be given to students at any stage of language learning.

7. Develop task-oriented writing assignments.

A task-oriented approach to teaching writing is founded on the idea that students need explicit guidelines in order to execute a writing assignment (Scott, 1995). Scott and Terry (1992) propose that a writing assignment consist of a general situation followed by a series of tasks that specify language functions, vocabulary, and grammar structures necessary to complete the assignment. In designing these assignments, teachers should bear in mind that the tasks should not be restrictive, but rather serve as guidelines for generating ideas and engaging in autonomous expression. Figures 2, 3, and 4 give examples of task-oriented writing assignments.

Figure 6: Prewriting Exercise for Narrative Composition

(to be done in the target language)

I.   **Subject of story.** Write one sentence telling what you plan to write about.

II. **Point of view.** Indicate whether your story will be in the first person (I, we), or in the third person (he, she, they).

III. **Place.** Write where your story takes place (in a plane, at home during a big family dinner, etc.).
     1) Write three sentences describing the place.

IV. **Characters.** Write who is in your story. (Limit it to three people.)
     1) Write two sentences describing the main character.
     2) Write a sentence describing each of the other characters.

V.   **Tone.** Write the tone you want to have (humorous, sad, serious, etc.)
     1) Write how you want your reader to feel after reading the story.

VI. **Tense.** What tenses will you use in your story?

VII. **Verbs.** Make a list of six to eight verbs that create a sense of the action in your story. (Do not list verbs like *to have* or *to be*.)

(Taken from pedagogical materials used by the author.)

In *Teacher's Handbook: Contextualized Language Instruction* (1994), Shrum and Glisan include writing activities that are very similar to task-oriented writing assignments. In describing middle school FL instruction, they include an example of Nerenz's fixed-form writing assignment:

Monument Poem
Line 1: Name of the monument
Line 2: Four adjectives describing the monument
Line 3: Constructed in (date, century)
Line 4: Constructed by
Line 5: Which is (on the right bank, left bank, in Paris, . . .)
Line 6: Which is near (another monument or landmark)
Line 7: Don't miss (the monument name) because _____
(Shrum and Glisan, 1994, 183).

8. Work on all four modes of discourse.

Students should be taught to write in all four modes of discourse (description, narration, exposition, and argumentation) from the first stages of language study. This approach helps students prepare for the kinds of writing assignments in upper-level courses as well as engage in different types of cognitive functioning. The developmental writing program in Figure 8 shows task-oriented writing

Figure 7: Prewriting Exercise for Literary Essay

(to be done in the target language)

After reading the text (short story, article, etc.), prepare your essay by doing the following exercise.

I. **Introduction.** For the introduction of your essay, write down the following information:

1) The name of the author and the date of the text

2) Two sentences summarizing the content

II. **Personal reaction to the content.** For this section of the essay, you will analyze and explain how you feel about this text.

1) List the things you like about the content of this text (characters, place, etc.).

2) List the things you do **not** like about the content of this text.

3) From the two lists above, choose the **one** aspect of the content that you find most compelling and explain why.

III. **Analysis of the style.**

1) Write the point of view used in the story (first, third, etc.).

2) List five verbs, five nouns, and five adjectives that are crucial to creating the ambiance in the text.

3) Write how you felt after reading the text (sad, happy, pensive, etc.).

IV. **Conclusion.** For the conclusion of your essay, you will evaluate the overall merit of this text.

1) Write who should read/should not read this text and explain why.

(Taken from pedagogical materials used by the author.)

guidelines for each mode of discourse designed for students in first-, second-, and third-year FL courses.[6]

9. Be aware of learner differences.

The fact that every student has a different learning style is widely accepted among FL teachers. However, it is important to consider learner differences in the context of the writing class. Some students will benefit most from linguistic exercises, such as sentence combining or reformulation; others will benefit from pre-writing exercises or task-oriented guidelines; and some will feel more comfortable writing with computers than with pencil and paper. Teachers need to be open about individual student differences.

Another factor that may influence learners is their ethnic backgrounds. McKay (1993) points out that ESL students from non-Western cultures may have very different concepts about writing. For example, she notes that in some cultures reaching a conclusion about a matter of controversy is not valued. She suggests that L2 composition professionals need to examine the writing process "as it is affected by a culturally influenced set of values and beliefs" (p. 74).

Figure 8: Developmental Writing Program

DESCRIPTION

Situation: You have been asked to write a description of yourself for the new student files.

First Year Tasks

1. Give name, age, nationality.
2. Describe yourself physically.
3. Tell three things you like and three things you don't like to do.

Second Year Tasks

1. Give name, age, nationality.
2. Describe your appearance and personality.
3. Tell at least five things you like and five things you do not like about your academic and leisure activities.

Third Year Tasks

1. Give name, age, nationality.
2. Describe yourself in detail.
3. Indicate your likes and dislikes.
4. Tell what you will do after finishing school.

NARRATION

Situation: Imagine that you went on a trip to _____ last year. You are writing to a pen pal telling about the event.

First Year Tasks

1. Tell where you went.
2. Tell three things you did.
3. Tell three things you did not do.

Second Year Tasks

1. Tell where you went and how you felt.
2. Tell what happened and how you felt.
3. Tell what you will do on your next visit.

Third Year Tasks

1. Tell where you went and why.
2. Tell what happened, whom you were with and how you felt.
3. Tell what you would have done if you had had more money.

Figure 8: Developmental Writing Program (cont.)

EXPOSITION

Situation: Read the following poem (short story, article) and write a short paper.

First Year Tasks	Second Year Tasks	Third Year Tasks
1. Write a sentence summarizing the main idea.	1. Write 2 sentences summarizing the main idea.	1. Summarize the main idea.
2. Write three reasons why you think this is the main idea.	2. Discuss the specific aspects of the text that you like/do not like.	2. Explain specifically how the author communicates the message.
3. Conclude with a personal opinion about the text.	3. Conclude with a personal opinion about the text and explain your opinion.	3. Discuss the specific language and imagery in the text.
		4. Conclude with an evaluation of the text.

ARGUMENTATION

Situation: Write an article arguing for or against the following statement: Americans are obsessed with physical exercise.

First Year Tasks	Second Year Tasks	Third Year Tasks
1. Introduce the subject.	1. Introduce the subject and state your opinion.	1. Introduce the subject, state your opinion, and explain why you believe this.
2. State your opinion.	2. Support your opinion with three facts.	2. Support your opinion by citing facts.
3. Exlain why you believe this.	3. Suggest why Americans are (not) this way.	3. Suggest why Americans are (not) this way and give another informed opinion (i.e., a coach, a doctor).
4. Conclude with a restatement of the subject.	4. Conclude by showing how your argument proves your point.	4. Give an opposing view.
		5. Conclude with persuasive statements which prove your point.

Personality differences may also play a role in how students write. Carrell and Monroe's (1993) study of students in both native language and ESL composition classes provides insight into how personality types can affect writing. Using the Myers-Briggs Type Indicator they found that students who were "intuitive," "feeling," and "perceiving" performed differently on writing tasks than students who were "sensing," "thinking," and "judging." They posit that students with different personality traits will have different learning styles and will therefore benefit from different approaches to teaching writing. If teachers begin to teach writing from the start, these kinds of issues can be addressed early, thereby helping students to achieve success in writing throughout their FL studies.

10. *Teach writing from the start.*

Research and experience show that high school and college students are able to write extended compositions after as few as four weeks of FL study.

Figure 9: Composition Topic for *Système-D*

You have just received the name of your new French-speaking pen pal in the mail. You want to write him or her a letter, telling something about you and your family, and finding out a little about him or her.

Tasks

1. Use the appropriate letter format.
   PHRASES: Writing a letter (informal)

2. Introduce yourself, giving your name, age, and where you live.
   GRAMMAR: Prepositions with geographical places; *Avoir* expressions

3. Talk about your family.
   GRAMMAR: Possessive adjectives (*mon, ma, mes; son, sa, ses; ton, ta, tes; notre votre*)
   VOCABULARY: Family members; Animals

4. Write four things about yourself to describe your personality—including what you like and/or dislike.
   VOCABULARY: Personality
   GRAMMAR: Verb + infinitive

5. Write four things that you are not, including things that you do not like.
   GRAMMAR: Negation with *ne . . . pas*; Verb + infinitive

6. Ask three questions.
   GRAMMAR: Interrogative *est-ce que*; Interrogative adverbs

7. End your letter with the appropriate closing.

(Designed by R. M. Terry for students at the University of Richmond.)

CASE STUDY

At the University of Richmond, students in first- and second-year French are learning to write using ***Système-D*** (Noblitt et al., 1992).[7] This computer writing assistant (reviewed in chapter 3) is particularly well-suited for beginning students, since it provides linguistic support when students need it. This immediate response to linguistic queries gives the novice FL writer a sense of confidence. It is important to note that students writing with ***Système-D*** make errors typical of their level of study; use of this software does not guarantee error-free compositions.

Students in first-year and second-year French were given the composition topic shown in Figure 9. The following compositions are representative examples of work done by the students in these courses. The first composition was written by a student after four weeks of French study, and the second one was written by a student who had one year of French study. The brackets indicate incorrect spelling, grammar, or use of language structures.

Student #1 (four weeks of French):

[Chére] amie,

Salut! [Ca] va? [Je suis tres bien.] S'il vous plaît, je permets [dire une peu] de moi-même. Je m'appelle Amanda Breziner et j'ai dix-huit ans. J'habite à Dover, Massachusetts aux Etats-Unis. Qu'est-ce qu'il y a dans votre ville? Dover est très petit mais très beau.

J'ai une [petit] famille: ma mère, ma soeur, ma grand-mère. Avez-vous des soeurs ou des frères? Aussi j'ai deux chattes. [Ils appellent] Buttercup et Snowy. Ils sont intelligents et énergiques.

Je suis sportive, je joue [] tennis en été. J'aime l'été! Je suis toujours heureuse sauf quand je suis fatiguée. Je suis enthousiaste de [la école] et [ambitieux à mes cours]. J'aime chanter et jouer [à la théâtre musicale]. Quand je suis seule, j'aime lire et écouter la radio. [Usually] j'écoute la radio chaque matin avant [] école.

Je n'aime pas [veiller en retard] quand [j'ai devoir]. Quelquefois je regarde la télévision [tout nuit]. Je déteste des [réclames à nuit]. Des gens sont très stupides. Aussi, je n'aime pas beaucoup de bruit, spécialement lorsque je dors. J'aime voyager mais je déteste dormir [à] les avions.

[Comment-vous] aimez voyager? Aimes-tu ton cours? Quel [temp] fait-il? [Ecries moi] bientôt.

Sincèrement, Amanda[8]

[Dear friend,

Hello! How are you? I am very good. Please, I permit to say a little about myself. My name is Amanda Breziner and I am eighteen years old. I live in

Dover, Massachusetts in the United States. What is there in your town? Dover is very little but very beautiful.

I have a little family: my mother, my sister, my grandmother. Do you have sisters or brothers? Also I have two cats. Their names are Buttercup and Snowy. They are intelligent and energetic.

I am athletic, I play tennis in the summer. I like the summer! I am always happy except when I am tired. I am enthusiastic about school and ambitious in my courses. I like to sing and perform in musical theater. When I am alone, I like to read and listen to the radio. Usually I listen to the radio every morning before school.

I don't like to stay up late when I have homework. Sometimes I watch television all night. I hate advertisements at night. Some people are very stupid. Also, I don't like a lot of noise, especially when I am sleeping. I like to travel but I hate to sleep in airplanes.

How do you like to travel? Do you like you course. What is the weather like? Write me soon.

Sincerely, Amanda]

Student # 2 (one year of French):

[Cher] Angelique,
   Bonjour! Je m'appelle Owen. Je suis ton nouveau "stylo copain." J'ai [vingt et un] ans, et j'habite à Arlington, Virginia. Je pense que je suis sympathique, mais je suis très [orienté] aussi! J'aime jouer [tout] les sports, mais j'adore jouer [] golf. (Je joue au golf mal pourtant!) J'aime regarder [] baseball, [] football, et [] football américain à la télévision, et j'aime jouer [ils] aussi. J'aime fêter avec mes amis [sur] les week-ends.
   Je n'aime pas [] gens qui sont impolis ou embêtants. Je [deteste] [] gens qui visitent mon appartement et partent quand l'appartement est sale! [Je [deteste] que j'ai une blessure à ma poitrine aussi (elle blesse).] Je n'aime pas les New York Yankees.
   Ma famille est très sympathique d'habitude. Ma mère, Laurie, a quarante-huit ans (!) et elle est infirmière. Mon père, Dwight, a quarante-[nuef] ans et il aura cinquante ans [à] novembre. Il adore les Boston Red Sox. Mon frère, Peter, a dix-neuf ans. Il [alla] à un college à West Virginia pour un an, mais il [travailler] à la "Sept-Onze" maintenant. Ma [chiene], Sasha, est très âgée.
   Je désire [connaître de toi]. Est-ce que tu parles anglais bien? Est-ce [] tu penses que O.J. Simpson est coupable? Ou, est-ce que tu penses que Cato [] tué Nicole et Ronald? Ecrivez bientôt!

Ton ami, Owen[9]

[Dear Angelique,
   Hello! My name is Owen. I am your new "pen pal." I am twenty-one years old, and I live in Arlington, Virginia. I think that I am nice, but I am very oriented [?] also! I like all sports, but I love to play golf. (I play golf badly

however!) I like to watch baseball, soccer, and football on television, and I like to play them too. I like to party with my friends on the week-ends.

I don't like people who are impolite or bothersome. I hate people who visit my apartment and leave when the apartment is dirty! I hate when I have a wound on my chest also (it wounds) [?] I don't like the New York Yankees.

My family is very nice generally. My mother, Laurie, is forty-eight years old (!) and she is a nurse. My father, Dwight, is forty-nine years old and he will be fifty in November. He loves the Boston Red Sox. My brother, Peter, is nineteen years old. He went to a college in West Virginia for a year, but he to work at the "Seven-Eleven" now. My dog, Sasha, is very old.

I desire (want) to know of you. Do you speak English well? Do you think that O.J. Simpson is guilty? Or, do you think that Cato killed Nicole and Ronald? Write soon!

Your friend, Owen]

Despite the relatively short amount of time spent studying French, both of these students succeeded in writing compositions that show originality and are comprehensible. In addition to being able to write from the earliest stages of language study, elementary- and intermediate-level students are overwhelmingly positive in their reaction to using this computer writing assistant.[10]

CONCLUSIONS

As stated in the hypothesis of this chapter, FL writing should be taught at all stages of language study. Our students are members of an academic community that frequently measures students' performance by their writing. Therefore, it is critical that we foster the development of this skill in the FL curriculum.

> . . . teachers cannot expect students to produce communicatively complex language without practice. Students need opportunities to reflect in terms of that language's propositions or idea units. The ability to engage in discourse beyond descriptive or factual sentence series, to articulate wishes, requests, gratitude, or irritation in a manner that reveals sensitivity to the foreign norms, commences with cognitive practice. FL students need early, consistent opportunities for such practice, because sophisticated language can only develop from sophisticated thought (Swaffar, 1991, 270).

In defining a coherent approach to teaching FL writing, it is important to recognize both the short- and long-term goals of this endeavor. In the short term, we want students to practice the target language in a modality other than speech so that they are able to communicate a message to a designated community as well as to perform adequately in courses that focus on academic writing. In the long term, we want to increase students' overall cognitive functioning. The act of writing in the FL, just as writing in L1, requires students to think critically. When FL students are required to write beyond the sentence level from the start, they learn to communicate ideas with a reader without the pressure of face-to-face communication, to record experience, to explore a subject, to become familiar with the conventions of written discourse in the target language, and to discover the link between writing and thinking (Raimes, 1983).

Finally, in rethinking we need to reinvent. FL teachers need to recognize: 1) that students are often cognitively mature adults whose writing competence is already fairly well defined, 2) that teaching must take into account the complexity of the FL writing process, 3) that writing with computers can help students engage in FL writing process from the start, and 4) that teaching writing is more than evaluating the product. The traditional paradigm, which included writing in the FL curriculum after students had already attained some mastery of the target language, is no longer valid. This book offers a challenge to the traditional paradigm, proposing that teaching FL writing is a pedagogical imperative at all levels of language study.

TOPICS FOR DISCUSSION AND RESEARCH

1. Analyze the strategies that teachers use for teaching writing in lower-level language courses as well as upper-level literature and civilization courses.

2. Compare the writing of advanced-level language students who had an opportunity to write expository and argumentative essays from the beginning of their language study to those who did not.

3. Compare the writing of students at all levels who complete formal prewriting exercises to those who do not.

4. Determine whether sentence combining and reformulation exercises help elementary-level language students increase the syntactic complexity of their writing.

5. Devise a measurement instrument for evaluating task difficulty. Then, analyze the relationship between task difficulty and student performance.

6. Compare the writing of elementary-level language students who use a computer writing assistant and those who do not.

Notes

1. In a study involving 1,373 students and 59 teachers of French and Spanish from 12 universities, Harlow and Muyskens ("Priorities for Intermediate-Level Language Instruction," *The Modern Language Journal* 78(2):141–154,

1994) found that writing ranked relatively low on a list of priorities for inter-mediate year university instruction. Both students and teachers responded to questionnaires designed to assess immediate goals and the importance of activities to achieve those goals. Speaking, listening, and developing self-confidence were top-priority goals for both students and teachers. With regard to the activities for achieving goals, students and teachers ranked speaking in the target language as most important, however, they had differing views about writing. Teachers ranked writing third on the list of 19 activities, whereas students ranked writing 10th. Given the low ranking that students give to writing activities, the authors suggest that there is a need to reevaluate the approach to writing.

2. Stephen Krashen's Monitor Theory is described in detail in his book entitled *Principles and Practice in Second Language Acquisition* (New York: Pergamon Press, 1982).

3. The Army Specialized Training Program came into being during the 1940s in response to the international threat of war. First used at the Defense Language Institute, this program sought to train young men for work in defense and espionage. The goal of instruction was to achieve superior listening comprehension and native-like speech.

4. It is important to note that any approach to FL teaching may incorporate a proficiency orientation.

5. The traditional French *explication de texte* is an excellent tool for teaching students how to do a close reading of a text as well as a way of teaching them to developing an awareness of various textual features when they write.

6. This developmental writing program was first described in Scott's "Write From the Start: A Task-oriented Developmental Writing Program for Foreign Language Students," in R. M. Terry, (Ed.), *Dimension: Language '91*, Valdosta, GA: The Southern Conference on Language Teaching.

7. Professor Robert Terry at the University of Richmond provided the material for this case study.

8. Thanks to Amanda Breziner at the University of Richmond for allowing her composition to be published in this study.

9. Thanks to Owen Rodgers at the University of Richmond for allowing his composition to be published in this study.

10. Surveys regarding the use of **Système-D** are given to students every semester at Vanderbilt University. An average of 350 elementary- and intermediate-level students use the software during the fall semester and an average of 250 elementary- and intermediate-level students use the software during the spring semester. Responses indicate that more than 95 percent of the students like the software and feel that they learn a great deal when they use it.

REFERENCES

ACTFL Proficiency Guidelines. (1986). Hastings-on-Hudson, NY: American Council on the Teaching of Foreign Languages.

Carnicelli, Thomas A. (1980). "The Writing Conference: A One-to-One Conversation." In T. R. Donovan and B. W. McClelland, (Eds.), *Eight Approaches to Teaching Composition.* Urbana, IL: National Council of Teachers of English.

Carrell, Patricia L. and Laura B. Monroe. (1993). "Learning Styles and Composition." *The Modern Language Journal* 77(2):148–162.

Cumming, Alister. (1992). "Instructional Routines in ESL Composition Teaching: A Case Study of Three Teachers." *Journal of Second Language Writing* 1(1):17–35.

Donovan, Timothy R. and B. W. McClelland, (Eds.). (1980). *Eight Approaches to Teaching Composition.* Urbana, IL: National Council of Teachers of English.

Dowst, Kenneth. (1980). "The Epistemic Approach: Writing, Knowing, and Learning." In T. R. Donovan and B. W. McClelland, (Eds.), *Eight Approaches to Teaching Composition.* Urbana, IL: National Council of Teachers of English.

Eschholz, Paul A. (1980). "The Prose Models Approach: Using Products as Process." In T. R. Donovan and B. W. McClelland, (Eds.), *Eight Approaches to Teaching Composition.* Urbana, IL: National Council of Teachers of English.

Faigley, Lester. (1992). *Fragments of Rationality.* Pittsburgh: University of Pittsburgh Press.

Freed, Barbara, (Ed.). (1991). *Foreign Language Acquisition Research and the Classroom.* Lexington, MA: D. C. Heath.

Gaudiani, Claire. (1981). *Teaching Writing in the Foreign Language Curriculum.* Washington D.C.: Center for Applied Linguistics.

Hadley, Alice Omaggio. (1993). *Teaching Language in Context.* Boston, MA: Heinle & Heinle Publishers.

Hamp-Lyons, Liz and Sheila Prochnow Mathias. (1994). "Examining Expert Judgments of Task Difficulty on Essay Tests." *Journal of Second Language Writing* 3(1):49–68.

Harlow, Linda L. and Judith A. Muyskens. (1994). "Priorities for Intermediate-Level Language Instruction." *The Modern Language Journal* 78(2):141–154.

Horning, Alice S. (1987). *Teaching Writing as a Second Language.* Carbondale and Edwardsville, IL: Southern Illinois University Press.

Johnson, Karen E. (1992). "Cognitive Strategies and Second Language Writers: A Re-evaluation of Sentence Combining." *Journal of Second Language Writing* 1(1):61–75.

Kern, Richard and Jean Marie Schultz. (1992). "The Effects of Composition Instruction on Intermediate Level French Students' Writing Performance: Some Preliminary Findings." *The Modern Language Journal* 76(1):1–13.

Knoblauch, C. H. and Lil Brannon. (1984). *Rhetorical Traditions and the Teaching of Writing.* Upper Montclair, NJ: Boynton/Cook Publishers, Inc.

Koda, Keiko. (1993). "Task-Induced Variability in FL Composition: Language-Specific Perspectives." *Foreign Language Annals* 26(3):332–346.

Kroll, Barbara, (Ed.). (1990). *Second Language Writing: Research Insights for the Classroom.* New York: Cambridge University Press.

——— and Joy Reid. (1994). "Guidelines for Designing Writing Prompts: Clarifications, Caveats, and Cautions." *Journal of Second Language Writing* 3(3):231–255.

Lauer, Janice M. (1980). "The Rhetorical Approach: Stages of Writing and Strategies for Writers." In T. R. Donovan and B. W. McClelland, (Eds.), *Eight Approaches to Teaching Composition*. Urbana, IL: National Council of Teachers of English.

Leki, Ilona. (1992). *Understanding ESL Writers: A Guide for Teachers*. Portsmouth, NH: Boynton/Cook Publishers.

McKay, Sandra Lee. (1993). "Examining L2 Composition Ideology: A Look at Literacy Education." *Journal of Second Language Writing* 2(1):65–81.

Murray, Donald M. (1980). "Writing as Process: How Writing Finds Its Own Meaning." In T. R. Donovan and B. W. McClelland, (Eds.), *Eight Approaches to Teaching Composition*. Urbana, IL: National Council of Teachers of English.

Noblitt, James S., Willem J. A. Pet and Donald Solá. (1992). ***Système-D***. Boston, MA: Heinle & Heinle Publishers.

Raimes, Ann. (1983). *Techniques in Teaching Writing*. New York: Oxford University Press.

Schrum, Judith L. and Eileen W. Glisan. (1994). *Teacher's Handbook: Contextualized Language Instruction*. Boston, MA: Heinle & Heinle Publishers.

Schultz, Jean M. (1991a). "Mapping and Cognitive Development in the Teaching of Foreign Language Writing." *French Review* 64(6):978–988.

———. (1991b). "Writing Mode in the Articulation of Language and Literature Classes: Theory and Practice." *The Modern Language Journal* 75(4):411–417.

———. (1994). "Stylistic Reformulation: Theoretical Premises and Practical Applications." *The Modern Language Journal* 78(2):169–178.

Scott, Virginia M. (1990). "Task-Oriented Creative Writing with ***Système-D***." *CALICO Journal* 7(3):58–67.

———. (1992). "Write From the Start: A Task-Oriented Developmental Writing Program for Foreign Language Students." In R. M. Terry, (Ed.), *Dimension: Language '91*. Valdosta, GA: Southern Conference on Language Teaching.

———. (1995). "Writing." In V. Galloway and C. Herron, (Eds.), *Research Within Reach II*. Valdosta, GA: Southern Conference on Language Teaching.

——— and Robert M. Terry. (1992). *Teacher's Guide:* **Système-D** *Writing Assistant for French*. Boston, MA: Heinle & Heinle Publishers.

Selfe, Cynthia L. (1986). *Computer-Assisted Instruction in Composition*. Urbana, IL: National Council of Teachers of English.

Shakir, Abdullah. (1991). "Coherence in EFL Student Written Texts: Two Perspectives." *Foreign Language Annals* 24(5):399–411.

Silva, Tony. (1990). "Second Language Composition Instruction: Developments, Issues, and Directions." In B. Kroll, (Ed.), *Second Language Writing: Research Insights for the Classroom*. New York: Cambridge University Press.

Stephen, Judy. (1980). "The Experiential Approach: Inner Worlds to Outer Worlds." In T. R. Donovan and B. W. McClelland, (Eds.), *Eight Approaches to Teaching Composition*. Urbana, IL: National Council of Teachers of English.

Swaffar, Janet K. (1991). "Language Learning is More than Learning Language: Rethinking Reading and Writing Tasks in Textbooks for Beginning Language Study." In B. Freed, (Ed.), *Foreign Language Acquisition Research and the Classroom*. Lexington, MA: D. C. Heath.

Appendix A

ACTFL Proficiency Guidelines
generic descriptions for writing

Novice-Low Able to form some letters in an alphabetic system. In languages whose writing systems use syllabaries or characters, writer is able to both copy and produce the basic strokes. Can produce romanization of isolated characters, where applicable.

Novice-Mid Able to copy or transcribe familiar words or phrases and reproduce some from memory. No practical communicative writing skills.

Novice-High Able to write simple fixed expressions and limited memorized material and some recombinations thereof. Can supply information on simple forms and documents. Can write names, numbers, dates, own nationality, and other simple autobiographical information as well as some short phrases and simple lists. Can write all the symbols in an alphabetic or syllable system or 50–100 characters or compounds in a character writing system. Spelling and representation of symbols (letters, syllables, characters) may be partially correct.

Intermediate-Low Able to meet limited practical writing needs. Can write short messages, postcards, and take down simple notes, such as telephone messages. Can create statements or questions within the scope of limited language experience. Material produced consists of recombinations of learned vocabulary and structures into simple sentences on very familiar topics. Languge is inadequate to express in writing anything but elementary needs. Frequent errors in grammar, vocabulary, punctuation, spelling and information of nonalphabetic symbols, but writing can be understood by natives used to the writing of nonnatives.

Intermediate-Mid Able to meet a number of practical writing needs. Can write short, simple letters. Content involves personal preferences, daily routine, everyday events, and other topics grounded in personal experience. Can express present time or at least one other time frame or aspect consistently, e.g., nonpast, habitual, imperfect. Evidence of control of the syntax of noncomplex sentences and basic inflectional morphology, such as declensions and conjugation. Writing tends to be a loose collection of sentences or sentence fragments on a given topic and provides little evidence of conscious organization. Can be understood by natives used to the writing of nonnatives.

Intermediate-High   Able to meet most practical writing needs and limited social demands. Can take notes in some detail on familiar topics and respond in writing to personal questions. Can write simple letters, brief synopses and paraphrases, summaries of biographical data, work and school experience. In those languages relying primarily on content words and time expressions to express time, tense, or aspect, some precision is displayed; where tense and/or aspect is expressed through verbal inflections, forms are produced rather consistently, but not always accurately. An ability to describe and narrate in paragraphs is emerging. Rarely uses basic cohesive elements, such as pronominal substitutions or synonyms in written discourse. Writing, though faulty, is generally comprehensible to natives used to the writing of nonnatives.

Advanced   Able to write routine social correspondence and join sentences in simple discourse of at least several paragraphs in length on familiar topics. Can write simple social correspondence, take notes, write cohesive summaries and resumes, as well as narratives and descriptions of a factual nature. Has sufficient writing vocabulary to express self simply with some circumlocution. May still make errors in punctuation, spelling, or the formation of nonalphabetic symbols. Good control of the morphology and the most frequently used syntactic structures, e.g., common word order patterns, coordination, subordination, but makes frequent errors in producing complex sentences. Uses a limited number of cohesive devices, such as pronouns, accurately. Writing may resemble literal translations from the native language, but a sense of organization (rhetorical structure) is emerging. Writing is understandable to natives not used to the writing of nonnatives.

Advanced-Plus   Able to write about a variety of topics with significant precision and in detail. Can write most social and informal business correspondence. Can describe and narrate personal experiences fully but has difficulty supporting points of view in written discourse. Can write about the concrete aspects of topics relating to particular interests and special fields of competence. Often shows remarkable fluency and ease of expression, but under time constraints and pressure writing may be inaccurate. Generally strong in either grammar or vocabulary, but not in both. Weakness and unevenness in one of the foregoing or in spelling or character writing formation may result in occasional miscommunication. Some misuse of vocabulary may still be evident. Style may still be obviously foreign.

Superior   Able to express self effectively in most formal and informal writing on practical, social and professional topics. Can write most types of correspondence, such as memos as well as social and business letters, and short research papers and statements of position in areas of special interest or in special fields. Good control of a full range of structures, spelling or nonalphabetic symbol production, and wide general vocabulary allow the writer to hypothesize and present arguments or points of view accurately and effectively. An underlying organization, such as chronological ordering, logical ordering, cause and effect, comparison, and thematic development is strongly evident, although not thoroughly executed and/or not totally reflecting target language patterns. Although sensitive to differences in formal and informal style, still may not tailor writing precisely to a variety of purposes and/or readers. Errors in writing rarely disturb natives or cause miscommunication.

INDEX